# Reshaping Social Work Series

*Series Editors*: **Robert Adams, Lena Dominelli and Malcolm Payne**

The **Reshaping Social Work** series aims to develop the knowledge base for critical, reflective practitioners. Each book is designed to support students on qualifying social work programmes and update practitioners on crucial issues in today's social work, strengthening research knowledge, critical analysis and skilled practice to shape social work to meet future challenges.

## Published titles

*Social Work Research for Social Justice* Beth Humphries
*Social Care Practice in Context* Malcolm Payne
*Critical Issues in Social Work with Older People* Mo Ray, Miriam Bernard and
    Judith Phillips
*Social Work and Power* Roger Smith

## Forthcoming titles

*Anti-Racist practice in Social Work* Kish Bhatti-Sinclair
*Social Work and Spirituality* Margaret Holloway and Bernard Moss

**Invitation to authors**
The Series Editors welcome proposals for new books within the *Reshaping Social Work* series. Please contact one of the series editors for an initial discussion:

- Robert Adams at rvadams@rvadams.karoo.co.uk
- Lena Dominelli at lena.dominelli@durham.ac.uk
- Malcolm Payne at M.Payne@stchristophers.org.uk

**Reshaping Social Work**
*Series Editors*: **Robert Adams, Lena Dominelli and Malcolm Payne**
Series Standing Order ISBN 1–4039–4878–X
(outside North America only)

You can receive future titles in this series as they are published by placing a standing order. Please contact your bookseller or, in the case of difficulty, write to us at the address below with your name and address, the title of the series and the ISBN quoted above.

Customer Services Department
Macmillan Distribution Ltd
Houndmills
Basingstoke
Hampshire
RG21 6XS
England

# Critical Issues in Social Work with Older People

Mo Ray, Miriam Bernard and Judith Phillips

© Mo Ray, Miriam Bernard and Judith Phillips 2009

All rights reserved. No reproduction, copy or transmission of this publication may be made without written permission.

No portion of this publication may be reproduced, copied or transmitted save with written permission or in accordance with the provisions of the Copyright, Designs and Patents Act 1988, or under the terms of any licence permitting limited copying issued by the Copyright Licensing Agency, Saffron House, 6–10 Kirby Street, London EC1N 8TS.

Any person who does any unauthorized act in relation to this publication may be liable to criminal prosecution and civil claims for damages.

The authors have asserted their rights to be identified as the authors of this work in accordance with the Copyright, Designs and Patents Act 1988.

First published 2009 by
PALGRAVE MACMILLAN

Palgrave Macmillan in the UK is an imprint of Macmillan Publishers Limited, registered in England, company number 785998, of Houndmills, Basingstoke, Hampshire RG21 6XS.

Palgrave Macmillan in the US is a division of St Martin's Press LLC, 175 Fifth Avenue, New York, NY 10010.

Palgrave Macmillan is the global academic imprint of the above companies and has companies and representatives throughout the world.

Palgrave® and Macmillan® are registered trademarks in the United States, the United Kingdom, Europe and other countries.

ISBN-13: 978–1–4039–9125–6
ISBN-10: 1–4039–9125–1

This book is printed on paper suitable for recycling and made from fully managed and sustained forest sources. Logging, pulping and manufacturing processes are expected to conform to the environmental regulations of the country of origin.

A catalogue record for this book is available from the British Library.

Library of Congress Cataloging-in-Publication Data
Ray, Mo.
  Critical issues in social work with older people / Mo Ray, Miriam Bernard, Judith Phillips.
    p. cm.
  Includes bibliographical references and index.
  ISBN-13: 978-1-4039-9125-6 (alk. paper)
  ISBN-10: 1-4039-9125-1 (alk. paper)
  1. Social work with older people—Great Britain. I. Bernard, Miriam. II. Phillips, Judith (Judith E.) III. Title.
  HV1481.G7R39 2008
  362.6—dc22                                    2008030655

10   9   8   7   6   5   4   3   2   1
18  17  16  15  14  13  12  11  10  09

Printed and bound in China

Learning Resource
Centre

13848704

For our students – past, present and future

# Contents

# List of tables, boxes and extracts

## Tables

## Boxes

## Extracts

# Acknowledgements

The completion of this book could not have been accomplished so easily without the valuable support, advice and practical assistance of friends and colleagues.

Thanks to Catherine Gray and her support team, especially Sarah Lodge, Tina Graham and Keith Povey, for providing us with timely and helpful editorial assistance and advice.

Thanks to the many colleagues who have supported us in our endeavours, especially the members of the Centre for Social Gerontology at Keele University.

Mo Ray would particularly like to thank her colleague, friend and mentor Professor Miriam Bernard for her steadfast assistance and support throughout the process of writing this book.

We would like to thank those academic colleagues, practitioners and social work students who keep the flag flying for social work practice with older people through their researches, practice and commitment. Thanks to the many older people we have met in the course of our own practice, research and personal lives who have taught us much about what sort of help really matters when faced with change and transitions.

Finally, special thanks to Margaret Forster for writing a novel that continues to resonate almost twenty years after its publication.

The authors and publishers wish to thank Random House and the Sayle Literary Agency for permission to use the following extracts from Margaret Forster's book *Have the Men Had Enough?* (published by Chatto & Windus, reprinted by permission of The Random House Group Ltd and the Sayle Literary Agency):

3.1   Being at risk?
3.2   Occupational poverty and quality of life
4.1   Diagnosing dementia
4.2   Loss of personhood/objectification
4.3   Biographical understandings
4.4   Life story work and identity

# List of abbreviations

| | |
|---|---|
| CCW | Care Council for Wales |
| CSIP | Care Services Improvement Partnership |
| CSCI | Commission for Social Care Inspection |
| DH | Department of Health |
| DWP | Department of Work and Pensions |
| FAC | Fair access to care |
| GSCC | General Social Care Council |
| MRC | Making Research Count |
| NHS | National Health Service |
| NICE | National Institute for Clinical Excellence |
| NISCC | Northern Ireland Social Care Council |
| NSF | National Services Framework |
| ODPM | Office of the Deputy Prime Minister |
| ONS | Office of National Statistics |
| POVA | Protection of vulnerable adults |
| PQ award | Post-qualifying award |
| SAP | Single assessment process |
| SCIE | Social Care Institute for Excellence |
| SPT | Simulated presence therapy |
| SSSC | Scottish Social Services Council |
| WAG | Welsh Assembly Government |

# Key legislation

The legislation set out below reflects the major pieces of legislation referred to throughout the book. Please refer to the suggested reading for a more detailed analysis of these legislative frameworks.

Care Standards Act 2000
Carers and Disabled Children Act 2000
Carers (Equal Opportunities) Act 2004
Carers (Recognition and Services) Act 1995
Local Authority Social Services Act 1970
Mental Capacity Act 2005
Mental Health (Care and Treatment) Scotland Act 2003
National Health Service and Community Care Act 1990
Protection of Vulnerable Adults (Scotland) Act 2007

## Table of Cases

*R.* v. *Gloucestershire County Council*, ex parte Barry [1997] 2 All ER 1

# 1 Social work with older people: changing times, changing contexts

## main points

■ Social work with older people has undergone unprecedented change since the NHS and Community Care Act, 1990.

■ These changes have resulted in a greater emphasis on administrative processes at the expense of valued social work skills and practice knowledge.

■ There are significant tensions between policy which on the one hand seeks to manage finite resources effectively and efficiently and, on the other, aspires to provide person-centred and proactive services for older people.

■ Social work with older people has not been underpinned by the developing gerontological research base.

■ There is a gap between research and practice, which means that social workers may not be aware of, or informed about, the current gerontological and social work research base.

■ Older people have expressed dissatisfaction with administrative approaches to social work and social care, and have articulated clear aspirations for a quality social service.

## Introduction

Gerontology is a multi-disciplinary study of ageing. Adopting a critical gerontological perspective implies that research, writing and practice should make visible the social, economic and political forces that shape and influence the experience of ageing. Commentators have argued that critical gerontology should seek to change the social construction of ageing as well as to understand it (Phillipson and Walker,

1987). This emphasis on change and action will doubtless resonate with social work practitioners, and indeed any other practitioners working with older people.

As social work lecturers and practitioners, and as gerontologists, it is important first to establish the authors' own intellectual and value positions, to enable readers to know from what basis this exploration of critical gerontological social work with older people is being approached. The central argument in the two opening chapters is that building on the things the authors value about good social work with older people (but developing them into a more robust and critical approach drawing explicitly on research and theorizing from within critical gerontology) is imperative in the current context of welfare provision. The basis for this contention lies in a combination of historical, organizational and policy concerns, alongside developments in gerontological and social work practice, education and research. In developing this argument, this book aims to explore the historical, theoretical and conceptual foundations of a critical gerontological social work approach. This is premised on the authors' belief that there is a widening gap that needs to be bridged between traditional understandings and orientations of social work research and practice with older people, and the insights that can now be gleaned from more critical and gerontological approaches.

The book addresses primarily the policy and practice context of social work in England. Scotland, Wales and Northern Ireland have devolved powers in social policy and social care, and operate social work there within this framework. However, while there are differences in the ways in which social work functions in these countries, the principles and approaches encompassed by a critical gerontological social work approach can be applied across the UK. For example, principles around combating ageism, developing a healthy strategy for later life, promoting social inclusion, enabling flexible working lives and working in partnership to achieve change, are relevant regardless of the country in which one is practising. Indeed, in Wales, the strategies and aspirations outlined in *The Strategy for Older People in Wales* (Welsh Assembly Government, 2003) and *Fulfilled Lives: Supportive Communities* (Welsh Assembly Government, 2006), manifestly support the development of the approach taken in this book.

The book is organized as follows: Chapters 1 and 2 review the relationship between gerontology and social work, and set the agenda for critical gerontological social work practice. The central chapters (Chapters 3 to 7) then seek to apply this perspective to contemporary areas of practice. Here, there is a focus on risk, dementia, end-of-life issues and palliative care; key transitions around loss and bereavement and moving into a care home; and informal care giving.

Attention turns in the last two chapters to a consideration of the potential for critical gerontological social work in the future. In Chapter 8, post-traumatic stress, depression and the mistreatment of older people are examined through three case studies. Between them, they illustrate the importance of developing social work practice that challenges the conventional tendency to focus on care packages addressing physical needs. Finally, Chapter 9 draws together the discussions and arguments introduced in the preceding chapters into a re-evaluation of social work with older people, highlighting again the necessity of adopting critical perspectives in educational approaches, the research and evidence base, and in practice.

## Social work in context

In outlining the current situation in social work with older people, it is necessary first to set this against an historical and policy background that has seen social work develop in three ways: as a discipline; as a profession; and as a public service activity. Despite being a contested area, we would argue that social work has developed rapidly as a profession since its inception, and has subsequently undergone profound changes, particularly over the years since the passing of the NHS and Community Care Act 1990 (Gorman and Postle, 2003). We further argue that the fundamental changes in ideology and organization associated with a managerialist model of social care (Waine and Henderson, 2003) have led to an erosion of the traditional values, skills and knowledge base of social work in which the personal and human elements have been marginalized, and the roles and identities of social workers fundamentally altered and weakened (Lymbery, 2001). In the first half of this chapter, we therefore examine what these changes have meant for social work practice with older people in the twenty-first century.

At the same time as social work in general has been undergoing profound changes, older people as a section of society have become ever more visible in simple demographic terms. Demographic data confirms that the population will never be much 'younger' than it is now, and there are currently more people aged over 65 than under 16 in the population (ONS, 2006a). Alongside this, knowledge and research about older people has flourished. Yet it has to be conceded that much of the advance in research knowledge has come from disciplines other than social work. Consequently, the second half of this chapter discusses the reasons for what we call 'the social work–gerontology research gap', and then moves on to consider issues surrounding the training and educational needs that underpin social work practice with older people. The chapter concludes by arguing that, if those things that are valued about good social work with older people are not to be lost, then there is an urgent need to revisit its values, skills and knowledge base, and to develop a far more robust and critical gerontological social work practice (Neysmith and MacAdam, 1999).

Historically, there is also a need to be mindful of the differing policy and practice contexts of social work. While the drivers for policy change in the devolved administrations of the UK are similar, with social, health and demographic pressures fuelling the move to greater integration of health and social care, it has led to important differences in emphasis. In Scotland, for example, trusts have merged into single health systems, while in England competition and choice are seen as the way forward to provide more responsive care. A number of Scottish policy documents (Scottish Assembly, 1999, 2001, 2005) have placed a duty on Health Boards and local councils to work together at both strategic and practice levels and, importantly, have introduced free personal care for older people. In contrast to the situation in England, the emphasis in Scotland is on a single 'whole' system in which private sector provision is at the margins of activity.

In Northern Ireland too, the emphasis is on a joined-up system of organization, with acute care being delivered through hospital Trusts, and personal social services through Trusts collaborating with private and voluntary organizations. As in other areas of the UK, Northern Ireland has a strategy for older people focusing on promoting social inclusion; see *Ageing in an Inclusive Society* (Northern Ireland Assembly, 2005). This echoes the broader perspective on ageing embodied in the Welsh Assembly Government's *The Strategy for Older People in Wales* (2003) which is now in its second five-year phase. Older people have been one of the Welsh Assembly Government's priority areas for some time, but the strength of its approach is that it goes beyond traditional health and social care territory to take a more rounded view of older people, focusing on their citizenship, participation and ability to help build capacity within their local communities. The policy context in which social work operates in Wales, Northern Ireland and Scotland is therefore rather different from that in England: there is a greater emphasis on the citizen rather than on the consumer; on co-operation rather than competition; and on aligning health services with local councils to meet local needs.

## Social work practice with older people

Given the changing historical and policy contexts, it is perhaps not surprising that social work with older people, in common with other areas of social work practice, has been in a state of constant flux since the early 1990s, and is now often perceived as being beleaguered and under threat. From a national policy perspective, Butler and Drakeford (2005) have argued that it is difficult to ascertain with certainty any clear vision as to the role and purpose of social work. Furthermore, while calls have been made within the academic and practice community to re-evaluate the knowledge and skills that social work can contribute to the current practice landscape (see, for example, Lymbery, 1998; Neysmith and MacAdam, 1999), it remains the case that social work with older people has undergone unprecedented change without public debate, and with apparently little resistance from practitioners (Postle, 2002).

In attempting to understand the situation at present, we first explore some of the key practice changes that have arisen in the wake of the NHS and Community Care Act of 1990, which have fundamentally altered the nature of social work with older people. Rather than provide a long-winded historical description of how social work evolved during the twentieth century, we have chosen to look critically at developments since the 1990 Act because, in our view, this marks a crucial turning point in how services for older people have been conceived, viewed and delivered. Insightful historical accounts can be found elsewhere (see, for example, Means and Smith, 1998; Gorman and Postle, 2003; Means *et al.*, 2003), but an understanding of key issues arising from the 1990 Act, such as the management of finite resources, the nature of the interventions it is possible to offer, fundamental alterations to social work as a profession, and service-user participation and involvement, underpin our argument for the development of a critical gerontological social work practice.

## The NHS and Community Care Act, care management and managerialism

The NHS and Community Care Act 1990 heralded root-and-branch change in the way that adult social care was organized in the UK. The Conservative government in power had long championed market principles as a means of managing health and social care effectively and efficiently in a climate where there were limited public finances to spend on social care. Targeting resources such as home care services on those people defined as being in the greatest need (Gorman and Postle, 2003) was also a crucial element in the developing policy. However, an over-concentration on the measurement and assessment of need has in turn led to older people being seen increasingly in terms of crisis, risk, dependency and frailty. These terms, even where appropriate, are often used in an uncritical way, and reinforce the potential for practitioners to emphasize judgements about risk in order to secure scarce resources for an older person (Pritchard, 1997), and to focus on an older person's difficulties at the expense of his/her strengths as a means of proving eligibility for services (Saleeby, 2002).

Moreover, despite commentators such as Hughes (1995) highlighting the potential dangers of a market economy in social care, both social work and social care have moved steadily towards this type of organization. This means that, under the guise of the care management process, social work practitioners have experienced the erosion of their professional skills. The inherent complexity of work with older people has been reduced all too often to being a primarily technical exercise, as illustrated, for example, by standardized approaches to assessment. One consequence is that the social work knowledge base, never very well developed, has become even more indistinct, calling into question the role, status, direction and identity of social work with older people. To re-establish itself, social work with older people needs to re-engage with wider policy and research agendas, and employ methods and values that highlight its distinctiveness and complexity. Various authors have highlighted these key attributes of social work, including:

- Non-stigmatizing help, assistance and access to services (for example, Gilbert, 2004; Small, 2001);
- Training in social science perspectives, and an applied understanding of social perspectives and individual experience in social contexts (for example, Foster, 2005);
- Responding to loss, change and transition (Small, 2001); and
- Taking a 'whole system' view (Small, 2001).

The so-called 'reformed' managerialism of the Labour government also places greater emphasis on accountability and quality evidenced through defining the standards that agencies should achieve, and the priorities upon which they should focus (Waine and Henderson, 2003). The underpinning assumption is that robust standards – and being required to provide evidence of achievement via performance indicators – will lead to an accountable, efficient and effective organization. Systems of inspection, regulation and monitoring have also been introduced as a fundamental building block in the government's modernization agenda. Such regulatory systems have had a fundamental effect on the culture and role of councils, social care managers and front-line staff, to the extent that the language of performance measurement and audit now permeates social care organizations, and has an impact on supervision practice and on the ways in which practice dialogues are constructed (Sawdon and Sawdon, 2003).

## Social work as a profession

The pervasive culture of managerialism has also had a profound effect on the way that social work is constructed and delivered, with a growing separation between the notion of social work as a professional project, and an administrative model commonly associated with care management. While these changes have distanced social work from its professional aspirations, historically social workers have had a long-standing ambivalence about professionalizing their role. Fook (2002, p. 26) comments:

> On the one hand it is seen as a route for better social recognition and therefore better service provision. On the other it is seen as a grab for power at the expense of service users. So it has never been clear whether it is a good thing to foster and develop a professional social work identity.

If one accepts this critique of a professional social work identity in general terms, then we would further argue that it is even more the case where social work with (older) adults is concerned. As we shall show later, this is a devalued and undervalued area of practice, with students rarely opting freely to undertake training in work with older people.

Services are also reorganizing into multi-professional teams, with the aim of improving joint working, and standards of service delivery and development. This may have a further impact on the identities, roles and tasks of different professional groups as they merge. As Davies (2003, p. 204) argues:

> Today's practitioner does not need to be someone with a sense of self as possessor of a clearly bounded expertise. Instead they need to be someone who can value and connect with others, using the multiplicity of experiences of the client and team members to develop adaptive and creative solutions.

Nevertheless, traditional knowledge and power hierarchies may impede the potential for developing teams based on more collaborative lines of organization and culture. Social workers need to be able to articulate the contribution they can make and added value they bring to an interprofessional team, including the fact that their knowledge, skills and values are likely to challenge and bring alternative perspectives to other established viewpoints.

A consideration of the context for practice also raises crucial questions about the ways in which social work practitioners can manage the difficulties and ambiguities of their practice environment. Typically, social work practitioners with older people continue to work in situations of great complexity, balancing conflicting needs and aspirations, working creatively with risk, seeking to preserve autonomy, and working with systems with diverse and contradictory opinions and views. The complexity inherent in the social work role is supported by the Green Paper (Department of Health, 2005, p. 27) on the future of social care for adults, which reinforced the need for social workers to use their particular knowledge and skills in complex practice situations:

> For too long social work has been perceived as a gatekeeper or rationer of services and has been accused, sometimes unfairly, of fostering dependence rather than independence. We want to create a different environment, which reinforces the core social work values of supporting individuals to take control of their own lives and to make the choices which matter to them.

This aspiration for the future of social care has been further reinforced in the shared statement 'Putting People First' (Department of Health, 2007) which suggests a need for social work practitioners to spend less time on assessment and more time on support, brokerage and advocacy. Here, the deployment of key social work skills such as exercising judgement and supporting people to make positive choices, may well come into direct conflict with the frameworks of a managerialist agenda such as performance monitoring, audit processes and standard setting. The extent to which these priorities detract from engaging with the dilemmas inherent in practice is critical.

### Management of limited resources

One crucial priority for local councils is to demonstrate effective management of finite resources. The 'Duty of Best Value' (Department of Health, 2002a) highlights the imperative to deliver 'quality' services to clear standards, by the most effective, economic and efficient means available. Eligibility criteria as a means of targeting services for those people deemed most 'in need', is a well established feature of social care. While assessment practices highlight the importance of holistic assessment of need, financial expediency may result in what Aronson (1999, p. 51) describes as 'thinning of need', whereby needs are reduced to those deemed to be essential for survival. The present arrangements organized under 'Fair Access to Care' (Department of Health, 2002b) are most likely to result in councils responding to eligible need within the 'critical' band. Consequently, it is not surprising that, under these constraints, service responses are most likely to identify only a relatively small group of older women and men as being in the most acute need. Indeed, the Commission for Social Care Inspection (2006a, 2008) confirms that, increasingly, only older people identified as being in 'critical' or 'substantial' need receive any services at all. As a result, growing numbers of older people are left with unmet needs, and family members have to fill the gaps.

Paradoxically, this means that evidence highlighting the value (and benefit) that older people place on low-intensity support services, both as contributions to quality of life and as a preventative intervention, remains substantially overlooked by social services (Tanner, 2001). This is despite the fact that, from a national policy perspective, the importance of proactive and preventative services for older people has been increasingly recognized (Department of Health, 2005). However, evidence suggests that local councils, pressed to manage limited resources, can only respond to those deemed to be the most 'in need', and struggle to respond to the prevention agenda in any significant way. Frontline social workers therefore find themselves trying to work at the interface between the aspirations of policies highlighting the importance of older people having access to services that promote their choice, control and independence, against policies that focus on managing limited resources and achieving externally set targets.

Furthermore, the effective management of restricted resources has led to the development of assessment models that typically focus on dysfunction and problems as a means of identifying priority 'need'. This approach to assessment can reinforce the tendency to consider older people who require support as being 'dependent', 'frail' or 'at risk', defined or implied as absolute states. We see this tendency as having two major consequences. First, developing a critical understanding of the use of such terms and the possible consequences is in danger of being sidelined. Second, a focus on such concepts as absolute states minimizes the potential to consider older people's strengths and resources, together with the strategies they use to manage change and transition. One implication of an 'activities of daily living' audit of 'deficiencies' is that it embraces and reinforces a loss model of ageing and contributes to constructions of older service users as 'problems', and essentially as passive recipients (Horowitz, 1999; Grenier, 2007). This may serve to reinforce the gap that has been reported between older people's narratives about what is important and what makes for lives of quality, and the differing concerns of professionals (Older People's Steering Group, 2004). Moreover, a failure to grasp the complexity of older people's lives severely limits the potential of social workers to develop interventions that are geared to individual needs and circumstances.

## The nature of interventions

Even in the face of assessment that may be driven by eligibility, there is no doubt that interventions providing practical support, personal care and physical assistance offer vital help to (eligible) older women and men experiencing chronic illness and disability. Nevertheless, comprehensive and creative services focusing on assisting people with complex needs to, for example, remain at home, have not historically been considered a high priority. It remains the case that older people with complex needs are often offered care home placements because services or a range of other housing options are simply not available (Vallely *et al.*, 2006).

An administrative model of care management, with its emphasis on care brokerage, also leaves little or no room for interventions aimed at reducing difficulties such as emotional stress. Such an omission begs the question as to how care managers are able effectively to assess, care plan and intervene in the lives of those older people troubled, for example, by personal and emotional difficulties, or who live in the context of complex family or social systems. Moreover, this omission contributes little to challenging a view that older people's needs are essentially homogeneous. As with any other part of the life course, some older people may use alcohol or substances to help them cope; may experience feelings of helplessness and depression; have long-standing and unresolved difficulties; have to come to terms with a diagnosis of a progressive condition; have difficult and unstable family relationships; live in abusive situations at times; and struggle to cope with loss. These difficulties may be life-course experiences, or have developed as a result of changing circumstances in older age. Nevertheless, whatever these difficulties, it is the older person who needs to be central to any considerations about what support is or is not needed. As such, their involvement and participation are crucial.

## Service user participation and involvement

The service user movement has grown inexorably in the wake of the NHS and Community Care Act (1990) and has made ever more visible the perspectives and lived experience of both service users and carers. There is increasing acceptance that people who are effectively on the receiving end of policies and practices are in fact experts in defining their own experience and needs (CSCI, 2006a). Government policy addressing social care for older people (see, for example, Department of Health, 2005, 2007), highlights the importance of developing services that focus on maintaining independence, encouraging choice and promoting autonomy, and is underpinned by a number of important key principles:

- People should have the right to control their own lives.
- Services should be seamless, easy to access and person-centred.
- Services should have a shared agenda towards maintaining independence.
- People with the greatest/most complex needs should receive priority to ensure well-being and protection.

- The risks of independence are shared with people and balanced openly against benefits.
- Barriers to services should be challenged.
- Work with diversity.
- Emphasis on those people who are most excluded benefiting from improvements in services.

Policy further highlights the importance of user participation in risk management and risk-taking, as well as the importance of transparent practice in discussing the potential risks alongside the benefits of, for example, independent community living for older adults.

One mechanism for enhancing independent living is through the introduction of direct payments. Direct payments have been seen as a way of improving choice and autonomy for all service users, with older people being identified as a particular group who would benefit from an increase in this area of provision (Clark *et al.*, 2004). Ensuring that there are opportunities for older people with complex needs to access direct payments requires confident and comprehensive social work skills when older people face situations of considerable complexity, change and uncertainty; and there is a need to cut through complex organizational procedures and provide confident and ongoing support. Crucially too, social workers have a moral obligation to ensure that direct payments, when offered, do in fact provide a *better* opportunity for older people to meet their needs in creative ways and that this is not subverted as a means of further reduction of resources in the guise of choice and independence.

These developments in service user participation and involvement also chime with wider government agendas around social inclusion and exclusion, developing community cohesion, and the abilities of people (older people included) to take more control of their lives and exercise more choice (Department of Work and Pensions, 2005; CSIP, 2006). Here, local councils are envisaged as playing a crucial role in both challenging social exclusion and participating in the development of preventative services for older people. These strategies and developments in turn embrace key messages from research with older people and carers, which has highlighted the importance of preserving autonomy, enjoying a life of quality and continuing to be involved in one's own life, social and family networks and the wider community (Tanner, 2001; Gorman and Postle, 2003; Patmore and McNulty, 2005). Nevertheless, it is evident that there has not always been an easy or simple relationship between research and practice, nor between what we might distinguish as social work research and gerontological research. It is therefore to 'the social work–gerontology research gap' that we now turn our attention.

# The social work–gerontology research gap

In reviewing the recent history of social work with older people, it is evident that a gerontological approach – and in particular a critical gerontological approach – has been significant in its absence from both practice and education (Quinn, 1999; Chambers, 2004). We would argue that the two worlds of social work and gerontology have largely developed separately, with little commonality and cross-over between disciplines. Research agendas have mirrored this, with the two disciplines developing in very different directions, and the wider gerontological research perspective being absent from the narrow concentration on health and social care issues evident in social work research on older people (Phillips, 2000). We would further argue that (critical) gerontological research has much to offer social work and social workers with older people yet, until recently, it has had only a marginal influence on the social work profession. Chapter 2 concentrates in more detail on the development of what has come to be known as critical gerontology, so here we briefly review the historically divergent pathways followed by social work research and gerontology since the Second World War.

Social work research in most areas of practice, but in particular in respect of older people, took a considerable time to become established in the post-war period. In the early years of the profession, generic social workers carried mixed caseloads, and direct social work with older people was rare. Where it did exist, it tended to be allocated to unqualified workers and was perceived by qualified staff as being low-status work (Neill, 1976). One consequence of this perception was that (social) gerontological research at the time effectively mirrored – but did not challenge – what was happening in practice arenas: where community care services were sparse and admission to residential care was seen as being the only option for older people who showed any sign that they might struggle to cope at home (Means and Smith, 1998).

By the early 1970s, evaluative research that sought to examine the effectiveness of social work practice was gaining impetus (for example, Mayer and Timms, 1970). However, these so-called 'client opinion' research studies of social work interventions found, for example, that users lacked an understanding of the assessment process, and were unclear when assessment was completed and what its conclusions were. There was also a lack of fit between user perspectives and social work perspectives about the nature of a problem or difficulty, and differences of opinion between user and social worker as to the most appropriate means of intervening (Mayer and

Timms, 1976). Critically, then, the results of such research tended to highlight a paucity of demonstrable outcomes linked to social work interventions (Mullen and Dumpson, 1972; Fischer, 1973).

Despite this inauspicious start, it is important to note that evaluative research studies have since demonstrated increasingly positive results from social work interventions (MacDonald and Sheldon, 1992). In addition, other social work research that appeared in the 1980s showed that older people may have emotional needs, and experience trauma and distress, that would indeed benefit from appropriate intervention (Rowlings, 1981; Marshall, 1983). However, as the principles of the market-place developed in social care through the 1980s, fundamental changes in social work practice occurred, and social work with older people got swept up in the drive towards care management. Social work research in such a climate was directed increasingly towards examining the effectiveness and efficiency of the new community care arrangements and the role of care management as the practice arm of the reforms. The focus inevitably moved away from the *needs* of older people and concentrated instead on evaluating the effectiveness (and costs) of services in health and social care (Challis and Davies, 1986), with an associated emphasis on care markets, resources, needs and outcomes in the production of welfare.

In contrast to the evaluative and service focus evident in much social work research, social gerontological research from the 1980s onwards began to adopt a more eclectic mix of methodological approaches, and to draw on a wide variety of disciplines and theoretical perspectives to explore a range of pertinent issues. For example, those working within a political economy perspective (see Chapter 2) turned their attention increasingly towards a critique of public policies and health and social services provisions, and looked instead at how the welfare system was effectively transforming ageing into a dependent status (Townsend 1981). Another crucial strand of research began to highlight the strengths and resources people bring to old age, and to move away from pathologizing older people (Reinharz, 1986; Russell, 1987; Minkler and Fadem, 2002). Drawing on both feminist and humanist foundations, there was also a growing recognition and acceptance of the importance of qualitative and biographical methods in making visible the lived experience of older people (Butler, 1963; Gearing and Dant, 1990): a recognition that has continued up to the present day (Bornat, 2000; R. E. Ray, 2007).

Over the years, these research strands have increasingly come together to inform and contribute to social work/health care research with older people. This offers a forceful critique of the limitations of a welfare agenda characterized by the principles of the market-place and effective management (see, for example, Postle, 2002) and has been supported widely by the voice of older people (Older People's Steering Group, 2004). However, it is our contention that a clear opportunity was lost in the 1980s to underpin and inform social work practice with older people with the rapidly developing, and ever more critical, gerontological research base. Even where research was, for example, demonstrating the importance of social work interventions with older people, the results of that research still seemingly failed to reach those frontline workers and educationalists who were best placed to make a difference. As Sheldon and Chilvers (2000, p. 3) comment, social workers 'inhabiting a workplace culture favouring action over reflection, and much pre-occupied with the new commercial principles which accompanied the Community Care reforms, appear rarely to have heard of these more promising findings'. In the context of this book, it is precisely this gap between research and practice – and between research, practice and education – that we are seeking to address as we mount the case for critical gerontological social work.

## Social work training, education and continuing professional development

The final and related feature of social work developments to draw attention to here has been the consistently low level of interest in social work practice with older people, and the underlying educational and training needs this raises. In recent years, American research has explored comprehensively what does and does not attract students to social work with older people. Negative views of ageing (Anderson and Wiscott, 2004); a lack of appropriate coverage in social work curricula leading to lack of competence in social work with older people (Scharlach et al., 2000); and perceptions that the curriculum is too full to embrace any gerontological additions (Olson, 2002); have all been implicated. Moreover, research has also shown that negative attitudes held by students towards older people have been substantially unaffected by social work training, especially when that training failed to work specifically with students on the issue of age-based discriminatory attitudes and stereotypes (Rosen et al., 2002).

A similar picture emerges in the UK context. Here, there is a danger that social work training courses will focus on 'community care' rather than on older adults per se, with the added danger that the specific knowledge, skills and values that social work with older people requires, will be substantially overlooked. Quinn (1999) reported that social work students tend to perceive old age as desolation, underpinned by a fear that it constitutes a distressing vision of one's future self. However, we argue that a failure to address the whole life course adequately in social work education not only disadvantages practitioners who wish to specialize in gerontological practice, but also ultimately risks impoverishing the practice ability of *all* social work students, regardless of their area of practice. Consider, as illustration, the research summarized in Box 1.1. This focuses on the importance of grandparents in the provision of child care, support and assistance. It gives one example as to why all social work practitioners, regardless of their area of practice, should have an understanding of a life-course perspective, including ageing.

There is a need to ensure that gerontological knowledge and the theoretical basis of social work with older people has equal value to that of other service-user groups in social work education

---

### Box 1.1 Research into practice: grandparents caring for children

It is estimated that, each week, around a quarter of families with children under 15 use grandparents to provide child care (Age Concern England, 2004). Changing family structures mean that growing numbers of children are being brought up outside traditional ideas of the nuclear family (Age Concern England, 2004; Farmer and Meyers, 2005).

In a study of four local authorities, the care arrangements for 270 looked after children were examined (Farmer and Meyers, 2005); 45 per cent of kin carers were grandparents. The sample of kin carers included 31 per cent with an identified disability or chronic illness, and 75 per cent were experiencing financial hardship, and a number of specific needs relating to older kin carers were identified:

> older relative carers could feel socially dislocated as they did not fit with parents of the child's age or with their own friends who no longer looked after dependent children. Many found looking after children tiring when they were older, had less energy and had limited financial resources. Some too had other caring responsibilities for their own elderly parents or sick partner.
> (Farmer and Meyers, 2005, p. 4)

(Chambers and Ray, 2006). This aspiration must apply not only to students of social work but also to practitioners working in the field of social work, care management and health care with older people.

Moreover, we noted earlier that in addition to the gap between social work research and social gerontology research, there is also a more general research–practice gap. This gap is well documented in social work, and various authors (for example, Neysmith and MacAdam, 1999; Needham, 2000; Sheldon and Chilvers, 2000; Trinder and Reynolds, 2000) have identified reasons for its existence, including:

- Research often being presented in inaccessible ways and not user/practitioner friendly.
- Lack of commitment and strategies to develop research-mindedness and dissemination of key research in social work/social care agencies.
- Lack of fit between research and practice concerns.
- Insufficient time and resources to enable practitioners to assimilate key research findings.
- Practitioners do not have the skills to evaluate the quality of research.
- Practitioners feel threatened by the potential for research to change established and preferred patterns of practice.
- Disagreements and debates about what should constitute evidence-based practice.
- From the perspective of social work with older people, a sparse and poorly developed pool of research from which to draw.

More recently, there have been concerted efforts to draw attention to both the importance of social-work-led research and the dissemination of research relevant to social work practice, via, for example, the Social Care Institute for Excellence (SCIE) and Making Research Count (MRC). At the time of writing, the newly launched post-qualifying (PQ) award provides a framework for evidencing practice competence in 'adult social work', which includes older people but makes no specific reference to gerontological knowledge. Nor does it refer to the specialist skills and knowledge that might inform social work practice with older people. Established practitioners working with older people and engaged on a PQ award must, in our view, have appropriate access to gerontological research and knowledge, as well as appropriate support to consider its application to practice.

## Conclusion

On the face of it, the discussions in this chapter could be seen as painting a rather bleak picture of social work with older people. However, we would argue that what it in fact shows is that there is an urgent need to rethink how we support some of the most vulnerable people in society, and how students and practitioners can best be trained and supported to carry out this vital work. As we have seen, the reality for today's social workers is that they have to work within an organizational environment geared towards a managerialist framework. At the same time, their practice can and should be grounded in a commitment to working with older people in ways that not only enhance their ability to cope with change, but also create opportunities for older people to take an active role in determining their own support needs, how these may be met, and what counts as a life 'worth living' (Older People's Steering Group, 2004). Older age is a multi-dimensional experience with multiple explanations, so that recognizing the complexity of social work with older people is essential.

Rethinking social work with older people has to address not only practice issues, but also to ensure that it is underpinned by attention to education and training, and to the knowledge that social work and social workers can derive from research and theory. Social workers have a vitally important role to play in practice with older people, and in responding to what older people value in social work relationships.

## stop and think

- To what extent (as a student social worker or as a qualified practitioner) are you able to learn about key research about older people?
- What easily available resources could you access to learn more about research which focuses on ageing and older people?
- What do you think are the benefits and potential obstacles to promoting the active involvement of older people in developing appropriate services and resources?

taking it further

- Department of Health (2007) *Putting People First: A Shared Vision and Commitment to the Transformation of Adult Social Care;* available at www.dh.gov.uk.
- Older People's Steering Group (2004) *Older People Shaping Policy and Practice*, York, Joseph Rowntree Foundation; available at www.jrf.org.uk.
- Postle, K. (2002) '"Working between the Idea and the Reality": Ambiguities and Tensions in Care Managers' Work', *British Journal of Social Work*, 32, pp. 335–51.
- Tanner, D. (2005) 'Promoting the Well-being of Older People: Messages for Social Workers', *Practice*, 17(3), pp. 191–205.

# 2 Developing critical gerontological social work

**main points**

■ There is a need for social workers who work with older people to preserve the knowledge, skills and values that have traditionally been valued by the older people who are users of services.

■ A gerontological knowledge base will strengthen the knowledge and practice base of social work practitioners.

■ There is a clear agenda for the development of future practice in social work with older people.

■ There is an urgent need to articulate what social workers offer to older people, and the added value they can contribute to integrated or multi-disciplinary teams.

## Introduction

Having explored some of the profound changes to social work that followed in the wake of the NHS and Community Care Act 1990, this chapter moves on to consider the steps that need to be taken to develop an explicitly critical approach to social work with older people. Chapter 1 argued that while a crucial role for social work with older people persists, other forces and pressures within and beyond the profession have tended to erode professional skills and autonomy, and to marginalize older people. At the same time, social work theory and research on, about and with older people, has struggled to forge its own identity. The gap between what has been happening in social work research and in gerontological research has widened. This, we contend, has had detrimental effects not only on education and training, but also on practice and research.

One solution to these complex dilemmas lies in building on the features we value about good social work with older people, but developing a more robust and critical approach to them. It is therefore the task of this chapter to spell out what we mean by critical gerontological social work, and articulate what such an approach might look like. To do this, we begin by revisiting the values, skills and knowledge base underlying good social work practice with older people. Since many social workers will be unfamiliar with gerontology as a discipline, we then explore what critical gerontology is, and how it has developed. Drawing the two areas together, the chapter concludes by arguing that we need to make critical gerontology central to social work with older people. To do so, we identify a framework for gerontological social work. This framework provides the basis for exploring, in the remainder of the book, some of the crucial areas that such an approach urgently needs to address.

## Social work with older people: values, skills and knowledge

Regardless of their area of practice, social workers are likely to encounter older people, and there is no doubt that interventions that provide practical support, personal care and physical assistance offer vital help to older people experiencing long-term illness and disability. However, what is it precisely that underpins good social work practice with vulnerable older people? By 'social work practice' we mean all the elements that go to make up good social work: beginning with initial training and education, and including day-to-day practice in the field; continuing professional development; awareness of the wider policy and practice context; and the incorporation of relevant theory and research. The values, skills and knowledge that social workers with older people need, draw on all these elements.

Traditionally, critical and anti-oppressive practice with older people involves:
- *A value base* that recognizes the value and ethical conflicts inherent in enabling older people to preserve autonomy and agency against the reality of, for example, declining cognitive powers, or family members who seek to protect the older person by shielding them from risk (see, for example, Stevenson, 1989; Phillips *et al.*, 2006).
- *Skills* such as supporting people to take control of their lives; genuine engagement with older people and their carers as service users; interprofessional working; the ability to challenge established structures and procedures; advocacy; professional assessment skills; management of the complexities and ambiguities

of the practice environment; working creatively with risk; and management of resources (see Lymbery, 2005).

■ *Knowledge* derived from research (that is, evidence-based practice), together with knowledge from policy, practice and experience.

Traditionally, social work practice is underpinned by *a value base* expressed as a code of practice. The registering bodies for Scotland (Scottish Social Services Council – SSSC), Wales (Care Council for Wales – CCW), England (General Social Care Council – GSCC) and Northern Ireland (Northern Ireland Social Care Council – NISCC) have a code of practice for social care workers contained in a series of statements defining what social workers (and social care workers) *must* do (see, for example, General Social Care Council, 2004, p. 2). Perhaps surprisingly, traditionally accepted values such as social justice are not included in these statements. The British Association of Social Work (BASW) also identifies five basic values underpinning social work: human dignity and worth; social justice; service to humanity; integrity; and competence (BASW, 2002), as well as drawing attention to guidance on principles of practice and issues of ethical conduct (Beckett and Maynard, 2005). However, the extent to which codes of practice, value statements or ethical position statements can really assist social workers in the complexity of their daily practice is open to question. Social workers, for example, are required regularly to take into account the interests, expectations and obligations of people other than service users (Dalrymple and Burke, 2006).

That said, Dalrymple and Burke (2006, p. 39) argue that codes should be seen more appropriately as a framework for practice, to be used in conjunction with legislation, policy and procedures and, crucially, critical reflection, discussion and supervision, to explore the ethical dilemmas faced in practice. From the perspective of social work with older people, a critical perspective would assume a commitment to recognizing both the complexities of day-to-day practice with older women and men, and the need to consider value positions from a gerontological perspective. For example, the potential for ageism to influence the ways in which older people who use services are treated, is fundamentally important to practice. Moreover, age-based discrimination may be compounded by other forms of oppression such as sexism, racism or disablism experienced through the life course. This awareness could be manifested in practice by, for example, using research evidence to resist and challenge policy and practice which reinforces oppressions, or which is underpinned by inappropriate assumptions and beliefs about older people (Townsend, 2007). Such an understanding can assist practitioners to challenge the potential to individualize needs when, in reality, life-long structural inequalities have contributed to the circumstances faced by an older person.

Critical practice also necessitates practitioners having a sound *knowledge base* of the theories, policies and practices relevant to their practice context (Brechin, 2000). Historically, social work with older people may have been justifiably accused of lacking in well-established theoretical perspectives. It has also been the case that theories that have informed social work practice have tended to focus more on dysfunction and reinforcing perceptions of older people as dependent. As already noted in Chapter 1, there remains a tendency to construct social work with older people around the 'problem' of ageing. In order to avoid replicating experiences of oppression and discrimination grounded in assumptions about inevitable dependency, critical practice seeks to avoid operating in a framework dominated by pre-prescribed and proceduralized tasks.

Moreover, older service users are well placed to reflect on the experience of social work practice, and to ask questions about practices that may have a fundamental influence on their lives (Beresford, 2007a). Developments in listening to the opinions of older people, as a vital component in the growing evidence base for social care, exemplify such positive practice (Allan, 2001). However, the silence of some older people who are particularly vulnerable to life course inequalities becoming more acute in older age remains a crucial issue (Scharf *et al.*, 2005). Consequently, given some of the limitations of traditional social work with older people, we would argue the need for it to draw more extensively than it has to date on the insights from social gerontology in general, and from critical gerontology in particular. It is to these perspectives that we now turn.

## Critical gerontology

As with many labels, critical gerontology, like critical social work, is a contested term, and there is as yet no universal agreement on its definition. One definition that we suggest captures the essence of this approach comes from the work of Ruth Ray (1996, p. 675), who defines critical gerontology as: 'a critique of the social influences, philosophical foundations and empirical methodologies on which gerontology as a field has been historically constructed'. This alerts us to the importance of understanding the kinds of social, economic and political forces that promote critical perspectives (in whatever field), as well as the values that might underlie such approaches. It also sensitizes us to consider what might be the most appropriate ways of engaging with, and researching, the lives and needs of older people. In addition, back in the late 1980s, Phillipson and Walker (1987, p. 12) defined critical gerontology as 'a more value-committed approach to social gerontology – a commitment not just to understand the social construction of ageing but to change it'. This emphasis on 'change' and, indeed on action, is one with which social work practitioners, as well as (some) researchers, might well identify.

However, these apparently simple conceptions belie the complexity of critical gerontology's origins and its implicit value base. Critical gerontology, like critical social work, has grown out of the broader critical social science movement and builds on a variety of intellectual traditions and foundations (Achenbaum, 1995; Estes *et al.*, 2003). A critical perspective suggests that we are often unaware of just how much society, and societal structures, oppress us as individuals. With respect to older people, critical gerontology argues that they have long been marginalized and ignored; that we need to look afresh at our beliefs about old age, old people and the ways in which we as individuals, and society in general, respond to them; and that the traditional theories and methods we have used to study ageing and old age might need to alter (Estes *et al.*, 2003; Baars *et al.*, 2006; Holstein and Minkler, 2007). A critical gerontological perspective seeks to explain how oppression and injustice occur, and how they affect older people; it attempts to make the voices of oppressed and very diverse groups heard (for example, older women, black older people, people with dementia and so on); and it tackles problems and issues that have largely been ignored by mainstream social gerontological work (Baars, 1991).

## *The origins of critical gerontology*

Gerontology itself has only been recognized as a field of study for a little over a century, the term first being used in 1903 by the Russian-born biologist Elie Metchnikoff (Achenbaum and Levin, 1989). However, it was not until the 1940s that the first professional and academic society, the Gerontological Society of America, was founded. This society brought together researchers, teachers and practitioners who worked with, or studied, older people and old age. These early developments during the first half of the twentieth century also spawned a whole range of what Achenbaum and Levin (1989) have called 'gerontology's specialties', including applied gerontology, experimental gerontology and social gerontology. Critical gerontology followed these developments and emerged in 1988, largely as a response to concerns about mainstream social gerontology's failure to challenge adequately the dominant decline and loss paradigm (Holstein and Minkler, 2007).

Paradoxically, then, gerontology is still a relatively new and developing field, and critical gerontology, as defined above, is an even more recent development. This means that it is sometimes difficult to reach a consensus on what we may or may not consider comes within the scope of gerontology or critical gerontology. More accurately, perhaps, critical gerontology can be viewed as a set of perspectives that draw attention to the need to look at issues that go above and beyond conventional concerns and analyses (Baars, 1991; Achenbaum, 1997).

## The development of critical gerontology

For much of the twentieth century, (social) gerontological research was couched within a primarily quantitative tradition with an emphasis on how older people should adjust to the challenges (and problems) associated with ageing (Estes *et al.*, 2003). Driven by demographic imperatives and the concerns associated with a developing welfare state, a primary aim of much early social gerontological research in the UK was to highlight and address the 'problem' of 'the elderly' and the 'burdens' posed by ever-increasing numbers of older people. Against a background of a 'secure welfare contract' between the generations (Means and Smith, 1998) and an expectation that the state would be the dominant provider of welfare, research began to document the poor living conditions and maltreatment of older people (Townsend, 1962, 2007) and particular concerns were raised about those living in special circumstances such as residential or psychiatric care. At this time too, the first large-scale surveys of the needs and circumstances of older people living in the wider community were beginning to highlight the extent to which people were being cared for outside institutional settings (Harris, 1968).

However, it was not until the 1970s that those working from within a political economy perspective – and following the Marxist tradition – began to raise crucial questions about how growing old was being experienced, and to show how our welfare system was effectively transforming ageing into a dependent status (Townsend, 2006). Political economists saw long-term care and community care as systems that reflected and bolstered the power inequities between experts such as social workers and lay people (Estes *et al.*, 2003). They further argued that the systems and structures set up by society, including professions such as social work, were essentially about controlling and managing people rather than providing them – in this case, older people – with opportunities for self-determination, rehabilitation and participation in everyday social life. Drawing on an alternative theory that emphasized 'structured dependency', the political economy perspective also stressed the ways in which public policies, and health and social services, were reinforcing this control and management, and deepening the dependency of older people (Townsend,

2007). One consequence of this growing critique (on both sides of the Atlantic) was that (some) gerontological research began to diverge considerably from the evaluative and service focus that, as we noted in Chapter 1, was evident in traditional social work research.

Critical gerontology, then, is rooted first and foremost within the political economy perspective. However, the inherent narrowness of this approach, with its overriding emphasis on the relationship between ageing and economic life, and on class inequalities, was challenged in the 1980s and 1990s by those working from within feminist and humanist perspectives. Feminist perspectives helped us to acknowledge the profound effects of life-long gender inequalities on the experience of later life (Arber and Ginn, 1991, 1995) and also led to a greater examination of diversity and difference encompassing racial and ethnic dimensions, disability and sexuality, and the power relationships within and between various groups. Additionally, the humanist perspective, which to date has developed far more in the United States than in Britain, has provided 'an approach to ageing which puts a human face – and a human body and spirit – on ageing and growing old' and encouraged us to explore questions such as 'what makes for a good life in old age?' and 'how can society support different visions of old age?' (Minkler, 1996, p. 470). Critical geron-tology therefore seeks to raise vital questions, both about what we as a society *do* to older people, and about the *meanings* we attach to growing older and to old age itself.

Research from within a critical gerontology perspective has there-fore diverged from more traditional social work research on older people in a number of crucial ways. Instead of the predominant eval-uative and service focus we noted in the previous chapter, critical gerontology has provided us with research that has:

- Adopted a mix of methodological approaches and drawn on a wide variety of disciplines and theoretical perspectives to explore a range of issues pertinent to the experience of later life (Holstein and Minkler, 2007).
- Mounted a sustained critique of public policies and health and social services provisions affecting the lives of older people (Means and Smith, 1998; Townsend, 2007).
- Made the study of ageism, age discrimination and questions of intergenerational justice central to its research concerns (Bytheway *et al.*, 2007).
- Drawn attention to the significance of diversity and difference in later life (Estes *et al.*, 2003).
- Highlighted the strengths and resources people bring to old age, and moved away from pathologizing older people (Minkler and Fadem, 2002).

- Drawn attention to the search for meaning in old age and to what makes for a life of quality (Cole and Sierpena, 2006).
- Recognized and accepted the importance of qualitative and biographical methods in making visible the lived experience of older people (Bornat, 2000).
- Helped place older people at the centre of gerontological research and practice (R. E. Ray, 2007).

However, this is not to suggest that critical gerontology in and of itself provides all the answers to the challenges we face as social work practitioners and gerontological researchers. Consequently, before considering a framework for undertaking critical gerontological social work, we highlight some of the challenges that critical gerontology itself now faces.

## Challenges for critical gerontology

Despite the progress made in critical gerontology since the 1970s, one trenchant critique has been that its two pathways – one drawn from the humanities and the other from the political economy/critical social science perspective – have tended to remain distinct and have operated in different domains (Ovrebo and Minkler, 1993; Holstein and Minkler, 2007). Recent critiques suggest that the failure to bring the two together means that we have been unable to get to grips adequately with what a 'real' or 'proper' critical gerontology should entail: what it should concern itself with theoretically and conceptually; what the experience of ageing is really like in the twenty-first century, and what it might become; and what research strategies, approaches and tools are most appropriate to illuminate simultaneously both the structural and individual aspects of ageing (Estes *et al.*, 2003; Holstein and Minkler, 2007). Indeed, American commentators Holstein and Minkler (2007, p. 19) have put the case for what they term 'a richer critical gerontology', which

> Calls for a deeper understanding of how perception, standpoint and value commitments affect all our work ... [and] encouraging what we are calling methodological bricolage, which requires crossing disciplinary and methodological boundaries so that ... the different pathways in critical gerontology can together enlarge understanding and systematically challenge the status quo.

Consequently, the first and most obvious set of challenges for critical gerontology is to look at how these two pathways can be brought together more effectively. In other words, how can what might on the face of it seem to be an individualistic approach stressing personal growth, be seen as compatible with collective work tackling deeply embedded social, economic and structural inequalities? As Estes *et al.* (2003, p. 147) argue:

> Both require each other for a comprehensive understanding of contemporary ageing to take place. Structural approaches, without the humanistic element, offer limited insight into the humanity of the situations described. Without an understanding of social structure, however, an overly humanistic approach to ageing is isolated from context and history.

In the 1990s, Meredith Minkler (1996) suggested that one means of doing this might be to organize work in critical gerontology around a unifying concept such as 'empowerment' – a concept with which radical social work practice has also been associated. Despite empowerment being a much used and much abused term, Minkler (1996) and others (for example, Bernard, 2000) argue that it is useful precisely because it emphasizes notions of interdependence and is about acknowledging the ways in which we relate to, and can support, each other, as opposed to stressing independence or individual good above everything else. It impels us all to recognize that we live our lives in a social and political context, and that in order to fully understand both the commonalities and the disparities that exist, we need to look at the multiple ways in which people in general, and older people in particular, are disadvantaged and marginalized. If we can understand something of how environments and policies *disempower* people, we should be able to think more creatively (as researchers, educators and practitioners) about how we go about establishing situations in which older people can regain power and control over their lives. It means too that we can look at ways in which the capacity for empowerment and growth in old age can be facilitated and supported. This perhaps runs counter to how policy-makers might use the rhetoric of empowerment, where it is often seen as making individuals entirely responsible for their own actions, and a way of legitimizing cutbacks to communities and individuals.

More recently still, certain commentators have begun to argue for an approach to critical gerontological research and action that also lays greater emphasis on a 'human rights' perspective (for example, Feldman, 2002; Townsend, 2007). Such a perspective is premised on the unacceptability of discrimination against older people and the belief that all human beings, of whatever age and in whatever circumstances, have certain rights to things such as a reasonable standard of living. However, if bringing the two pathways in critical gerontology more closely together around a human rights perspective appears complex and difficult, then this is precisely because it *is* and because, as Townsend (2007, p. 32) cogently explains:

> Rights are 'human' and not only civil or political. Rights are multiple and inter-dependent. Corrective anti-discriminatory measures have to be directed not at the separate existence of racial, religious, gender, disability or ageist discrimination but in a comprehensive, connected and proportionate manner against all forms of discrimination.

He also urges us to attend to the methodologies we use to uncover, measure and understand the impacts of human rights violations on people: 'not those only that end life, or involve extreme abuse ... but those that represent affronts to human dignity and identity' (Townsend, 2007, p. 32).

Thus a second set of challenges for critical gerontology is related to *how* we conduct research. Townsend (2007) challenges us to reject – or at least look at and question – the continuing use of traditional, familiar and single indicators in favour of developing multiple indices that would expose more reliably and unambiguously violations of rights in later life (Walker, 2005). Alongside this, a critical gerontology, organized along human rights lines and with empowerment as a central organizing concept, allows us to engage in more detailed examinations of how ordinary, everyday people live out their lives. As we have noted elsewhere (Bernard *et al.*, 2000), a key tool in this endeavour is the increasing use of biographical and narrative approaches in extending our knowledge and understanding about individual and shared aspects of ageing (Bornat, 2000; R. E. Ray, 2007).

Embracing both human rights and empowerment in research terms also means that, just as we might espouse the centrality of older people's views in terms of social work practice, so must we seriously consider the involvement of older people in the entire research process: from deciding the research questions to taking part in the different stages of the fieldwork, and to analysis, writing up and dissemination (M. Ray, 2007). Allied to this is the need we have already noted, to be critically reflective and self-reflexive in both research *and* practice: what Chamberlayne and her colleagues (2000) have argued as the importance of understanding something of our own histories and how we have come to be what we are, if we are to fully understand those with whom we work.

Moreover, biographical, participatory and reflexive research practices are only some of the methodological elements needed to bring together the two pathways in critical gerontology. Beyond this, it is important not to dismiss the insights we might obtain from other kinds of research: what Holstein and Minkler (2007, p. 22) have argued as the necessity for 'methodological bricolage':

> Methodological bricolage means not ruling out knowledge that is gained from personal narratives, fiction, poetry, film, qualitative investigations, philosophical inquiries, participatory action research and any other method of inquiry we may discover that yields insights into fundamental questions about how, and why, we experience old age in very particular ways.

This call for methodological bricolage, in turn links closely with a third set of challenges that have to do with articulating our value base and how we work with older people in professional capacities. And this links directly back to the values, skills and knowledge needed for good social work with older people, providing a direct bridge to the framework for critical gerontological social work outlined below. Thus a critical gerontology perspective with human rights, empowerment and methodological bricolage at its centre means that instead of 'doing to' older people in a detached and value-free way, we need to look at ways of 'working with' them in effective partnerships: in research, education and practice contexts. This is vital not least because, unpalatable though it may be, ageism and discrimination is alive and well amongst those who care for older people in professional capacities (Stevenson, 1989; Help the Aged, 2007; Milne *et al.*, 2007). Indeed, professionals who work with older people often hold some of the most negative and ageist attitudes of all – compounded, in many instances, by this being inflicted on older women by other women (Bernard, 1998). It is therefore important not only to draw attention to the evidence for these attitudes and practices, but also to stress the crucial role that reflexivity plays in a critical gerontological perspective. As ageing women (and men), we argue that it is necessary to explore and question our own values, assumptions and motivations – not to be self-indulgent but to enable us to clarify our understandings about what we do and how we do it, in order to become better practitioners, educators and researchers.

## A framework for critical gerontological social work

By building on the things we value about good social work with older people, and drawing this together with critical gerontology, we can now begin to articulate what a more robust and critical gerontological social work approach might look like. The current requirements for social work training (Department of Health, 2002c) make clear that *all* students should gain an understanding of the life course, and of intergenerational and systemic perspectives. Requirements also stipulate that service users should be involved in the design, development, delivery and assessment of social work degrees. Clearly, then, there are opportunities for all levels and aspects of professional training, education and practice to address and be underpinned by the kinds of anti-oppressive, critical and gerontologically informed principles and evidence we have been discussing. Critical gerontological social work therefore needs to be both about what we do (in terms of content) and how we do it (both academically, and as professionals and practitioners). In subsequent chapters we focus on crucial areas of substantive concern, including risk and frailty, dementia, end-of-life issues and informal care. However, underlying these key areas, a framework for critical gerontological social work must first revisit the values, skills and knowledge necessary for working with older people in the twenty-first century. And these, in turn, have implications for practice, for research, and for education and training.

## *Underpinning values*

As has already been noted, leading proponents of the critical gerontology field have long argued for a more value-committed approach, and recognition that researchers, academics and practitioners cannot, and should not, stay aloof from involvement in social change (Phillipson and Walker, 1987; Estes *et al.*, 2003). These values have been articulated in our earlier writings (Bernard and Phillips, 1998, 2000; Bernard *et al.*, 2000; Bernard, 2001) but we reiterate them here so that readers are at least aware of – even though they might disagree with – our particular standpoint.

For us, the critical gerontological social work we engage in, whether it is from an educational, practice or research perspective has necessarily to be informed by commitments to:

- Social justice and intergenerational understanding.
- Countering stereotypes and combating myths and discrimination.
- Empowerment, citizenship and human rights.
- Pluralist and preventive views of ageing.
- Understanding oppression: its multiplicity and diversity (racial and ethnic, gender, disability, age and sexuality).
- Making experience visible through the words of older people themselves.
- Developing a critically reflective, and self-reflexive approach to ageing – both our own and that of those around us.
- Negotiating understandings and recognizing the existence of multiple perspectives.

- Working creatively with older people at the interface between preserving autonomy and independence in the face of declining physical and cognitive powers.
- Actively participating in making known policies, legislation and practices that are oppressive or which reinforce or maintain stereotypes, myths and discrimination relating to older people.

Clearly, articulating one's value base is a political act, since it locates social workers in a particular relationship to what and whom are being researched or worked with. In our view, this is a vital first step along the road to developing critical gerontological social work. It needs to be articulated, recognized and affirmed because, as Holstein and Minkler (2007, p. 19) argue, we all view the world and undertake our research, practice and educative work 'with a view from somewhere'.

## Skills for critical gerontological social work

Rather than delineating a shopping list of skills, it is our contention that critical gerontological social work needs to develop, preserve and build on the kinds of skills social workers already use to facilitate positive and beneficial outcomes for older people. We know from the research evidence that the skills that are vital for good social work with older people include being able to:
- Form and develop positive and effective relationships between a social worker and an older person.
- Challenge a focus on medical perspectives at the expense of other aspects of an older person's life.
- Provide information to older people to enable them to make choices and decisions.
- Work creatively with ethical dilemmas such as risk against rights and conflicting agendas between an older person and their carer.
- Remain committed to the well-being of older people in the face of very considerable change and uncertainty.
- Recognize diversity, and challenge the tendency to treat older men and women as a homogenous group.

These skills, underpinned by a gerontological knowledge base, can help to ensure, for example, that social work assessments and interventions are geared towards the individual person's needs, rather than merely offering 'off the shelf' solutions. This in turn is bound up with recognizing that older people do not simply become passive recipients of care and support services, but that they seek actively to manage the challenges that might be associated with increasing impairment. Older people often utilize strategies, strengths and resources that have served them well throughout their life course, and ensuring that these resources and strengths are considered alongside needs and difficulties creates the possibility for a different narrative about older people who use services. In order to create a different narrative, gerontological social workers must also have a sound understanding of terms that practitioners often use uncritically, such as frailty (Grenier, 2007); risk (Kemshall, 2002); and dependency (Johnson, 1979, 1990). These issues are returned to in detail in subsequent chapters, but lead us here into a consideration of the knowledge and skills that underpin practice. As an illustration, the example in Box 2.1 highlights ways in which social work practitioners can integrate an understanding of critical issues in social work with older people with achieving a user-centred approach to assessment practice.

---

## Box 2.1 Research into practice: assessment skills

Richards (2000) undertook ethnographic research that explored the ways in which social workers approached assessment with older people. Richards identified a number of key social work skills that were critical in facilitating older people to explore and clarify their situations, talk about their subjective experience, and be aware of the range of options potentially available to them. Crucially, she noted that skilful assessors used different skills, depending upon the context of the older person and the degree to which the older person knew what he or she wanted to gain from the process.

Additionally, Richards highlighted the importance of social workers being able to conceptualize and maintain a distinction between user-centred and agency-centred elements of assessment. Attention to narrative enabled practitioners to work positively with older people to identify needs accurately and reduce the power imbalance as the social worker strove to engage with the older person's perspective. Richards (2000) highlighted that:

 Working with elders in a way that recognizes the individuality and complexity of their needs, that deals appropriately with conflicts of interest between elders and their carers, that achieves an essential clarity of task and fulfils agency objectives is skilled social work indeed. (p. 48)

---

### Knowledge base

The final area to revisit in setting out a framework for critical gerontological social work is to look at its knowledge base and at the gerontological research and scholarship that underpins this approach. One example will serve here to illustrate what we mean by this. A recent study by the Older People's Steering Group (2004) highlighted that older people value practitioners who are able to:

■ Widen their approach from an assumption of the deficit model of assessment, and for intervention outcomes to move beyond the dysfunction perspective.
■ Work in partnership with an older person as a means of changing the balance of power.
■ Recognize and build-in the strengths and resources of an older person.
■ Value what older people value (and have proper regard for the subjective experiences of older people).
■ Facilitate active participation by older people.

These findings about what older men and women value in social work practitioners clearly resonate strongly with the themes coming from within critical gerontology. In turn, they suggest to us that practitioners might be able to strengthen their practice in a number of ways if they were to become more aware of, and could use the insights from, critical gerontology. If older people do indeed value practitioners who adopt these empowering ways of working, then these ways of working can be bolstered and reinforced by attention to the range of theories and perspectives which now provide a coherent critique of the multiple experiences of, and approaches to, ageing and old age. This body of evidence would assist practitioners to identify and challenge traditional myths about ageing and the stereotypical images younger people have about older people; to explore how society creates a sense of powerlessness in old age; and to understand how ageism manifests itself in all sorts of ways in our society – in the vocabulary used, in society's visual imagery, in institutional policies, and in discriminatory structures and practices (Butler, 1980; Johnson and Bytheway, 1993). The knowledge base underpinning critical gerontological social work also has implications for thinking about the kinds of ethical questions and dilemmas that practitioners face.

## Conclusion

Alongside the well-established skills we know are vital for good social work with older people, twenty-first-century critical gerontological social workers need to be able to articulate their values, and their knowledge and skill base, and be confident in the contributions that they make, both to the lives of older people who use services, and to other professionals they are likely to work alongside. We know what older men and women value in social workers, and we can use the ever-widening critical gerontological evidence base to reinforce and bolster best practice and education. We therefore see that developing the skills of research awareness and research mindedness, both at qualification and during later professional development, is a key component of critical gerontological social work. By bringing together theoretical and research insights from critical gerontology with the best elements of social work theory, research and practice with older people, it is our hope that the two can be integrated into a sound basis for creative practice with older people. In the following chapters of the book, we aim to show how we can no longer ignore these difficult challenges if, as we hope, social work with older people is to be accorded its rightful, but long overdue, place in the twenty-first century.

## stop and think

- What do you understand to be the key principles of 'critical gerontology'?
- How could the gerontological knowledge base contribute to and develop social work practice?
- What knowledge, skills and values can you identify that are crucial in developing your critical gerontological practice?
- In what ways might age-based discrimination impact on the quality and range of services an older person might receive?

## taking it further

- Bernard, M. and Phillips, J. (2000) 'The Challenge of Ageing in Tomorrow's Britain', *Ageing and Society*, 20(1), pp. 33–54.
- Lipman, V. (2005) 'Rights for the Invisible: Older People and the Human Rights Project', *Generations Review*, 15(4), pp. 42–7.
- Milne, A., Gearing, B. and Warner, J. (2007) *Ageism, Age Discrimination and Social Exclusion*, London, Social Care Institute for Excellence; available at www.scie.org.uk.
- Qureshi, H., Patmore, C., Nicolas, E. and Bamford, C. (2000) *Learning from Older Community Care Clients*, Research Findings from the Social Policy Research Unit, York University, Social Policy Research Unit.

# 3 Risk and older people

- Notions of risk are used to determine eligibility for services.

- Risk is a concept that may be used uncritically to label older people.

- Risk is often located at an individual level, whereas in reality, older people may be at risk from a range of structural, environmental and practical factors. These wider understandings of risk may be overlooked in practice.

- Critical practitioners have a duty to engage in a deep understanding of risk in order to enhance their interventions with older people.

## Introduction

The preceding chapters have presented the case for retaining what we most value about good social work with older people, but developing it into a more robust, challenging and explicitly critical approach. In this chapter, and the ones that follow, we now turn our attention to areas we regard as crucial to the practice of critical gerontological social work in the twenty-first century. We begin with an exploration of risk and, in subsequent chapters, go on to consider dementia, end-of-life care, transitions and care-giving.

Concern about risk has found heightened expression in the current context of health and social care practice and policy. Whether we are conscious of it or not, social work practice with older people often involves defining and constructing them as being 'at risk' and evidenced by conceptions such as 'frailty' or 'dependency'. Working in a climate of constrained resources, risk has inexorably become central to defining eligibility for receipt of support services, as well as shaping the activities of both staff and organizations (Kemshall *et al.*, 1997). As a result, defining an older person as being 'frail and at risk' can increase the likelihood of their gaining access to limited personal social services. Indeed, the presence of 'risk' may be used so frequently to define eligibility for resources that it is often treated as a relatively unproblematic concept.

By contrast, this chapter begins from the premise that 'risk' is a contested and ideologically loaded concept (Lupton, 1999), and that its *uncritical* use can have a number of potentially undesirable consequences. We explore risk in the context of social work reforms before turning our attention to the ways in which risk has been theorized and conceptualized. With this as a basis, the chapter goes on to argue for a widening of our understanding of risk. The second half of the chapter is devoted to a consideration of risk and critical gerontological social work, drawing attention to some of the crucial areas on which practice in the twenty-first century might most profitably focus.

## Critical reflection

In order to provide opportunities to think and critically reflect on how risk and other key concerns have an impact on older people and those around them, we use an ongoing case-study throughout the remainder of the book. This is taken from Margaret Forster's (1989) superbly written, but excruciatingly uncomfortable novel, *Have the Men Had Enough?* Although this novel was published some time ago, it conveys vividly many of the themes and issues we address in this book. Briefly, the novel examines the ways in which different members of the McKay family handle their relationships with each other, and with 'Grandma', who has dementia, among other things. Each chapter is written alternately from the viewpoint of two of the main female characters: Jenny – the middle-aged daughter-in-law; and Hannah – the 17-year-old granddaughter.

At the time the novel opens, Grandma McKay is aged 80 and living in the ground floor flat (of a converted house) adjacent to the flat belonging to her unmarried 43-year-old daughter, Bridget. She is Scottish by birth, is a Presbyterian and was brought up with two brothers and one sister. She was very much a homemaker and the linchpin of the family, bringing up the children on her own after her husband was killed in the war in 1945 (the year Bridget was born). Until she was diagnosed with moderate dementia four years previously, she lived on her own in Glasgow, but, following her diagnosis, her children decided to move her to be nearer to them in England. Mrs McKay is a feisty character, and even though her dementia has become more severe, she is clearly central to everyone's lives. She is a smoker, is given to reciting the poetry of Robert Burns, and is a lover of the novels of Charles Dickens.

Her daughter Bridget works full-time as a nurse in the local hospital and, while she is the 'co-resident' carer for her mother, she has two nights a week 'off', when Mildred, the night carer, comes to stay. Mrs McKay and Bridget live in the next street to her middle son, Charlie (aged 53) – a broker in the city, his wife, Jenny, who does not have a paid job, and their two teenage children, Hannah (aged 17) and Adrian (aged 18). Adrian is working but Hannah is studying for her A-levels and enjoys helping out as much as she can after school. Mrs McKay comes to their house three days a week and on Sundays so that Jenny can look after her, while Charlie looks after his mother's flat, and pays the bills.

Mrs McKay's eldest son, Stuart (aged 55), is a policeman and is married, to Paula, his second wife. They have two small boys, Alistair (aged 5) and Jamie (aged 3). Stuart has two older sons (both in their twenties) from his first marriage. Stuart and Paula live a car ride away, but it is Paula, rather than Stuart, who visits most often and who comes to Sunday lunch. In fact, Stuart is of the view that his mother is now too much of a risk to herself and should be 'in a home', and has absolved himself of all responsibility for her.

## The rise of risk

The historical and policy context detailed in Chapter 1 highlighted how the move away from institutional care for people using services was clearly one priority of the community care reforms of the 1980s and 1990s. However, from the outset, there were potential contradictions in these reforms. For example, policy guidance emphasized the importance of holistic assessments of need, starting from the service user's perspective and considering a wide range of potential options to meet need (Department of Health, 1991). At the same time, community care reforms were being targeted at people deemed to be most 'in need', to the extent that the importance of eligibility criteria and the targeting of resources to a relatively small group of people became an overriding concern. Moreover, while service users were encouraged to define their needs, the guidance made it clear that it was practitioners who were ultimately responsible for determining what needs could be considered to fall within agency eligibility criteria (Department of Health, 1991). The Gloucestershire judgement (1997), in particular, was important because it confirmed that need could be redefined dynamically and was dependent on the financial resources of any given social services department (see Box 3.1). From

## Box 3.1    The Gloucestershire judgment (1997)

The Gloucestershire judgment (*R* v. *Gloucestershire County Council, ex parte Barry* [1997] 2 All ER 1) resulted from a judicial review called for after services were summarily cut from service users (many of whom were older people). This decision was made by the council because it had inadequate funds to continue to provide the level of service. The decision to withdraw domiciliary care services was challenged by Mr Barry on the basis that, despite the alteration in the Local Authority's financial circumstances, his needs had remained the same. The judgment confirmed that local authorities could take resources into account in the assessment of service users' needs. The court recognized that eligibility was a key component in the management of finite resources. Following the judgment, if a local authority decides to alter its eligibility threshold on the basis of availability of resources, it *must* provide appropriate reassessment of people receiving services before any changes (that is, reduction) in services can be initiated.

(*R* v. *Gloucestershire County Council, ex parte Barry* [1997] 2)

the 1980s onwards, therefore, the concept of risk was used increasingly in locally developed eligibility criteria, both in an attempt to provide for those persons deemed to be most 'in need', and as a means of attempting to ensure that state penalties were not incurred as a result of the inadequate management of resources.

Kemshall (2002, p. 78) has further argued that the growing emphasis on risk as a means of determining eligibility has in effect replaced need, and that the assessments that professionals make are framed increasingly by notions of vulnerability and risk, rather than need:

> Gatekeeping was considerably simplified by replacing the inclusive and ambiguous concept of need with the exclusive and managerially defined concept of 'vulnerability' in which clearer priorities could be set.

Termed 'Fair Access to Care Services' (FACS) (Department of Health, 2002b), the current national eligibility criteria framework has been devised with the aim of equalizing access across local social services departments (see Box 3.2). However, evidence of 'risk' plays a significant part in the eligibility framework and the guidance suggests, for example, that by identifying the risks that fall within the eligibility criteria, professionals are thus able to identify eligible needs (Department of Health, 2002b, p. 9). In reality, financial pressures mean that many local councils are able to respond only to eligible needs that fall within the 'critical' and 'substantial' bands of the 'Fair Access to Care Services' framework.

---

**Box 3.2**   Fair Access to Care Services (FACS) (2002)

The eligibility framework is graded into four bands that analyse degrees of risk and the supposed consequences of those risks. The bands are:

Critical:

- Life is or will be threatened; and/or
- Significant health problems have developed or will develop; and/or
- There is, or will be, little or no choice and control over vital aspects of the immediate environment; and/or
- Serious abuse or neglect has occurred or will occur; and/or
- There is or will be, an inability to carry out vital personal care or domestic routines; and/or
- Vital activities in work, education or learning cannot or will not be sustained; and/or
- Vital social systems and relationships cannot or will not be sustained; and/or
- Vital family and other roles or responsibilities cannot or will not be undertaken.

Substantial:

- There is or will be, only partial choice or control over the immediate environment; and/or
- Abuse and neglect has occurred or will occur; and/or
- There is, or will be, an inability to carry out the majority of personal care or domestic routines; and/or
- Involvement in many aspects of work, education or learning cannot or will not be sustained; and/or
- The majority of family and other social roles and responsibilities cannot or will not be undertaken.

Moderate:

- There is or will be, an inability to carry out several personal care or domestic routines; and/or
- Involvement in several aspects of work, education or learning cannot or will not be sustained; and/or
- Several support systems cannot or will not be sustained; and/or
- Several family and other social roles and responsibilities cannot or will not be undertaken.

---

**Box 3.2** *continued*

Low:

■ There is or will be, an inability to carry out one or two personal care or domestic routines; and/or

■ Involvement in one or two aspects of work, education or learning cannot or will not be sustained; and/or

■ One or two social support systems and relationships cannot or will not be sustained; and/or

■ One or two family and other social roles and responsibilities cannot or will not be undertaken.

Strict application of such a framework results in an emphasis on a relatively small group of older people deemed to be at the greatest risk. Arguably too, the emphasis is on minimal intervention and a focus on what is required to secure safety, health and autonomy, rather than optimal interventions aimed at enhancing quality of life and promoting opportunities for positive citizenship (see, for example, Kemshall, 2002). It seems to us that in both policy and practice, 'risk', and its being linked with 'need' and eligibility criteria, has crept ever more uncritically and unchallenged into the language and practice of social work with older people. It is timely therefore to take stock and review what we mean by risk, how it is theorized and how we might widen our understanding of risk as the basis for practising critical gerontological social work with older people.

## Theorizing risk

Practitioners tend to talk about being 'at risk' as a unified idea or reality: a person is deemed to be 'at risk' or not. This may create or reinforce the perception that the idea of risk is a given or objective reality, whereas there are different ways of theorizing and conceptualizing risk (Lupton, 1999). Technical and scientific approaches define risks as absolute realities and seek to define and measure the degree of risk by linking hazard with probabilities (Lupton, 1999). Fox (1999, p. 13) has commented that, from this perspective, 'all risks may be evaluated and suitably managed, such that all may be predicted and countered, so risks, accidents and insecurities are minimised or prevented altogether'.

The conventional approach to risk assessment and management within social services utilizes a narrow and supposedly objective approach, characterized by an increase in what Webb (2006, p. 145) has described as 'technologies of care'. In this context, there is a preoccupation with *risk assessment* and *identifying risk factors*. which are then matched against *eligibility criteria*. This in turn drives what levels of need count as risks that are sufficiently high enough to warrant a response. In this sense, needs could be argued to be prede-termined, in particular given the reported difficulties of social service agencies in responding in any meaningful way to the prevention agenda (CSCI, 2006a). Kemshall (2002) also argues that the emphasis on using risk as a monitoring tool and mechanism for accountability, as a rationing device and case-prioritizing tool, and as a means of avoiding litigation and blame, all contribute to a move away from a deep to a surface analysis of risk, as well as reinforcing the potential to respond in a bureaucratic or administrative manner to the demands of the managerialist agenda.

One of the major difficulties with such an approach is that risks cannot easily be measured or known. The presumed threat of terrorist attack, for example, is located on a global scale, and Kemshall (2002) comments that, while being involved is a relatively low probability, the impact and consequences are huge. In reality, the risks in this instance and in many others are both unknown and unknowable. Paradoxically, however, legislation, policies and procedures still seek to deal with or address the risk and urge us to participate in manag-ing the risk (for example, by reporting unsupervised luggage in air-ports and railway stations). A critical response within this frame of reference would be that of the precautionary principle (Kemshall, 2002), which seeks to highlight a potential hazard or risk, and manage it, before the implications or consequences are known. With respect to older people, there is, for example, considerable media attention about the risks they face from crime and the ways in which this vulnerable group should be protected. In reality, however, it remains the case that younger people are far more likely to be the victims of crime than older men and women (ESDS, 2007).

Another critical weakness of an overly scientific approach to risk is that, beyond recognizing that people may respond subjectively (or irrationally) to information about risk, it fails to take any serious account of the notion that ideas about risk can be socially con-structed and defined (Lupton, 1999). Cultural theory, while acknowl-edging that risks or hazards do exist, is critical of scientific approaches to risk because they offer no explanation of the social or cultural influences that create attention to specific hazards (Douglas, 1992). Why, for example, does the narrative on crime and older people highlight the vulnerability of older people to crime, but is a fundamentally different narrative from that around crime and younger people? From a cultural perspective, certain groups of people are singled out as being particularly vulnerable to risk; for example,

Fox (1999) highlights how risk assessment practices target specific groups who are effectively put into the position of being 'other' (that is, not like 'us'). This is particularly evident when thinking about people with mental illness, or older people with dementia.

Green (1997) has further commented that the notion of 'illness prevention' inevitably includes ideas about blame or a lack of judgement when a person fails to avail themselves of preventative courses of action. As illustration, consider the current widespread emphasis on 'active ageing'. Here, it could be argued that blaming older people for their failure to 'age successfully', ensures a construction of them as 'other' and preserves the position of older people with chronic illness and disability as being different from, and apart from, the rest of the life course.

Douglas (1992) has also highlighted the relationship between risk and blame, and contends that, in any negative risk outcome, someone must be to blame. In a social work context, risk used in this sense can be seen as a means of deciding accountability, and demonstrated through procedures such as audit and externally derived performance criteria. As Kemshall (2002, p. 83) argues, audit has become 'an essential mechanism for holding practitioners to account and for eradicating the inherent uncertainties of social work. Such audits have replaced trust, thereby reducing the autonomy and professional status of workers'. Kemshall further develops her argument by highlighting the paradox between practitioners managing an often highly prescriptive set of risk management procedures, against the realities of risk assessment with individual service users, which is often characterized by uncertainty, or aspirations or motivations that do not correspond easily to risk management. An older person may wish, for example, to retain slip rugs and mats despite an assessment that they create a tripping hazard. Practice with older people is a complex and dynamic process when a practitioner has to balance the existence of risk on the one hand and, on the other, the right of an older person to retain autonomy and independence.

In summary, therefore, risk is a complex and difficult concept: it is contested and ideologically loaded and, moreover, the uncritical use of the concept may have potentially undesirable consequences both for older people and for those who seek to support them in a professional capacity. First, as we have seen, an over-reliance on scientific definitions of risk may reinforce inappropriately biomedical orientations and assumptions about the passivity of older women and men with physical and/or cognitive impairments. Such narrow definitions serve to promote a highly proceduralized approach to intervention. Second, a risk-dominated approach to assessment as a means of testing eligibility will reduce the potential for assessments and interventions to be grounded in strengths-based approaches, or approaches that take properly into account the perspectives, expertise and aspirations of older people. Third, terms like 'being at risk' or 'frail' or 'dependent' imply total states. The use of terms in this global way creates what Fook (2002) has coined as the tendency to define people in terms of 'binary opposites': thus a person is either 'dependent' or 'at risk', or they are not. However, it is rare for a person to be entirely 'dependent' or, for that matter, to be wholly at risk. This can set the scene for a label that effectively defines the person, as well as reducing opportunities to work with, for example, a person's strengths and resources. The widening of our understanding of risk is therefore a necessary prerequisite for developing critical gerontological social work with older people.

## Widening our understanding of risk

As we have argued, risk is often very narrowly defined in relation to service users (Tanner, 1998) and can carry with it a number of (unintended) consequences. Conventional assessments of older people and their levels of risk tend to focus attention on individual problems (for example, poor management of risk in the home) or pathology (for example, lack of capacity in making decisions about risk-taking). While it is imperative to consider how an individual's behaviour, environment or ability to assess degrees of risk may place them at risk, it is important not to assume that risk is located solely at the level of individual dysfunction or pathology. Such a superficial analysis would disregard the antecedents of the risk and fail to analyse how risks come to be constructed and defined. In developing a wider understanding of risk we therefore need to take into account a number of key aspects, including structural factors and life-course inequalities, and iatrogenic risks.

### Beyond individual pathology: structural factors that contribute to risk

In the practice environment current at the time of writing, an in-depth analysis of risk caused by structural factors such as life-long poverty, racism or sexism is in danger of being overlooked or reconstructed as an individual risk or problem state (Tanner, 1998; Kemshall, 2002). A failure to identify external factors that contribute to, or cause, risk may reinforce and promote ageist assumptions such as the inevitable decline or dependency of older people. Such an approach will limit inexorably the scope of interventions and their success in reducing risk. Feminist analysis on the use of physical space, for example, highlights that minority groups such as older women and men may be marginalized in their use of, and access to, space by dominant groups such that: 'this domination of space leads in turn to feelings of enhanced fear and anxiety of being "at risk" of intimidation, violence or coercion' (Lupton, 1999, p. 146).

Other research consistently highlights the ways in which older people feel restricted in their use of neighbourhood space because they are fearful of crime, have been the victims of crime, or experience the environment as being devoid of, or limited in, the resources it offers of relevance to them (Phillipson *et al.*, 2001). These issues are not confined to urban environments, and recent studies of multiple disadvantage in inner city areas (Scharf *et al.*, 2004) and of rural disadvantage and older people (Scharf and Bartlam, 2006), have highlighted the role played by socio-economic inequalities in contributing to older people's experiences of exclusion and marginalization from a range of social relationships and activities (ODPM, 2006). Assessment should therefore consider risks more widely and in relation to issues such as lack of access to transport, low income, poor housing, living alone and being childless.

Gathering wider information about unmet needs, such as transport difficulties, may also serve as evidence in building a case for a change in provision. In addition, social workers can (and indeed do) have a significant part to play in ensuring that older people are in receipt of benefits to which they are entitled, or to encourage (and assist) older people to apply for benefits. Providing help to apply for benefits is seen increasingly as being outside a social worker's remit. Nevertheless, it is our belief that social workers still use considerable skill in advocating for an older person to get their full benefit entitlements. At the very least, social workers should be able to refer an older person to a reliable, skilled benefits advice service, as well as follow up on the outcome of the referral. As an illustration of the necessity for social workers to retain such skills, consider the data in Box 3.3, which highlights the poor take-up of benefit entitlements.

## Box 3.3   Benefit take-up and older people

- Around two-fifths of pensioner households (one and a half million people) entitled to Pension Credit are not claiming it.
- Around two-fifths of pensioner households entitled to Council Tax Benefit (two million) are not claiming it.
- In 2005/6, unclaimed income-related benefits to which pensioner households were entitled, amounted to some three and a half billion pounds.

Source: www.poverty.org.uk (accessed 8 January 2008)

The challenges of living on a low income are further illustrated in the 'Just above the Breadline' report from Age Concern (2006b). In this study, low income was defined as a person who had savings of less than £20,000, and a weekly income of less than £150.00 (£200.00 for a couple). The experience of low income had a major impact on purchasing decisions made by participants: maintaining a strict budget for food, doing without holidays and social outings, and limiting socializing, are stark examples of the ways in which older people with limited resources work to make the money go round. Doubtless, the consequences of poverty and its impact on daily life may create or reinforce risks for older people. Consider, for example, the finding that fuel poverty is a significant factor in the 50,000 additional deaths of older people occurring in the winter months in England and Wales (www.poverty.org.uk), as well as the impact on well-being and quality of life that worrying about unexpected bills or unplanned emergencies in the context of uncertain or declining health might have.

## Iatrogenic risk

Research also draws our attention to the potential iatrogenic risks associated with being in particular environments (that is, those risks caused by interventions aimed at meeting a particular need or reducing a particular risk). For example, older people moving into a care home or hospital may in fact face risks associated with the move to an unfamiliar environment, with its associated unfamiliar routines. Research by Age Concern (2006a) also suggests that among hospital in-patients and residents of care homes, as many as 40 per cent of their populations could be suffering from malnutrition. According to the National Institute for Clinical Excellence (NICE) (National Institute for Clinical Excellence, 2006), the risk of malnutrition among older people in hospital could rise to 60 per cent, and the implications of malnourishment can include lowered immunity, secondary infections, bedsores and death.

Of course, older people may very well be admitted with eating and hydration needs, and the type or severity of their illness may be closely linked to the risk or presence of eating difficulties and malnourishment. Nevertheless, research has persistently highlighted the potential for poor practice, reinforced by ageist attitudes and lack of staff awareness, to contribute to poor nourishment profiles of older vulnerable patients (Age Concern, 2006a). In a busy medical environment it is possible for the complexity of nutritional need, the social and emotional significance of food, and individual support requirements, to be overlooked or marginalized. A report from the

Commission for Social Care Inspection (CSCI, 2006d) revealed that over 80 per cent of care homes for older people were achieving minimum standards in respect of food and nutrition. However, the report also pointed to examples of meals being taken away from some older people before they had a chance to eat them, and to a lack of staff support at mealtimes. While social workers may have only a limited role in this area of practice, they can contribute to a wider understanding of risks by alerting family and care workers to the nutritional needs of an older person in their assessment, discharge and care planning. This constitutes more than indicating on a care plan that an older person needs access to a 'good diet'. For example, likes and dislikes, preferences about meals and eating routines, cultural or religious requirements, ways to help an older person make choices about what to eat (for example, if a person has memory impairment), will all help to build a more comprehensive picture of an older person when they move into a new care environment.

## Risk and critical gerontological social work in practice

As we have shown, risk in relation to older people is often perceived as a negative or undesirable experience. Such perceptions are undoubtedly linked to the ways in which older people, especially those with complex needs, are constructed and perceived. Risk is then less likely to be seen as an experience that might carry highly desirable outcomes and which might add to quality of life, or a person's right to make decisions and choices about their life. Evidence also suggests that social work organizations may attach greater importance to certain types of risk, particularly those located at an individual level (for example, being at risk of self neglect) (see, for example, Kemshall, 2002). This may mean that other types of risk, including those that are well rehearsed in research/evidence terms do not attract the same amount of attention in terms of practice-based risk management (for example, the risk associated with depression, loneliness or poverty). To illustrate these points, consider Extract 3.1 and, as you read it, think about what these circumstances might say about the difficulties Mrs McKay is having. What too is your view of the consequences of a peremptory move for this person as a response to her apparent difficulties?

A critical gerontological social work approach would widen the risk agenda around the kinds of areas noted in the previous paragraphs as a means of recognizing, for example, the potential impact of life-course inequalities, health inequalities in older age, the potential for

## Extract 3.1  *Being at risk?*

It was Charlie the neighbours had rung because only Charlie had been thoughtful enough to leave a number with them. 'She's wandering at night,' they reported, breathless with the weight of their own virtue, 'wandering up and down the street in her nightie at two in the morning. Anything could happen.' And she shouted, opened her front door and shouted pointless things like, 'Awa' wi' you all.' Her milk bottles piled up on the doorstep and newspapers were never taken from the letter box. So Bridget went up and was shocked. There was food everywhere, a trail of buttered toast across every surface and puddles of tea poured onto the carpet and cushions. Then Charlie went up and together they brought her down from Glasgow because Bridget could not bear it. It seemed to her the only solution and no amount of Charlie's reasoning could persuade her otherwise.
(Margaret Forster, *Have the Men Had Enough?*)
Seen from Jenny's perspective, p. 34.

multiple exclusions, the social model of disability, and the impact of age-based discrimination. In other words, risk is intimately bound up with how we view older people, their value and place in society. A widening of the risk agenda in turn suggests a number of crucial areas on which practice might focus, including risk assessment, risk in institutional care, and living at home and risk.

### Assessing risk

Research on risk assessment, risk management and risk-taking in respect of older service users paints a rather gloomy picture. Kemshall's (2002) analysis of risk concludes that in a climate of risk assessment and managerialized practice, risk-taking is minimized and risk avoidance maximized. Older people with complex needs are often seen as being uniquely vulnerable and therefore may be particularly susceptible to risk avoidance – that is, risk-taking being actively discouraged on the basis that older people must be protected from danger. In reality, and regardless of how well-intentioned it might be, such an approach serves to promote and reinforce images of older people as passive and dependent, and to deny personhood. As we have also illustrated in this chapter, avoiding one risk does not inoculate an older person against the consequences of other risks that emerge as unanticipated consequences of interventions based on risk avoidance.

Risk assessment, as part of critical gerontological social work practice should therefore be based on clear analysis and grounded in theory and research in order to encourage a risk-taking rather than a risk-minimization approach (Tanner, 1998). This shifts the focus towards defensible rather than defensive practice and, unless there is some toleration of risk and uncertainty, practice will inevitably be oppressive and defensive (Braye and Preston-Shoot, 1995). Practice should also incorporate a broader approach to risk management which, Alaszewski (2000) argues, should seek to balance potential negatives/harmful consequences against anticipated benefits, taking into account relative probabilities. Furthermore, risk assessment should seek to work in partnership with an older person in order to establish the perceptions that older people have about the risks they face in their daily lives. It is also critically important to determine the strategies that older people use to cope and manage, and to identify what a person may wish to retain or hold on to in their daily lives. A partnership approach between an older person and the person undertaking an assessment, is more likely to establish the actual (or potential) strengths and resources an older person has that might either mitigate risk, or be used as part of a risk-taking/risk management strategy. Balancing people's rights to autonomy against the risks they face should be a product of multi-disciplinary assessment that includes service users. This broader view of risk and risk assessment will, in turn, feed into other areas where social workers come into contact with older people, in both institutional and community settings.

Good risk assessment practice should therefore:

- Evidence the risks a person experiences.
- Analyse the risks in relation to potentially desirable outcomes and against potentially negative outcomes.
- Analyse the risks in relation to the strengths and resources that do (or may) mitigate the risk.
- Garner evidence from the older person, relevant social networks and other people involved in the formal care system.
- Be able to make informed decisions and choices/capacity.
- Be carried out with the best interests of the older person uppermost.
- Identify the least disruptive intervention needed to manage/take risks.
- Properly record risk management/risk-taking strategy and intervention plan.
- Put in place a review and monitoring framework.
- Make appropriate use of the provision for the protection of vulnerable adults (see Chapter 8).

## Risk and institutional care

Although admission to care homes may be experienced by many older people as a positive choice and an opportunity to receive care and assistance in a supportive and homely environment, it is more commonly seen by professionals and family members as a way of managing unacceptably high levels of risk and ensuring the person's safety. All too often, older people with complex needs have moved to a care home because the inadequate or poorly developed resources to enable them to remain safely at home have been exhausted. Research by Housing 21 (Vallely *et al.*, 2006), examining housing biographies for older people with dementia, concluded that a diagnosis of dementia is not the primary reason for admission to residential care. Instead, premature admission is often caused by fragmented services, the complexities of long-term funding, and lack of expertise and experience in tackling so called 'challenging behaviour'.

In addition, moving into a care home can happen in situations of pressure or emergency, and it is perhaps easy to overlook the potential risks associated with the very course of action that was intended to reduce or remove risk. Pritchard (1997) cites a number of examples of what might happen to an older person who now finds him/herself in institutional care:

- Being in an unfamiliar environment (lost and disoriented).
- Loss of remaining skills.
- Emotional distress.
- Isolation and loneliness.
- Depression.
- Loss of existing social support networks.
- Inappropriate care.
- Abuse.
- Loss of identity.

As research has also shown, there are further risks associated with inappropriate medication of older people in care homes (CSCI, 2006c). Older people with dementia, for example, are one group of people who may be particularly vulnerable to the overuse of neuroleptic (anti-psychotic) medication as a way of treating symptoms such as agitation or aggression. The Alzheimer's Society comments that it: 'remains deeply concerned about the overuse of neuroleptic drugs for people with dementia in care homes. The over-reliance on pharmacological treatments for behaviour such as wandering or agitation, can be the result of lack of training in dementia care' (www.alzheimers.org.uk). Moreover, as recently as 2006, the Commission for Social Care Inspection (CSCI, 2006c) reported that half of all care homes in England, providing 210,000 places for residents, many of whom are older people, do not meet minimum standards in the management and administration of medication. Current poor practice constitutes significant risk and potential harm to older people, including:

- Evidence of wrong medication given to residents.
- Poor recording of medicines received and administered.
- Inappropriate handling of medicines by untrained staff.
- Medicines being stored inappropriately.
- Poor achievement of six-monthly reviews for people prescribed four or more medications.

Such practice is also now regarded as institutional abuse (Select Committee on Elder Abuse, 2004) and must therefore constitute a significant risk for older people and an area of practice concern for gerontological social workers. The potential for ageist attitudes grounded in assumptions that nothing much can be done, together with poorly resourced and inadequately trained staff groups, cannot be discounted as possible causes of such poor practice. Does it matter, for example, if someone who is very ill misses a tablet? Should we be concerned if a resident is asleep for most of the day and can barely be roused to eat or drink? Evidence suggests that organizational and cultural changes are necessary to develop practice, reduce institutional abuse (inappropriate medication) and promote safe practice (CSCI, 2006c). Again, gerontological social work practitioners cannot remain aloof from these issues. They actively participate in helping older people to move into residential facilities and, at the very least, prepare an initial care plan. They are also often responsible for undertaking reviews of the placement and may be called upon to participate in reassessing a person's care needs if it is felt that the person's needs cannot be met in the care home.

A further area of concern for practitioners is where care homes struggle to provide worthwhile and valued activity for older people. Older people with dementia may be particularly susceptible to being under-occupied, as Perrin and May (2000) show in their research. Based on observational data, they stress the extreme occupational poverty of many residents and draw important inferences about levels of 'ill-being' and poor quality of life. A person with dementia living in a care home may well be left alone for much of the day and respond by sleeping and appearing to be socially isolated and disengaged. Is that person at risk because of their failure to stimulate and occupy themselves or because, at some level, it remains acceptable for some older people who are sufficiently powerless and invisible to live in a situation of extreme under-occupation and, therefore, institutional abuse?

Extract 3.2 illustrates vividly some of the consequences of living in the kind of institutional environment where opportunities to do something interesting or worthwhile appear to be limited. As you read, consider what role you think social workers (and others) should have in ensuring that assessments and individual care plans include information about a person's lifestyle and interests? What action, if any, would you take if you came across the situation described in this extract?

## Extract 3.2    *Occupational poverty and quality of life*

On Tuesday when I first went I could not find her. I went into the sitting room, looked around, could not see Grandma, could not think of whom to ask and so went in search of her ... There was no one about in any of the corridors. Wherever I looked, there seemed to be old women asleep and I started tip-toeing instinctively ... She was sitting [in the dining room], on her own, at a table for four ... Grandma was motionless, staring straight ahead, slumped in an attitude of total dejection. I rushed up to her, saying her name, but there was not a flicker of response. I came right up to her and said, 'Hey, it's me,' and she looked straight at me with entirely blank eyes. It seemed to me that there was a faintly sickly odour about her and tiny flecks of what looked like foam in the corner of her mouth – but it was meringue, clinging to her incipient moustache. I wiped it away, far too energetically, still talking to her. It took a long time for any recognition to dawn and even then she did not know my name. I wanted to cry. I longed to go and shout at someone and blame them. But there was still no one about ...

Yesterday I went full of apprehension. I went later, reckoning I had gone at a bad time the day before, at the post-lunch time when most of the Birchholme ladies were snoozing. At least, this time, Grandma was not on her own. She was in the sitting room, ostensibly grouped with two other women, but they had pulled their chairs round so that their backs were to her. She seemed asleep when I arrived. When I whispered in her ear, she tried to swat me away as though I were a fly and said she couldn't be bothered. She told me to go away, she was fed up, she wanted to be left alone. I coaxed and wheedled and tried to humour her into opening her eyes. When she did, I was alarmed. Her eyes were red-looking and a small amount of pus leaked out of one corner. She looked at me as blankly as she had done the day before and then she said, 'How long is this going on?'
(Margaret Forster, *Have the Men Had Enough?*)
Seen from Jenny's perspective, pp. 182–4.

## Risk and living at home

Of course, older people may also experience risk and harm as a result of living at home and, again, professional interventions may unwittingly worsen rather than alleviate these risks. For example, McCarthy and Thomas (2004) highlight the ways in which an excessive focus on the principles in 'Best Value' can lead to interventions that create and reinforce experiences of social isolation and loneliness: delivering frozen food once a fortnight for an older person to reheat in their microwave may achieve a target for Best Value, but the potential hidden cost of loneliness and isolation may well outweigh any savings incurred from this intervention. Furthermore, social isolation, linked with a lack of meaningful activities and social opportunities, may contribute to earlier admissions to care homes, especially for older people with dementia (Vallely *et al.* 2006). Research has emphasized increasingly the importance of meaningful activity and occupational identity in person-centred care (Perrin and May; 2000; Bell and Troxel, 2001) but, it remains the case that, all too often, insufficient attention is paid to the occupational identity of older people, and in particular those persons with dementia. Social workers can make a vital contribution to identifying, in both assessment and care planning, the occupational identities and the sorts of things an older person likes to do with his or her time.

## Conclusion

The association of assessment and eligibility criteria has contributed to the biomedicalization of older people. Specifically, need is constructed as risk (and danger) as a means of confirming that a person is eligible to receive finite and limited services. Risk all too often is defined as 'individual risk', and being 'at risk'. This perspective fails to take into account the fact that older people may experience considerable risk from wider social and structural factors, and that the risks they face may have little to do with an individual orientation. Social workers' commitment to a critical perspective can be helpful in considering ways in which an anti-oppressive stance can resist practices which may increase or, at the very least, reinforce structural and socially situated risks.

Increased managerialism has also led to a tendency towards being 'risk averse'. This can create messages for practitioners about older people being essentially passive, and can discourage an acceptance that the right to take risks is part of the lives of all of us, and often adds to our quality of life and sense of identity. The importance of working in partnership with older service users who may experience a range of risks, as well as recognizing the existence of other perspectives that are likely to be at variance with these, calls for considerable social work skill. Risk-taking strategies require practitioners to assess evidence or information about the likelihood of the risk leading to an undesirable outcome, and the actual (or potential) resources that can be used to support the risk. This practice has to be undertaken with careful consideration of Human Rights legislation and capacity. The involvement of service users in evaluating services and professional support seems to be a critical factor in discouraging managers and practitioners from erring towards a risk avoidance approach to practice. The importance of evaluating practice and learning from such evaluations is also crucial, as it remains the case that the evidence base on risk-taking and ageing remains relatively under-developed. Social work practitioners, by using practice as an opportunity for learning and development, can augment local knowledge and expertise about 'what works' in risk-taking and risk management, as well as identifying areas for the commissioning of support services and resources.

## stop and think

- Reflect on how you like to spend your time (for example, the hobbies or activities you enjoy). What does participation in those activities contribute to your sense of well-being and a sense of who you are?
- How might you seek to address the risks that an older person might encounter in moving to a care home?
- How can social workers contribute to reducing the risks that might be associated with living on a low income?
- How can you find out how a care home approaches the role of activities and occupation in promoting quality of life and well-being?

taking it further

- Commission for Social Care Inspection (CSCI) (2006c) *Handled with Care? Managing Medication for Residents of Care Homes and Children's Homes – a Follow Up Study*, Newcastle, CSCI.
- Fine, M. and Glendinning, C. (2005) 'Dependence, Independence or Inter-dependence? Revisiting the Concepts of "Care" and "Dependency"', *Ageing and Society*, 25(4), pp. 601–21.
- Grenier, A. (2007) 'Constructions of Frailty in the English Language, Care Practice and the Lived Experience', *Ageing and Society*, 27(3), pp. 425–45.
- Lupton, D. (1999) *Risk*, London, Routledge.

# 4 Social work with older people with dementia

main points

- There has been a considerable development of interest in research, policy and practice relating to people with dementia. Nevertheless, people with dementia remain marginalized and often do not receive the range of support, services and interventions that they need to promote and maximize their well-being.

- Social workers have a crucial role to play in assessment, intervention and care planning with people with dementia and their carers.

- Social workers need to have an understanding of the knowledge and skill base that would support positive practice with people with dementia.

- Good practice means challenging the potential for practice to be reduced to bureaucratic procedures.

## Introduction

This chapter focuses on an area of growing concern, by exploring how a gerontological social work approach might help to address the needs of older people with dementia. Traditionally, dementia has been located within a biomedical perspective, influenced by the drive to diagnose the cause of the illness and provide medical treatment to address and manage symptoms. At the time of writing, however, dementia is not 'curable', leaving aside so-called 'arrestable' dementias. Dementia has also largely been understood in terms of irretrievable loss and impairment, and as a personal tragedy for the individual and those closest to them. In this context, people with dementia have been perceived and constructed as 'victims' of an incurable disease that would inevitably rob them of their personalities, identities, insight and abilities. As a result, traditional care cultures emphasize physical tending such as keeping the person with dementia clean, fed, warm and dry (Kitwood, 1997). Moreover, in policy and practice terms, people with dementia (and people involved in their care and support) have experienced a legacy of marginalization and oppression. Little attention has been paid, for example, to developing creative housing options for people with dementia (Vallely *et al.*, 2006), and social and health care services are often poorly developed, patchy and fragmented.

Since the mid-1990s, however, significant interest has developed in research, practice and policy around dementia and dementia care. It is this body of work that we draw on in this chapter, and that we argue should underpin critical gerontological social work with older people. Consequently, the chapter begins by reviewing briefly the biomedical approaches to dementia care, before discussing the development of interest in person-centred approaches. We then consider other key theoretical developments as well as structural, biographical and rehabilitative work, which, together, have widened our understanding of dementia and contribute to the agenda for future practice and service development. Finally, the chapter raises a number of important challenges around developing critical gerontological social work practice with older people with dementia.

## Biomedical perspectives

Dementia has long been located within a biomedical perspective and this, in turn, has often meant that a person's behaviour was most likely to be construed as a manifestation of cognitive decline. However, biomedical perspectives also differentiate between the normal changes in the brain associated with cell death, and impaired function of cells associated with a diagnosis of dementia (McKeith and Fairbairn, 2001). Alongside this, and given the greater preponderance of dementia in older age, it is also important to distinguish between 'normal' and 'abnormal' ageing. Clinical studies suggest, for example, that a 70-year-old, normally-ageing person will experience some cell death, but this will not have any impact on existing knowledge, although it may have some impact on learning new skills (McKeith and Fairbairn, 2001). Moreover, the prevalence of dementia at age 75 is currently estimated to be 10 per cent of the population, doubling every five years (for a full discussion, refer to Gauthier, 2006). However, these estimates fail to take into account people experiencing cognitive impairment who may be 'hidden' (for example, in care homes) and have not sought help or diagnosis, or who have not been referred for specialist assessments and diagnostic investigation. In addition, stigma associated with cognitive impairment may well prevent people from approaching general practitioners (GPs) for further investigation (Manthorpe and Iliffe, 2007). Once the GP has been consulted, however, research from the National Audit Office (formerly the Audit Commission) (2000) has shown that there is also evidence of GPs failing to refer older people with cognitive difficulties to secondary specialist sources, as well as failing to identify presenting symptoms such as memory loss, as potentially being caused by dementia.

These kinds of barriers are problematic, not least because we know that a diagnosis of dementia can be crucial in unlocking services, interventions and symptom modification, such as anticholinestarase medication (Marshall and Tibbs, 2006). At the time of writing, formal diagnostic procedures focus on clinical history, establishing the existence of treatable conditions, physical examinations and cognitive function tests. Cognitive function is also commonly tested alongside an assessment of the impact that cognitive impairment has on a person's daily living activities (Maciejewski, 2001). However, the perception of people with memory difficulties who have been cognitively assessed suggests that the process is often disempowering, frightening and confidence-sapping (Keady and Gilliard, 2001). Moreover, diagnosis may not be certain, and so follow-up may be necessary in order to assess the development of symptoms over time.

In addition, a diagnosis has other implications in that the diagnostic label 'dementia' may well influence the ways in which the person is subsequently responded to (Manthorpe and Adams, 2003). As an illustration of this, consider Extract 4.1, in which a diagnosis of dementia is given to Bridget about her mother. What principles of good practice do you think should underpin sharing a diagnosis of this nature? Once a diagnosis has been given, what are the implications of such a diagnosis for the person with dementia, and for their families/supporters?

Although multi-agency assessment, care planning and intervention are becoming increasingly better developed, sociological analysis still highlights the medicalization of dementia, the mandate to *treat* people with dementia, and the persisting monopoly of medical knowledge (Bond, 2001). The central focus of a biomedical model is therefore for disability to be located as *an individual* problem, evidenced by the functional limitations of people who are impaired (Swain *et al.*, 2003). Moreover, the collective experience of oppression that people with dementia may experience is overlooked in favour of identifying individual problem states and treating the individual.

## Extract 4.1  *Diagnosing dementia*

[Dr Carruthers – the geriatrician] came and spent an hour with Grandma on his own and then he wrote a report. Bridget said she could have written it herself, it was so obvious, but we found it helpful. Grandma, the report said, was suffering from moderate senile dementia. She knew her name, her age, the names of her children and grandchildren, and where she was living. She could feed herself, toilet herself and walk unaided. But her sense of time had gone. She did not know the date or the year or who was Prime Minister or Queen. She did not know whether she had eaten today or not. She had no sense of direction. The prognosis was carefully worded: with the family support she was getting it was perfectly possible that the dementia might get no worse for several years. Charlie rang up Dr Carruthers to ask the crucial questions: was it inevitable that eventually it would get worse? Yes. And how long did the process usually take? Five years. What happened after that? Death.
(Margaret Forster, *Have the Men Had Enough?*)
Seen from Jenny's perspective, pp. 35–6.

## Social models and dementia

In order to address some of the criticisms of the biomedical perspective, it has been argued that dementia should be seen in the context of a social model of disability. This alternative to the biomedical model was first developed by disabled people themselves (UPIAS, 1976) and defined impairment and disability in these terms:

- *Impairment*: Lacking part or all of a limb, or having a defective limb, organ or mechanism of the body (later, this definition extended to include cognitive impairment and emotional distress).
- *Disability*: The disadvantage or restriction of activity caused by a contemporary social organization which takes no or little account of people who have physical impairments and thus excludes them from participation in the mainstream of social activities.

These definitions highlight the fact that disability can constitute exclusion from full participation, which is neither inevitable nor necessary, and as a result disabled people are an oppressed social group

(Priestley, 2003). In a social model, disability is reconstructed as a social and political process, created by societies and the way they are organized to suit the needs and requirements of non-disabled people. The development and increasing acceptance of the social model of disability has been a powerful and important means of drawing attention to the experiences of oppression, marginalization and exclusion that are commonplace for many disabled people and, by extension, for many people with dementia and other socially disabling conditions.

A further achievement of this model is that it has highlighted the importance of a collective identity as a means of challenging oppression (Campbell and Oliver, 1996), which also acts as a foil to the focus on the individual in diagnosis and treatment within a biomedical model. Adams and Bartlett (2003) acknowledge that the notion of a collective identity for people with dementia may appear to be counter-intuitive to the efforts that have gone into promoting the importance of each person with dementia as having a unique biography and identity. However, they further argue that an understanding of the collective impact of oppression should not preclude the consideration of the individual person's journey in dementia, his/her unique identity, and individual care and support requirements. In other words, they espouse an approach that brings together the awareness engendered through the social model of disability, with the person-centred approaches to dementia that have gained considerable ground in recent years.

## The development of person-centred approaches to dementia

Person-centred approaches to dementia are synonymous with the work of Tom Kitwood, who, in the early 1990s, first began to offer a robust and critical challenge to the dominance of the biomedical perspective (Kitwood, 1993, 1997). While acknowledging the important contributions of medical science, Kitwood's concern was that, in the quest for medical dominance, personhood was often overlooked, particularly with regard to people who could not easily speak for themselves: 'It has become all too easy to ignore the suffering of a fellow human being, and see instead a merely biological problem, to be solved by some kind of technical intervention' (1997, p. 44). In Kitwood's analysis, the consequence was that dementia was constructed as a catastrophic loss of self, and care cultures developed to focus on physical elements of care with a focus on warehousing people in collective settings. The term 'malignant social psychology' was coined to signify the damaging and harmful effects of care environments that undermined or diminished and neglected individual personhood. Using a critical incident technique, Kitwood identified evidence of malignant social psychology in the everyday care of people with dementia (for a full discussion, see Kitwood, 1997, p. 46–49). As you read Extract 4.2, reflect on the potential for loss of personhood and the challenges for people with cognitive impairment in sharing communal spaces. How might we move towards developing more positive social and physical environments? Consider also what you would look for if you were going into a care home for the first time, in the physical layout and design, the atmosphere and the approach/attitude of staff?

## Extract 4.2 *Loss of personhood and objectification*

... it is the going into King's Wood which is the worst ... No one came forward to greet us but then it was tea time, everyone was busy. All the old women were seated round a table being fed. There were four staff for the twenty women. The noise was terrible – wild cawings as though a clutch of rooks had settled there. One woman banged all the time with a spoon on the table and another shouted, 'About bloody time! About bloody time!' over and over. I pushed Grandma to the table, glad that I was behind her and could not see her face. The four staff members, in yellow overalls, stared at us... I said we were expected. One of them went off, grudgingly it seemed, and came back with a small, squat woman in a blue and white uniform who said she was Sister Grice, and she was in charge ... While she addressed me, a white-haired, sweet-faced old woman got up from the end of the table and shuffled down to stand beside me. She put her hand on mine and made some sound I could not distinguish. 'Go away, Leah,' the Sister said. 'Go on, off with you, don't bother the lady.' I said she wasn't bothering me and asked Sister what she had been trying to say to me. 'She's deaf,' Sister said. 'Nothing she says makes sense, don't let her bother you. It doesn't bother us.'
(Margaret Forster, *Have the Men Had Enough?*)
Seen from Jenny's perspective, pp. 201–2.

Traditional ideas of personhood, such as those posed by Quinton (1973; cited in Kitwood, 1997) focused on consciousness, rationality, agency, morality and the capacity to form and maintain relationships. In contrast, Kitwood sought to embrace a definition of personhood characterized by attention to feelings, emotions and living in relationship to, and with, other people. In order to keep personhood at the centre of a positive culture of care, Kitwood proposed that the individual person should be considered first and foremost, as opposed to allowing the label 'dementia' to subsume and overwhelm the person.

The 'doing' of person-centred care was not worked out in detail by Kitwood, and others have sought to develop person-centred care practice and also to offer refinements on the definition, construction and meanings of person-centred care. Rather like 'empowerment', person-centred care is in danger of becoming a catch-all term incorporating a range of definitions and practices. Brooker (2004) has identified four key elements that encapsulate person-centred care, but comments that these may be used singly or in combination. The elements she identifies are:

- Valuing people;
- Treating people as individuals;
- Seeing things from the perspective of the person with dementia; and
- Creating a positive social environment.

An examination of these elements highlights the critical challenges posed in achieving a person-centred culture. Social work environments increasingly focus on, for example, fast throughput of assessment work which is of itself often limited by a focus on dysfunction and problem states; difficulties in providing proactive and preventative services caused by the current emphasis on the highest levels of risk and need as defined by Fair Access to Care criteria; and a limited potential for continuity by practices that fragment 'cases' into different teams with increasingly narrow functions (for example, screening teams and review teams). Consequently, it is important to reorientate our views and understanding of dementia if critical gerontological social workers are to be enabled to support and advocate for older people and those who care for them in the most effective ways.

## Widening our understanding of dementia care

Cantley (2001) has argued that, in a multi-agency context, the first essential step is for practitioners and managers to understand a range of theoretical perspectives relevant to their own and others' practice. Social work training and practice espouse the importance of working with individuals, but they are also concerned with the social, structural and economic systems within which individuals operate. Social workers wishing to engage in critical practice with older people should therefore be encouraged to consider additional theoretical developments beyond the traditional approaches discussed so far. In this context, we now discuss the more recent extension of attachment theory to informing our understanding of behaviours associated with dementia. This is followed by a brief consideration of structural aspects, with a focus on ethnicity, before outlining recent developments in biographical and rehabilitative work, which have both contributed to widening our understanding of dementia and dementia care.

## The role of attachment

The early work of Bowlby (1969) on attachment behaviours highlighted the ways in which attachment experiences between a child and his/her parent would have an impact on the child's emotional and behavioural development. In recent years, this work has been extended and developed to consider both the role of attachment in adult and later life (Antonucci, 1994) and the impact of childhood attachment experiences on later life attachment behaviours. Andersson and Stevens (1993), for example, argue that evidence suggests that early attachment experiences have an impact on attachment behaviours in later life. However, their research also indicated that the presence of important attachments formed in adulthood (such as a partner) could mitigate the effects of ambivalent/anxious or disrupted attachment experiences learnt through childhood experience.

Alongside these developments, there is growing interest in the role of attachment experience and behaviours in dementia. For example, Miesen (1992) has argued that, in severe dementia, the attachment behaviours a person may ordinarily have may be increasingly difficult to enact as memory, language and orientation become compromised. As a result, a person with dementia may seek comfort and security in past early relationships, which are often believed by the person to exist in the present. Deceased parents may therefore be identified as living, available and in a relationship with the person with dementia.

Other research has extended this understanding of attachment behaviours and explored the potential of simulated presence therapy (SPT) to provide comfort and security to people with dementia who are living in a nursing home (Woods and Ashley, 1995). SPT comprises audio-taped material, produced by a person close to the person with dementia. The material is made up of cherished memories, anecdotes and experience shared between the person with dementia and their loved one. Its rationale is that the voice of a person who represents a key attachment figure in the life of the person with dementia will promote well-being, encourage ongoing attachment behaviours and reduce separation anxiety. Woods and Ashley's (1995) research was carried out with twenty-seven participants, and they found that the use of SPT had a significant impact on emotional state, evidenced by the person exhibiting positive behaviours such as singing, smiling, laughing and verbalizing. Results also suggested a significant impact by SPT on reducing behaviour such as social isolation, agitation and anxiety. However, this is a small sample and there is clearly a need for further research in the area of attachment and simulated presence therapy.

While the research base examining attachment and dementia is clearly an evolving one, Browne and Shlosberg (2005) identified a number of potential practice implications. They contend that it can help practitioners to understand why a person may be behaving in a certain way, and assist carers in planning positive support strategies. In addition, by encouraging support staff and carers to consider a person with dementia and their attachment style and past attachment experiences, it can help in understanding how a person with dementia relates to staff and carers. Finally, a basic awareness of attachment through training may help both carers and staff to respond more appropriately to the emotional meanings of so-called 'challenging' or 'confused' behaviour (Mills *et al.*, 1999, cited in Brown and Shlosberg, 2006).

## Ethnicity and dementia

From both research and practice perspectives, it is important to acknowledge that people with dementia, like all older people, are also located in other structural contexts such as age, gender, sexuality, class and ethnic minority membership. A critical gerontological approach argues forcefully that an analysis of multi-faceted structural features is important to illustrate how other oppressions, such as racism, are experienced over the life course, and how these in turn impact on a person who is diagnosed with dementia. For example, there is now considerable evidence demonstrating a widespread lack of culturally appropriate services for older people from minority ethnic groups (Forbat and Nar, 2003). Members of minority ethnic communities may be rendered effectively invisible by services that are, in reality, geared to the needs of the dominant population. This, in turn, may be reinforced by a lack of understanding among such communities about what dementia is, and what it is like to live with, and care for, someone with dementia (Jutlla and Moreland, 2007).

Iliffe and Manthorpe (2004) further highlight the contested nature of terminology used to discuss ethnicity, and argue that the primary issue between ethnicity and dementia may relate more to the misunderstandings of professionals than to a precise relationship between the two. For example, services may be developed with an 'Asian' community in mind, but this generic term covers huge diversity and difference between and within religious and cultural groups. Citing the work of Alexander (2002), Iliffe and Manthorpe (2004) comment that notions of collectivity may render less visible the heterogeneity that exists within groups. In other words, attempts to provide culturally sensitive services based on an understanding of a group of people (for example, Sikh people) may result in promoting inappropriate assumptions about individuals, rather than addressing what is needed to provide 'tailored, wrap around services for diverse individuals' (Iliffe and Manthorpe, 2004, p. 289). This can further reinforce stereotypes such as 'Asian' people looking after their own. Anti-oppressive approaches support a practice that, rather than making professional assumptions, engages in a dialogue with the person. Such an approach recognizes the expertise and experience of 'the other' and seeks to ensure the inclusion of people in the process of negotiated interventions.

## Biographical understandings

One important way of facilitating dialogue, which has gained considerable ground over recent years, is to develop an understanding of the individual person's biography and identity. Awareness of individual biography is important for a number of reasons. First, recognizing an individual as a unique person may help practitioners to keep that person at the centre of what they are doing and help to maintain personhood in the ways envisaged by Kitwood and others. Such an approach challenges the potential to respond to a person with dementia as just another member of an essentially homogenous group, whatever their ethnic or cultural background. Second, biographical information may enhance understanding of the person's individual context. How long a person has lived in his/her house; the person's interests and achievements; his/her family history; experiences of migration; and relationships with friends constitute essential information that may illuminate areas of strength and resources as well as those of need. Biographical information is also likely to provide insights into which aspects of a person's life that person would wish to preserve or maintain. Third, biographical information is a vital component in care planning. It is important for a person with dementia to have his/her habits, routines and preferences respected in planning care or support. This may not only contribute to helping the person feel secure, but may also ensure that he or she continues to participate actively in their own lives. Finally, biographical information – especially where it can be linked with insights from attachment theory – can help to understand behaviour that may not be easy to understand, or is perceived as 'challenging'. Again, this may be crucial in helping formal and informal carers to provide sensitive support and assistance.

To illustrate the importance of biographical understandings, consider Extract 4.3. This reflects on the evocative power of smells, textures and sights in conjuring powerful images and memories of Mrs McKay from her granddaughter's perspective. If you were working with this family, how would you try to ensure that Grandma's memories were preserved? How could you capture some of this information in an assessment, and what would the challenges be of achieving this?

## Extract 4.3 *Biographical understandings*

The house smells of Grandma when I go in ... Grandma is kept very clean but she just smells of being old. Just old. She's forgotten her tartan shawl. I pick it up from the sofa and bury my face in it. Mum comes in and says to give the shawl to her, it needs washing, that she shudders to think how many times Grandma has blown her nose on it and mopped up tea and used it to wipe dishes. She will wash it in Lux flakes and rinse it in Comfort and hang it in the garden to dry in the wind. In fact, she'll help Grandma to wash it and hang it out herself tomorrow, she'll love that. It's perfectly true. Grandma is passionately happy scrubbing things. I look at her, when Mum has her standing at the sink up to her elbows in suds, and I can always see Mum is right. Washing is women's work. It doesn't take Grandma back to backbreaking days of unremitting labour, when she had to heat the water in a copper and stand in a freezing wash house, oh no, it takes her back to a house full and never a lonely moment and a sense of purpose.
(Margaret Forster, *Have the Men Had Enough?*)
Seen from Hannah's perspective, p. 20.

### A focus on rehabilitation

Alongside the now wider acceptance that biography and identity are important to our understanding of people with dementia, recent years have also witnessed much greater practice effort geared towards the rehabilitation of older people. Social work has contributed to the multi-disciplinary rehabilitative team in a number of ways; for example, undertaking components of multi-disciplinary assessment, participating in intermediate care plans, contributing to hospital discharge planning, and post-discharge care and support. Historically, however, people with dementia have not generally been linked to rehabilitative services. But there are some encouraging signs that this is beginning to change. Marshall (2005), for example, has identified four major strands of rehabilitation in respect of people with dementia which we regard as being crucial to widening our understanding of dementia and dementia care. She suggests that rehabilitation is important:

1. Following an acute illness, surgery or medical intervention.
2. After a period of 'challenging' behaviour (for example, a person being admitted for assessment to a specialist ward from a care home environment where their behaviour was identified as 'difficult to manage').
3. As a means of making the best use of brain function by cognitive rehabilitation; the emphasis is on an ability model rather than one of deficit.
4. As a positive approach to dementia care underpinned by the assumption that obtaining appropriate, timely and skilful assistance will contribute to better functioning and, potentially, quality of life.

However, while generic research examining outcomes and the effectiveness of rehabilitative effort is beginning to develop, there is still a paucity of research on the effectiveness of rehabilitation for people with dementia. Consequently, there is much that still needs to be done to continue to actively construct models of rehabilitation that are specific to the needs of people with dementia (Mountain, 2004). This, then, is one of many important tasks facing the development of critical gerontological social work practice.

## Dementia and critical gerontological social work practice

Good practice guidelines in dementia care have been published jointly by the National Centre for Clinical Excellence (NICE) and the Social Care Institute for Excellence (SCIE) (NICE/SCIE, 2006). These guidelines include a commitment to the principles of person-centred care as the underpinning knowledge, skill and value base in dementia care. Paradoxically, however, an increase in awareness of the needs of people with dementia has not generally coincided with increases in proactive support services. Consequently, those who subscribe to a critical gerontological practice orientation must contribute to making explicit the experience of dementia, and to promoting interventions that enhance quality of life and enable the active participation of older people with dementia in service development. In order to do this, we suggest that practice needs to focus on the challenges of improving communication, of appropriate assessment and care planning, and of effective partnership with informal carers: issues to which we now turn our attention.

## *The importance of communication*

Despite the limited contribution that speech makes to the totality of human interaction, we have a long socialization in the importance of verbal communication. In our day-to-day lives, value is placed on our ability to communicate verbally: we tend to value eloquent expression, the ability to build a coherent argument, debate a case and, as a result, receive positive outcomes such as validation of identity, respect and access to resources. Language also communicates information about power and the ways in which hierarchical relationships are maintained and characterized by the possession of resources such as particular or specialist knowledge.

Social work, along with most other areas of health and social care practice, relies heavily on the use of verbal communication in its construction of relationships, development of a therapeutic alliance and achievement of key processes such as assessment. The extent of our reliance on verbal communication is illustrated by the fact that we may feel discomfited and vulnerable when faced with communicating with a person with dementia who does not use words, or communicates in unexpected ways or ways that 'break the rules' (see, for example, Killick and Allan, 2001).

Traditionally then, people with dementia have been perceived as people who, as they become progressively 'engulfed' by the condition, inevitably lose the ability to communicate. A perceived loss of communication ability is then linked to loss of personhood, which in turn fuels paternalistic practice, where communication with carers and family members becomes *about*, rather than *with* the person with dementia, especially where, for example, social workers want to undertake an assessment or discuss possible care options (Brooker, 2004). One implication of such an approach to communication is that it privileges the voice of carers over the voice of the individual with dementia. Decisions can be made 'for' and 'about' a person with dementia because they are effectively silenced, both as individuals and collectively.

The importance of communication, and seeking different and appropriate ways to communicate, have become even more fundamental to good practice in England and Wales since the Mental Capacity Act (2005) came into force in April, 2007. In Scotland, mental capacity is addressed in the Adults with Incapacity (Scotland) Act, 2000, but there is no equivalent law on mental capacity in Northern Ireland at the time of writing. The principles of the Mental Capacity Act include the presumption that adults have capacity unless it is established that they lack capacity; and, moreover, that all practical steps must be taken to help the person make decisions (McDonald and Taylor, 2006). Consequently, critical gerontological social work practice would seek to wholeheartedly embrace the importance of utilizing and developing communication skills which ensure that people with dementia have continued opportunities for social engagement, participation and inclusion.

The basic principles of empathy, warmth and genuineness (Truax and Carkhuff, 1967) remain fundamentally important skills for effective communication. But, beyond that, communicating positively with people with dementia often requires a shift in emphasis away from traditional patterns of (verbal) communication and its associated rules, towards developing greater self awareness of, for example, our use of non-verbal communication (Killick and Allan, 2001). The principle of congruence must underpin communication if it is to be effective. That is, 'what we believe must match what we say (verbally) which must match what we do with our body and voice. Any discrepancy will engender a mixed message and mixed messages serve only to confuse and threaten' (Perrin and May, 2000, p. 88). For example, it would be difficult to believe that someone was listening to us if they persistently glanced around the room, checked their watch and fidgeted with their diary.

Research suggests that skills in non-verbal communication in people with dementia are comparable to those of people who are not known to have dementia. Killick and Allan (2001) have argued that people with dementia may in fact have a greater enhancement of non-verbal skills because of the need to assess peoples' moods and disposition towards offering help or assistance. Communicating with a person with dementia may mean that we use physical contact (such as appropriate touch) along with eye contact, a smile and voice tone to communicate interest and engagement. We may use physical gestures to emphasize a verbal message, or perhaps use a photograph or picture to communicate. For a person with severe dementia, singing, massage, mirroring body movements and hand holding may all help to communicate engagement and presence (for a full discussion, see Killick and Allan, 2001). It is not possible to be prescriptive about the best ways to use non-verbal communication, because what works with one person may not work well with another. Cultural factors, gender, personal preferences and the nature of the relationship will all influence ways in which communication develops and highlights the importance of thinking about interaction on the basis of the individual person, rather than trying to apply a 'blanket rule'. Consider, for example, the recent advancements in the use of Talking Mats™, described in Box 4.1.

---

**Box 4.1    Research into practice: the use of Talking Mats™ in communicating with older people with communication difficulties**

The use of Talking Mats™ has been assessed as a means of enhancing communication with older people with communication difficulties, living in a care home (Murphy *et al.*, 2005). Ten older people participated in the research, all of whom had communication difficulties as a result of dementia, stroke or other long-term illness. Talking Mats™ provide pictorial representations of everyday topics (for example, activities). The research project worked with older people to establish their views about topics such as activities in the care home and the environment. The researchers concluded that the Talking Mats™ enhanced the participants' ability to communicate, helped them to organize and express what they wanted to say and increased motivation to participate in communication. The researchers concluded that Talking Mats™ had a variety of applications (for example, for use with people with comprehension difficulties, hearing loss, unclear speech, people without speech). The mats could provide an important part of a repertoire of communication skills to enable people to participate in research, evaluate services and communicate individual wishes, preferences, likes and dislikes.

---

Person-centred communication of the kind described in Box 4.1 means that practitioners need also to be aware of their own communication styles, the ways in which social work shapes and constructs their language, and to reflect on their use of non-verbal communication (Perrin and May, 2000). For example, an emphasis on open-ended questions typically used as good practice to elicit fuller responses may be difficult to cope with by a person with a poor working memory. Again, it is vital to consider how such practices may be experienced from the perspective of the individual with dementia rather than on the basis of a set of prescribed communication 'rules'. However, Box 4.2 illustrates some general and encompassing principles of person-centred communication practices which

## Box 4.2  Research into practice: relationship-centred approaches

Relationship-centred practice seeks to highlight the importance of interdependences and the reciprocal nature of close personal relationships. Adams and Gardiner (2005) highlight that relationship-centred practice moves beyond Kitwood's conception of 'malignant social psychology', which focused essentially on the subjective experience of a person with dementia. From a social constructionist perspective, the impact of structural factors such as identity, power, role and social location construct different sets of meaning within dementia care triads (Adams and Gardiner, 2005, p. 188). Other writers have commented on the likelihood of triadic interaction between social work or health care professionals, the person with dementia and their caregiver or supporter (for example, Biggs, 1993). Communication in triads can often create alliances that may effectively exclude one person from the encounter. People with dementia may be particularly susceptible to exclusion or marginalization in an encounter between a professional worker and care giver. On this basis, the authors identify the conditions for 'enabling dementia communication and disabling dementia communication', as highlighted below.

| Enabling dementia communication | Disabling dementia communication |
| --- | --- |
| Removing unwanted stimuli | Interrupting |
| Getting in the right position | Speaking on behalf of the person with dementia |
| Promoting equal participation | Reinterpreting what the person with dementia was saying which undermines the credibility of accounts given by the person with dementia |
| Demonstrating (modelling) inclusive and enabling communication to the care giver and person with dementia | Using technical or professional language and jargon |
| Providing opportunities (and time) to talk and communicate | Talking out of earshot of the person with dementia (for example, on the way out to the front door) |
| Being sensitive to non-verbal cues | Taking sides by verbal utterances or non-verbal behaviour (e.g. body positioning, proximity) |
| Valuing and respecting the contributions of people with dementia | Ignoring the person and making no effort to communicate or include the person with dementia |
| Developing appropriate strategies to overcome communication difficulties | Ridicule |
| Promoting and encouraging joint decision-making | Not inviting the person with dementia to meetings or discussions that are about them |

are important aide-memoires for gerontological social work practitioners (adapted from Adams and Gardiner, 2005).

Importantly too, it may take time for you as a practitioner to build up a relationship with a person who struggles to remember who you are, and may feel afraid or suspicious of you. It is likely that the interaction will need to be slowed down to maximize the opportunity for a person with dementia to participate and not be outpaced. For example, it may take time for a person to answer a question or formulate a response; deciding too quickly that a person cannot or will not respond may, in effect, stymie every attempt the person makes to communicate (Innes and Capstick, 2001). Like all of us, a person with dementia may also be better able to participate at some times of the day than others, while sensory issues such as acquired hearing loss are woefully neglected as a factor inhibiting communication with a person with dementia (Allen *et al.*, 2003), as are other physical conditions that might be painful and debilitating.

### Assessment and care planning

Communication is clearly important when it comes to assessment and care planning for people with dementia. Yet critical questions remain about how social work practitioners communicate the purpose of assessment and, indeed, undertake an assessment with a person with memory impairment and communication difficulties. While, in our view, the kind of biographical approach discussed earlier clearly constitutes good practice where comprehensive, and indeed specialist, assessment is concerned, there are often tensions between what may constitute sound and inclusive practice, and the pressures created by the requirement for a speedy turnover of assessments (Gorman and Postle, 2003); an over-reliance on check lists that focus on medical models; and performance indicators that require assessments to begin within 48 hours of initial contact and for 70 per cent to be completed within two weeks, and the remaining 30 per cent within four weeks (McDonald and Taylor, 2006).

Care planning is also a vital component in the provision of services and support, and the link between the person's assessment and statement of need and the subsequent care plan should be clear. Of course, care plans do not just address the needs of the individual person with dementia; they also identify goals for the provision of support or services to carers or the wider family/support system. Like assessment, care plans should make use of biographical understandings as a way of assisting gerontological social workers to deliver personalized and sensitive care and support. Most importantly, care plans should also make visible the involvement and participation of the people for whom they are intended; identify the outcomes that will be achieved by specific interventions; what steps will be taken or services/resources used to achieve outcomes; who will undertake different aspects of the intervention; and what needs to happen for the goal to be successful. They should also be physically accessible and, in keeping with the aspiration of improved communication, should be written in clear, jargon-free language and available in different formats if required (such as audio tape). People with dementia do not just (or indeed always) have physical care needs, and care plans should reflect this.

In addition, people with dementia may experience rapid change and transition, and Tibbs (2001) makes the point that care plans often need frequent adjustment if they are to remain meaningful to the experience of the person. The importance of continuity in the person leading care planning is crucial: it is problematic trying to adjust a care plan when a practitioner is new to the situation and has little insight into the changes that have taken place, or the baseline from which change has happened. This, of course, raises further issues for social workers who may find themselves organized into teams with discrete activities such as 'intake and assessment', 'complex care' and 'review and monitoring' teams. While this may address the organizational difficulty of practitioners holding large numbers of 'cases', it detracts from the possibility of people with dementia experiencing continuity by, for example, having the same gerontological social worker over a period of time.

### Working with informal carers

Although we address the difficult issues practitioners face in working with informal carers later in the book (see Chapter 7), it is important to highlight here some of the ways that gerontological social workers can support the carers of people with dementia. First, in relation to assessment and care planning, it is evident that social workers are very well placed to provide a valuable source of support, assistance and advice to carers during the whole process. Provided they have taken the time to build sound relationships with the person with dementia and his or her carers, gerontological social workers will be able to address the concerns and worries of families in appropriate and supportive ways. Second, and of particular importance, gerontological social workers should be able to identify specific needs of carers in the process of assessment, and enable the carers to access appropriate support and resources to meet their own needs. Third, they may participate in group support/education for carers (and potentially, individuals with dementia); and fourth, they can be instrumental in finding ways of encouraging those carers who wish to participate in the active care and support of people with dementia.

One practical example of this latter point is the potential afforded by life-story work. Life-story work has been identified as an important element in ensuring that individual biography is made visible by helping people to recall and record their personal history (Gibson, 1994). Gerontological social workers may contribute positively to this by, for example, helping a person with dementia and his or her family members/informal carers to begin a life-story book. Bell and Troxel (2001) highlight a number of significant ways in which life-story work may be used positively to enhance well-being:

- It is helpful in acting as a remembrance book for people with memory difficulties.
- Relationships between family members and a person with dementia can become unsettled or altered as a result of the declining cognitive powers of the person with dementia. Helping a person with dementia can be a very positive way of finding new ways of engaging with the person – providing a new source of interest and a positive relationship experience.
- It provides a framework to which people can refer when experiencing some form of transition, such as receiving new care or support at home, or moving to a residential setting.
- A life-story book can provide a source of communication; validate and celebrate achievements; keep the person at the centre of their own lives; and help with the development of new relationships.

As an illustration, Extract 4.4 highlights an important aspect of Grandma McKay's identity and her biography. How would you capture this information in life-story work? How could you try to ensure that these important parts of her life are identified as strengths and maintained as continuities?

In working with informal carers, we recognize the complexity and difficulties of these tasks and acknowledge that gerontological social workers have a fine line to tread between addressing and meeting the needs of the person with dementia, and ensuring that the needs of informal carers are also given adequate consideration. As we discussed in Chapter 2, access to services is often linked to diagnosis and to eligibility criteria and, as a result, one (unintended) consequence has been that carers who lack practical and emotional support and assistance have often come to the attention of formal services when

## Extract 4.4   Life-story work and identity

Adrian looks how Grandma thinks real men should look. Grandma is appallingly sexist. Men should be tall, men should be broad, men should be strong. If I ask her why, she says feeble things like 'for working' ...

Adrian slobbily asks Grandma if she would like a cup of tea ... yes she would like some fresh. Adrian makes it with the maximum of fuss. Then he says he had better go and rest before the next shift. Grandma says he's done well and he's a fine worker and to get his head down at once and she'll wake him for his dinner. Very slowly, when he's gone, she gets up and lifts the pan of water into which she has mistakenly put the potato scrapings. She carries it carefully to the sink while Mum and I watch. Slowly she puts it down, accurately, on the draining board and then starts searching. Neither of us ask what she is looking for. We know she wouldn't be able to tell us. It becomes quite fascinating watching as drawer after drawer is opened, cupboard after cupboard inspected. She is in a trance. Probably she's already forgotten what she was looking for, but no. She locates a sieve. That's it. Back she goes to the sink and strains the potato scrapings through the sieve then lifts the pan onto the cooker. She sighs with contentment and tells us the soup will not be long, it'll be ready when the men come in.

(Margaret Forster, *Have the Men Had Enough?*)
Seen from Hannah's perspective, pp. 39–40.

effectively it is too late. A carer who becomes exhausted and over-burdened to the point that the person with dementia is then admitted to a care home, is an all too familiar tale. Moreover, the long-term consequences for the emotional health of informal carers involved in these kinds of circumstances remains relatively invisible and under-researched. This situation persists despite the fact that legislation now (theoretically) ensures that people who either do provide regular and substantial care, or who plan to provide regular and substantial care, are entitled to an assessment in their own right (Carers [Recognition and Services] Act, 1995; Carers and Disabled Children Act, 2000; Carers (Equal Opportunities) Act, 2004). Furthermore, the NICE/SCIE (2006) good practice guidelines in dementia care also emphasize the support needs of carers (see Box 4.3).

## Box 4.3 Research into practice: NICE/SCIE clinical guidelines on supporting people with dementia and their carers (2006)

Evidence from research about interventions and services for carers was reviewed systematically. Evidence reviews highlighted:

- Misperceptions and misunderstandings by carers about dementia and its potential implications.
- A lack of supportive and proactive services directed at carers of people with dementia.
- The potential for information and knowledge to decrease the risk of depression in carers of people with dementia.
- The difficulties for carers from black and minority ethnic groups to access help and information.

Interventions involving training of carers and stress management which involved the person with dementia appeared to have the largest effect on carers' psychological health and well-being (Brodaty et al., 2003).

Recommendations for carers of people with dementia included:

Care plans should include tailored interventions for carers of people with dementia, which should consider:

- Individual and group psycho-education.
- Peer support groups.
- Other forms of indirect support (e.g. telephone/internet).
- Training for carers about dementia, services and benefits.
- Involvement of other family members.
- The potential involvement of the person with dementia.
- Provision of transport, respite care and short breaks to enable carers to participation in such interventions.
- Specialist therapeutic support for carers experiencing psychological distress.

## Conclusion

Since the early 1990s, the developing managerialist agenda has emphasized progressively the importance of managing effectively within finite resources, with a narrow focus on eligibility criteria. Increasingly, the assessment of risk and risk management has been utilized as a means of managing finite resources (see Chapter 3). As a consequence, people with dementia and their carers all too often come to the attention of social workers and health care workers only in a crisis, having already coped with the experience of dementia and its implications and consequences for a considerable period of time. While there is evidence of the benefits of preventative, small-scale interventions having a positive impact on the quality of life of older people (Tanner, 2001), the ability of social services and health care departments to provide comprehensive and integrated preventative services remains largely aspirational. A critical approach, under-pinned by the values, skills and knowledge we have discussed above, would assist practitioners and formal services to recognize the importance of early intervention and respond to people with dementia and their carers in more sensitive and effective ways. However, how agencies geared to eligibility criteria that define those 'most in need' can respond to such a development remains open to question (CSCI, 2006a).

## stop and think

- What support services and resources are available in your area for older people recently diagnosed with dementia?
- How can practitioners support and assist people with dementia to actively participate in decisions about their support, care and housing needs?
- How can you find ways of keeping abreast of the research and developing knowledge about dementia?
- What are the potential benefits of life-story work for people with dementia?
- Are there any risks or difficulties that you would need to be aware of?

## taking it further

- Adams, T. and Manthorpe, J. (eds) (2003) *Dementia Care*, London, Arnold.
- Friedell, M. (2002) 'Awareness: A Personal Memoir on the Declining Quality of Life in Alzheimer's', *Dementia*, 1(3), pp. 359–66.
- Marshall, M. and Tibbs, M. A. (2006) *Social Work with People with Dementia: Partnerships, Practice and Persistence*, Bristol, BASW/Policy Press.
- National Institute for Clinical Excellence (NICE)/Social Care Institute for Excellence (SCIE) (2006) *Dementia: Supporting People with Dementia and their Carers in Health and Social Care: Clinical Guidelines 42*, London, NICE/SCIE; available at www.nice.org.uk.

# 5 Older people and end-of-life care

**main points**

- Despite the fact that death is most likely to occur in old age, considerable inequalities persist in the experience of death and dying for older people.

- Older people will often die after a period of deterioration; end of life is therefore often characterized by uncertainty as to when death is likely to occur.

- A reconceptualization of end of life and older people may help to promote positive, person-centred practices that embrace both life and living, and end of life/death.

- The need to promote awareness of palliative approaches to end of life in a range of non-specialist settings is highlighted as a means of improving end-of-life care for older people.

## Introduction

Death means, of course, the inevitable end of all our lives. While it is true that most people in our society die in older age, significant inequalities persist in experiences of the end of life. Such inequalities are evidenced by, for example, differential mortality rates in relation to factors such as social class as well as different experiences of dying between younger people and older people. Older people have also been particularly disadvantaged in their ability to access palliative care services, even though traditional approaches to palliative care are now being challenged by a developing knowledge base which reveals that the end of life for many older people often does not have a predictable pattern (Froggatt, 2004). There has also been a widening appreciation that, for the very many older people who do not die of cancer (a traditional area for palliative care), palliative care approaches would be particularly beneficial in the last years of their lives (Froggatt, 2004). Such research has contributed to the National Council for Palliative Care developing policy and practice initiatives specifically addressing the end-of-life treatment and care needs of older people (National Council for Palliative Care, 2005).

We argue in this chapter that this developing knowledge base is just as important to social workers who work with older people in non-specialist settings, as to those professionals practising in specialist environments. Social workers regularly work with older people who have long-term and deteriorating or changeable conditions. They may be called upon to assist older people with help and support at home, to help them access other types of support (for example, in a care home), and to participate in planning safe and effective discharges from hospital. Social workers, alongside other care professionals, therefore work with older people who need help to continue to live a life of quality, but who are also living out the last phase of their lives. Given the demonstrated differences between end-of-life care for older people compared with younger people who are dying, a sound knowledge base is essential when working with older people with serious physical and/or cognitive impairments and co-morbidities.

Consequently, this chapter begins by considering the environments in which older people are likely to die. Here, we look at the hard evidence, and at what key theorists have said about how contemporary society marginalizes and treats death. We discuss the notion of 'disadvantaged dying' and, in order to widen our understanding, discuss the argument that we should reconceptualize end-of-life care (Froggatt and Payne, 2006) in recognition that the end of life is uncertain for many older people living with deteriorating and long-term illness and disability. The importance of promoting an awareness of palliative approaches to end-of-life care in non-specialist settings is also highlighted. Finally, we turn our attention to the implications for critical gerontological social work practice with older people.

## Where do older people die?

Despite the widespread belief that people prefer to die at home, in a place of familiarity and in close contact with family and friends, it is evident that significant numbers of older men and women die in environments outside their home. Table 5.1 illustrates the number of older people who die in hospitals or other collective care settings (ONS, 2006c). At the time of writing, older people are most likely to die in hospital, followed by care home settings, then their own home and, finally, in a hospice (Age Concern, 2005).

**Table 5.1   Place of death (2005)**

| Age range | Hospitals | | Hospices | | Home | | Communal establishments | |
|---|---|---|---|---|---|---|---|---|
| | M | F | M | F | M | F | M | F |
| 65–74 | 31,437 | 22,310 | 3,684 | 3,076 | 13,416 | 8,282 | 2,645 | 2,592 |
| 75–84 | 55,085 | 53,622 | 3,976 | 3,370 | 16,857 | 14,124 | 9,689 | 15,578 |
| 85+ | 31,395 | 56,640 | 970 | 1,108 | 6,718 | 10,404 | 11,474 | 39,700 |

Source: ONS (2006c).

As Table 5.1 shows, over half the deaths of older people took place in a hospital setting, yet meeting the needs of people who are dying in hospital presents considerable challenges. In an early study, Field (1989) observed how nurses demonstrated 'detached concern' caused by a range of organizational factors, including poor stress management and the low status of nursing. A more recent ethnographic study examining the care of dying older people concluded that contact with patients was characterized by a lack of emotional engagement and poor communication about diagnosis, treatment and outcomes (Costello, 2001). Individualized care continued to focus on the demands of physical care, despite nursing staff highlighting the importance of psychosocial needs in end-of-life care (Costello, 2001). The research concluded that the still-dominant biomedical perspectives on care contributed to the less than satisfactory experiences of older people dying in hospital. Moreover, tensions have also been identified in the gap between nurses' perceptions of an 'ideal' death and their experiences of the realities of people dying in hospital (Hopkinson *et al.*, 2003).This research also reports the difficulties of meeting the needs of dying people in hospital, where the tendency to focus on physical needs takes precedence over addressing psychosocial needs.

In addition, older people may be wholly reliant on family and friends to support them in hospital. Family members may have to face the dilemmas associated with participating in complex ethical decisions about treatments, as well as trying to provide appropriate care and attention to the dying person while also acting as an intermediary between the dying person and medical practitioners (Seymour *et al.*, 2002). In these situations, family members are called upon to manage concerns that go beyond notions of autonomy and choice for the dying person, but which also involve a range of complex responsibilities and duties around preserving the personhood of their dying relative (Seymour *et al.*, 2002).

In Extract 5.1, Mrs McKay's family are faced with a number of dilemmas in respect of the care of their mother/grandmother. As you read, consider what you think the challenges are of providing individualized

## Extract 5.1 Dilemmas, complexities and care in an acute setting

I don't say a word. There's nothing to say. Nobody is thinking of poor Grandma lying in pain in hospital – we're all far too busy thinking of our own inconvenience …

We all visit every day. That is the easy part. No family could be more devoted. Mum goes at two o'clock and stays until four when I arrive and I stay until five when Adrian arrives and Adrian either leaves at half past or stays a little longer if Dad isn't going to be able to get there until seven. Adrian asks me what I do. I say I talk. Adrian says he talks but Grandma doesn't seem to hear him and he finds it embarrassing. I can just see him. He'll mutter and mumble and then he'll just sit looking gloomy and watching the clock …

Nurses are supposed to be angels. Maybe they are angels in other wards but not in this one. Or maybe they just don't think Grandma needs any angel-ling when she has this devoted family. They hardly seem to come near her. They always seem to be in the office or sluice room having private jokes. Grandma loves jokes – if they only knew. Grandma will laugh at anything, she would love their jokes. … Nurses have come while I've been there, twice, and tried to get Grandma up. It was pitiful, I thought, but they didn't seem to think so. They spoke loudly, telling Grandma to 'come *on*' and warning her this 'will not *do*.' If that's how they speak to her when I'm there, how do they treat her when I'm not?

(Margaret Forster, *Have the Men Had Enough?*)
Seen from Hannah's perspective, pp. 190–1.

care for a person with dementia in an acute setting such as a hospital. How can families be supported in these situations, when they are often coping with anxiety and uncertainty about their relative's condition and treatment, as well as being potentially in an unfamiliar or intimidating environment?

In contrast to the numbers of older people dying in hospital, only one in five older people dies in a care home (Froggatt, 2001). We also know that age, gender and social class are factors likely to influence whether or not an older person moves into such a setting. However, being in one's own home is usually identified as the preferred and ideal place to die (Bowling, 1983). But, for older people in particular, there may be a considerable gap between this aspiration and the reality, especially given the fact that many older people live alone. The prospect of dying alone is characterized by fear and anxiety (Seale, 1995) and often perceived as the 'worst case scenario' (Gott *et al.*, 2004). Qualitative research conducted with older people (Gott *et al.*, 2004) has also highlighted a number of practical and moral concerns associated with dying at home, both for the older person and for those who might be caring for him or her:

- Concern about being a burden to family and friends and concern about loved ones witnessing the older person's suffering.
- Anxiety and reluctance for family members to deliver care that was unduly intimate.
- Concerns about the quality of care that could be provided at home; for example, the availability of reliable symptom relief.
- The automatic exclusion from being cared for at home of widows, people living alone or people without close relatives.
- Awareness that an older person may live in very poor material circumstances which would not be a comfortable or appropriate place to die.

Regardless of where people die, however, there has also been considerable debate about whether Western societies are 'death denying'. This reflects a change from the familiarity of death across the life course in pre-industrial society towards increased concealment of death and the location of death in one part of the life course (that is, older age) in modern society. In the 1950s, Gorer (1955) argued that death had already become a taboo, as fewer and fewer people experienced it as a commonplace part of life. Ariès (1983) also suggested that Western societies view death with shame, and increasingly seek to move those who are dying out of the public view. It is only comparatively recently that the notion of death as a taboo subject in Western industrialized nations has been challenged by the growth of research, academic commentary and further theorizing about this complex issue (Mellor and Shilling, 1993).

## Theoretical perspectives

Giddens (1991) argues that death is a social process that is hidden and separated (what is often termed 'sequestered') from public space as a means of preserving what he calls our ontological security. Ontological security refers to people being able to preserve a sense of meaning, order and continuity in their day-to-day lives (Mellor, 1993). Death, by its very nature, has the potential to challenge ontological security profoundly by calling into question the meanings we ascribe to our social worlds. In fact, Mellor (1993: 13) comments that death is:

> *Always* a problem for *all* societies, since every social system must in some ways accept death, because human beings inevitably die, but at the same time social systems must to a certain extend deny death to allow people to go on in day-to-day life with some sense of commitment.

It is difficult to create and integrate a social acceptance of death, precisely because it cannot be contained or controlled (Giddens, 1991). Sickness and death are therefore experiences set apart from the routines of ordinary life. Mellor and Shilling (1993), among others, highlight the ways in which society copes with the realities of death and ageing, by physically setting apart people who are dying, and thus reinforcing the boundaries between the living and the dying. Residential homes have been viewed in this way and defined as 'dying spaces' (Hockey, 1990), where evidence of physical and cognitive decline, sickness and death are hidden. This negative and bleak view of life in an institutional setting is well illustrated in Extract 5.2. Once again, as you read, consider how we can counter the view that living in a care home is simply a final resting place before death? To what extent do you think we can create a view that care homes can be pleasant and enjoyable places to live, as well as comfortable and safe places to die?

In developing theoretical understandings, Froggatt (2001) has helpfully identified three elements of separation and segregation in respect of older people at the end of their lives. First, as we have already seen, at the societal level, contemporary society sets death apart from non-dying people. Second, at the local level, we see a further separation of groups of people within institutional settings. For example, more active people may separate themselves or be separated from, frail or dying older people as a means of continued assertion of their own social existence (Mulkay, 1993). This has associated implications for the social relationships they continue to encounter, for their physical location within the care home, and for the care and support received (Hockey, 1990). Froggatt (2001) also notes how residents are spatially separated, depending on their ability to interact and their level of cognitive impairment. In her research, less able residents were, for example, placed on the margins of activities in the role of passive bystanders, rather than being seen as meaningful participants. Readers too may be familiar with the experience of visiting some care homes where people with the most 'complex' needs are located furthest away from public spaces such as entrance halls and adjacent sitting rooms.

Third, Mulkay (1993) draws attention to the notion of 'social death', whereby an individual ceases to be perceived as a person with

## Extract 5.2   *Dying spaces*

I took Grandma back to her original chair, once more running the ordeal of what I was already thinking of as the Six Death Chairs and settled her down. I knew I must try to make friends for her – it was foolish to isolate her and make others jealous. I sat at her feet, holding her hand, and tried to talk to the women either side. One seemed remarkably sensible. She said her name was Ellen and that she had been in King's Wood a year and liked it very much thank you but missed her children ... The woman on the other side, to whom I turned for some relief, had very clear, alert eyes but could not talk. She tried to but all that came out was a mm-mm-mm sound, her lips working away desperately. Grandma said she wished this woman, on her left, would shut up and give her some peace ... All the other women sat there staring at me hungrily. When Charlie rang the door bell I leapt up and had kissed Grandma and gone all in a flash.

We did not speak on the way home. There was no need to. Depression filled our car like a fog. I found myself thinking of that inane question which turns up in women's magazine quizzes or on radio shows: how would you define happiness? I had just defined it and wished to be asked: happiness is coming out of King's Wood. It was sickening, the feeling of liberation. Of relief. Not to be in King's Wood was bliss. To breathe fresh air, see the trees, hear ordinary conversation. Not to be confronted by hopeless, despairing people waiting to die. Not to have to tussle with the hideous moral dilemma: why is this allowed? Why don't I do something? Oh, happiness was leaving King's Wood behind all right.

(Margaret Forster, *Have the Men Had Enough?*)
Seen from Jenny's perspective, pp. 204–6.

agency who can continue to act in, and on, relationships with others. Mulkay (1993) also highlights the ways in which care homes can create a physical separation between older people and 'full social actors' as part of their progressive exclusion from the social world. Social death increasingly reflects the breaking down of social bonds as physical and cognitive impairment, together with physical segregation, fundamentally challenge the usual elements that make up human relationships (Seale, 1995). Importantly too, Froggatt (2001) concludes that segregation and separation is influenced less by a clear separation of those people who are dying, but rather by 'transitional states' between living and dying that residents can occupy, temporarily or permanently, and sometimes for many weeks or months. This reflects the uncertainties often inherent in the end of life for older people, and will be returned to in the discussion below.

In contrast to transitional states, the development of Kübler-Ross's (1969) stage theory of responses to being terminally ill was, historically, a hugely influential model. Kübler-Ross proposed that terminally ill people progressed through a series of emotional stages as they reached the ends of their lives:

- denial;
- anger;
- bargaining;
- depression; and finally,
- acceptance.

These ideas were ground-breaking in highlighting the complex emotions that people faced when experiencing loss relating to their own life, or to the loss of a loved one. However, as a theory based on the premise of 'stages' of grief or reaction to loss, it has since been critiqued on a number of fronts. For example, the theory implies that reaction to grief or loss is a linear or staged process. As such, it offers little scope for diversity, and a person who does not progress through the stages in an appropriate manner might be perceived as reacting 'abnormally' (Kastenbaum, 1975). Nor does the theory address adequately cultural diversity. Deviation from the 'norm' can thus be perceived as being dysfunctional rather than being an appropriate reflection of cultural orientation. It is now accepted more widely that it is inappropriate to regard such stages as a prescription or rulebook for grief reactions. Rather, emotional reactions overlap, entangle and are visited and revisited over time (Stroebe *et al.*, 2001). New models of grief, such as the dual process model (Stroebe and Schut, 2001), emphasize two dimensions in the experience of loss: the first focusing on the experience of the loss, and the second concentrating on the present and the future. Grief reactions involve moving between these two dimensions and are discussed in detail in Chapter 6. For our purposes now, we refocus attention on the care needs of older people, and on the actual experience of dying and end-of-life care.

## Widening understanding of end-of-life care

End of life, and death and dying, is often characterized for older people by uncertainty as to when death will occur (National Council for Palliative Care, 2005). This has led to the necessity of reconceptualizing the end of life period for older people with complex physical and/or cognitive needs. Such a reconceptualization involves acknowledging the importance of considering end of life alongside a commitment to support and interventions that promote quality of life. A widening of access to palliative care services, and the importance of developing palliative skills and approaches in wider settings and circumstances, has also been highlighted.

## 'Disadvantaged dying' and older people

The term 'disadvantaged dying' was coined by Clarke and Seymour (1999), and refers to the persistent inequalities that are experienced by particular groups of people, especially those people who are marginalized, experience wider disadvantages throughout the life course, or are particularly susceptible for some reason to discriminatory practices. Older people, particularly the 'oldest old', are particularly susceptible to inequalities in end-of-life care. In our society, death is most likely to occur in older age. At the beginning of the twentieth century, deaths at age 75 and over occurred in only 12 per cent of the population. However, this figure has risen exponentially; it reached 39 per cent of the population by 1951, and 66 per cent in 2005 (ONS, 2006c).

Despite this considerable growth in longevity, a relationship has been consistently demonstrated between social inequalities, health inequalities and differential mortality rates (Scharf et al., 2005). Research shows that the more deprived a geographical area, the greater is its incidence of premature mortality (Eams et al., 1993). Structural factors such as class, poverty and housing quality have also been found to have an impact on where people die, as well as their experience of end-of-life care. For example, people from the highest socio-economic groups (1 and 2) are more likely to be able to choose where they die, and to have access to palliative care and hospice facilities. As an illustration of this, in an annual sample of people dying of cancer in Doncaster, Yorkshire, it was found that in socio-economic groups 1 and 2, only 14 per cent died in hospital, compared with 77 per cent of people in socio-economic groups 4 and 5 (Sims et al., 1997).

In reality, though, older people die of many causes other than cancer. The National Council for Palliative Care (2005) has observed that many other older people would have benefited from palliative care interventions in the last year of their life, including the two-thirds (approximately 260,000 people a year) who die from a range of causes such as chronic heart failure, vascular disease and respiratory conditions. Box 5.1 highlights this issue in respect of the unrecognized needs of older people with chronic heart failure.

**Box 5.1** Research into practice: advanced heart failure – impact on patients and informal carers

Heart failure has an increased prevalence with age, and following diagnosis, more than a third of the diagnosed population die within 12 months. It is generally recognized that older people suffering heart failure receive fewer health, social and palliative care services, and that such services are often poorly co-ordinated. A small-scale qualitative study (Aldred *et al.*, 2005) sought to explore perceptions and experiences of living with heart failure from the perspective of older people with the condition, and their informal carers. In-depth interviews were conducted with ten people with advanced heart failure, and with their primary carer.

Findings highlighted that primary symptoms focused on breathlessness, fatigue and physical debility, which had an impact on a person's ability to undertake everyday roles and responsibilities. People with heart failure have to cope with unpredictable symptoms, which are sometimes very severe. Participants therefore highlighted the difficulties of planning activities or having reliable social contact. This gave participants a feeling of isolation. These difficulties were often compounded by what participants experienced as inadequate and poorly co-ordinated service responses, including having poor or inadequate information about their condition and its implications.

Although this was a small study, the researchers highlighted the apparent importance of a palliative approach to this condition. Such an approach would aim to improve the co-ordination of services as well as providing for psychosocial support and appropriate interventions. A more appropriate focus of care and support should be directed towards promoting comfort and security, rather than the current emphasis on choice.

*Source*: Aldred *et al.*, 2005.

Moreover, diseases such as coronary heart disease and diabetes, which are of particular concern to older people from specific minority ethnic groups, do not yet fall within the remit of palliative care. This, Firth (2001) argues, raises critical questions about equity of both access and provision, while other research (Gunuratnam, 2006) has also reported a number of barriers to minority ethnic older people accessing palliative care:

- Lack of knowledge by older people from minority ethnic groups about the services that might be available. This is often reinforced by a lack of accessible information provided in appropriate languages and formats.

- Lack of confidence that services have the ability to meet cultural and religious needs.
- Inappropriate cultural assumptions about the needs and requirements of older people of different ethnicities, reinforced by a lack of training in developing culturally appropriate practice.

The widespread marginalization of older people in accessing palliative care services has also, at least in part, been influenced by assumptions about how older people themselves view death and dying. Death in older age is understood by many to be 'on time': occurring at the end of a 'good innings' (Lloyd, 2004). This notion may reinforce beliefs that older people are more accepting of death, are less troubled by a diagnosis of illness that may spell the end of their life, and that their symptoms are somehow less severe (Catt *et al.*, 2005). This in turn feeds into assumptions that older people are less in need of palliative care services than are younger people with terminal illnesses. However, research that seeks to challenge these assumptions and explore the attitudes, views and opinions of older people about end-of-life issues remains sparse.

Catt *et al.* (2005) are among the few researchers who have set out to test some of the assumptions that may underlie unequal provision. Using qualitative interviews and focus groups with older people, they examined views about the needs of older people for palliative care (when compared with younger people); the extent to which older people may be more accepting of death; and the extent of knowledge about palliative care (which may influence an older person's readiness to accept services of this type). The research concluded that, while respondents supported the view that it was 'easier' to die in older age, they refuted the notion that palliative and specialist services should be prioritized for younger people. In fact, they saw it as both fair and appropriate for older people to receive the same level of service as younger ones. In addition, respondents in this study had a good understanding of palliative care, and so, for this group, knowledge or lack of it could not be identified as an issue affecting preparedness to seek or accept palliative care. Despite being only a small-scale study, it nevertheless highlights that older people are well aware of the potential for unequal access to specialist and general palliative care.

### Palliative care and older people

Palliative care has been defined by the National Council for Palliative Care (2005, p. 3) as:

> The active holistic care of patients with advanced progressive illness. Management of pain and other symptoms and provision of psychological, social and spiritual support is paramount. The goal of palliative care is achievement of the best quality of life for patients and their families. Many aspects of palliative care are also applicable earlier in the course of the illness in conjunction with other treatments.

There is a differentiation between general and specialist palliative care services. General palliative care is defined as being provided by professional carers who are *informed* by the knowledge and practice of palliative care. By contrast, specialist palliative care is defined as the provision of specialized health and social care professionals who specialize in palliative treatment and work in specialist, multi-disciplinary teams. The National Council for Palliative Care argues that specialist services should in fact be available for people with complex palliative care needs in all care settings.

The World Health Organization (Davis and Higginson, 2004, p. 14) also highlights the importance of palliative care approaches in affirming life, regarding death as a normal process, and seeking neither to hasten nor prolong dying. In addition, the WHO recognizes that older people may have a wide range of complex care needs caused by:

- the impact of iatrogenic illness;
- coping with additional acute illness;
- the psychological impact of complex needs, characterized by fluctuating health and abilities and uncertainty; and
- structural factors such as the impact of economic hardship and social isolation.

These factors, together with an awareness of the reality that it is often difficult to predict the course of many chronic conditions affecting older people, build the case for a gerontological knowledge and skill base, specifically geared towards understanding the complexities of end-of-life issues for *all* older people.

Froggatt (2001) also argues that the commonly used term 'end of life' has different meanings and that, in the context of dying in a care home, it can be characterized by uncertainty as to when a person might die. This is because, for older people in care homes, death often comes after a time of deterioration or declining health (Davies and Higginson, 2004). Nevertheless, research has demonstrated that care home managers will often perceive and define 'end-of-life' care as relating to the last days or hours of a person's life (Froggatt, 2004). This understanding is also encapsulated in Standard 11 of the Care Standards Act (2000) which focuses on the immediate period before death, the person's actual death, and the processes to be undertaken immediately following a death. The result of this emphasis, Froggatt and Payne (2006) found, was that this standard was not addressed significantly in inspections because no one in the care homes being inspected had recently died.

Evidence also suggests that older people with complex needs may not always receive appropriate support. Sometimes this is because an older person dies very soon after admission and there is insufficient time to build a relationship with that person, or to grasp fully the complexity of his/her care needs. However, it remains the case that issues such as pain assessment and pain management are not always well recognized. Barriers to the identification of pain have been identified by Allcock *et al.* (2002) as including:

- Attitudes of professionals – it is 'expected', 'natural or 'normal' for an older, ill person to experience pain and discomfort – 'What can you expect, at your age?'
- Difficulties and anxieties about recognizing, assessing and treating pain correctly in people who have communication difficulties, or cognitive or sensory impairments.
- Older people may believe that they must be stoical or uncomplaining in a collective care setting, where their needs are likely, at least at times, to compete with the needs of others.

Allcock *et al.* (2002) further argue that the emphasis in the National Service Framework for Older People (Department of Health, 2001) is directed towards acute care and prevention, and that the needs of older people with serious chronic and life-limiting illness are less well recognized. These authors have also critiqued the National Minimum Standards for being almost 'pain neutral'. This means that the presence of pain, and the importance of pain assessment and management, is only detailed to any extent in Standard 11 (Dying and Death).

Despite repeated calls for older people to be enabled to die at home, the gap between aspiration and reality, as we have highlighted, is often considerable. Outside of the moral concerns raised with regard to burdens placed on informal carers, there is also the issue of the extent to which a person's home can remain a 'defensible space' when, in effect, it has become the site of formal care provision. Milligan (2000) highlights the potential tensions and blurring of roles when domestic space is merged with formal service provision. She argues that, in this arrangement, people can be as confined at home as they might be in an institutional setting. Issues of body management and disembodiment (for example, loss of continence) are also likely to create anxieties about the ability both to achieve a comfortable death, and to cope with ambivalence, fear or distaste

**Box 5.2    Research into practice: Standard 11 – Dying and Death**

11.1  Care and comfort are given to service users who are dying, their death is handled with dignity and propriety, and their spiritual needs, rites and functions observed.

11.2  Care staff make every effort to ensure that the service user receives appropriate attention and pain relief.

11.3  The service user's wishes concerning terminal care and arrangements after death are discussed and carried out.

11.4  The service user's family and friends are involved (if that is what the service user wants) in planning for and dealing with increasing infirmity, terminal illness and death.

11.5  The privacy and dignity of the service user who is dying are maintained at all times.

11.6  Service users are able to spend their final days in their own rooms, surrounded by their personal belongings, unless there are strong medical reasons to prevent this.

11.7  The registered person ensures that staff and service users who wish to offer comfort to a service user who is dying are enabled and supported to do so.

11.8  Palliative care, practical assistance and advice, and bereavement counselling are provided by trained professionals /specialist agencies if the service user wishes.

11.9  The changing needs of service users with deteriorating conditions or dementia – for personal support or technical aids – are reviewed and met swiftly to ensure the individual retains maximum control.

11.10  Relatives and friends of a service user who is dying are able to stay with him/her, unless the service user makes it clear that he or she does not want them to, for as long as they wish.

11.11  The body of a service user who has died is handled with dignity, and time is allowed for family and friends to pay their respects.

11.12  Policies and procedures for handling dying and death are in place and observed by staff.

*Source*: Care Homes for Older People: National Minimum Standards (Department of Health, 2000d p. 13)

often associated with managing the discharge of bodily fluids and other visible deterioration of the body. Indeed, continence difficulties as well as severe pain have been identified as specific triggers to promote a move from home to another form of collective care setting (Gott *et al.*, 2004).

In a climate of cost containment, it is unlikely that a person living alone would receive sufficient support from the formal services to make dying at home a feasible prospect (Lloyd, 2004). The impact too of age-based discrimination, and underlying assumptions about where and how older people should die, are likely to have an impact on people's perceptions of the desirability of dying at home. Lock and Higginson (2005) argue that notions of choice are confounded by realism: for a group who are already disadvantaged, choice becomes a less relevant concept to inform current discussions about end of life and older people. On this basis, it is argued that dying in hospital should not be 'demonized' but, instead, effort should be made to find ways to improve the experience of dying in an institutional setting (Gott *et al.*, 2004).

## Reconceptualizing end of life

There is, then, a clear case for reconsidering what is meant by a 'good death' with respect to older people with complex needs, whose transition between living and dying is both unclear and uncertain. This, according to Lloyd (2004), means moving beyond the current preoccupation with rights and control, towards an ethic of care. This would recognize the connectedness and interdependence of human beings, and consciously seek to develop practice concerned with care and well-being. Lloyd (2004, p. 253) argues that:

> A social policy based on the centrality of care to social life in general would be an important corrective to the current depiction of older dependent people as a separate group whose rights as individual citizens must be subjected to the political imperative of maintaining limits on expenditure.

In Western society, we place huge value on independence. The notion of independence is translated into social and health care policies current at the time of writing: policy goals now focus on older people being able to maintain autonomy, independence and choice. However, a policy emphasis on 'successful ageing', for example, offers little to an older person experiencing chronic ill-health who is in the last phase of their life. Lloyd (2004, p. 236) further argues that, in respect of older people and end-of-life care, the language of emancipation in fact offers a limited view of well-being. The language of a 'good death' tends to emphasize choice and control, with an expectation that dying can be pinpointed as a specific transition. One example of this orientation is provided in Box 5.3, which details Age Concern England's (2005) 'Principles of a Good Death'.

## Box 5.3 Research into practice: 'Principles of a Good Death'

The principles of a 'good death' are to:

■ Know when death is coming and to understand what can be expected;
■ Retain control over what happens;
■ Be afforded dignity and privacy;
■ Control over pain relief and other symptoms;
■ Choice and control over where death occurs;
■ Access spiritual and emotional support required;
■ Access hospice care in any location, not just in hospice;
■ Control over who is present and who shares the end;
■ Issue advance directives;
■ Have time to say goodbye and control over other aspects of timing; and
■ To be able to leave when it is time to go and not to have life prolonged pointlessly

*Source*: Age Concern England, 2005.

While these principles are in many ways laudable, they do not easily reflect the complexities and ethical issues inherent in end-of-life care for an older person who has, for example, a severe cognitive impairment. Lloyd (2004) has also questioned whether these principles stretch a desire for autonomy beyond the limits of possibility.

Given these complexities, Froggatt (2004) has suggested that a reconceptualization of end-of-life issues is necessary. Her reconceptualization seeks to integrate living and dying in three phases, which appear to us to resonate more closely with the experience of older people. Although this work focuses on care in residential homes, it is likely to be of relevance in other settings, such as the care of older people with complex needs who live at home. The three phases Froggatt (2004) identifies are:

■ Support directed at openly acknowledging the losses associated with a transition into a care home, or as a result of declining physical and cognitive abilities; support directed at helping people to live a life of quality.
■ Care focused on the time of dying and death.
■ Support with the bereavement/s that follow the person's death.

At the heart of this reconceptualization lie notions of person-centred practice (Kitwood, 1997; Brooker, 2007), but a person-centred

## Box 5.4 Research into practice: The Senses Framework

| | |
|---|---|
| A sense of security | To feel safe and receive competent and sensitive care |
| A sense of belonging | Opportunities to form new relationships and to feel part of the place |
| A sense of continuity | Recognition of the importance of biography. Recollection of past events; use of biography to inform current care; ongoing evolution of biography |
| A sense of achievement | Opportunities to engage in purposeful activity; to be able to set goals and make progress towards desired goals |
| A sense of significance | That you matter and that you are a person of worth and value |

*Source*: Nolan *et al.*, 2006.

practice that embraces a more complex approach than that defining Standard One of the National Service Framework for Older People (Department of Health, 2001). Such an approach actively seeks to work with the whole person (compared to focusing only on physical needs); celebrates and recognizes diversity; considers each person as a unique human being; and provides interventions that build on people's strengths, resources and coping strategies, and which are aimed at reducing the impact of cognitive, functional and behavioural needs (Kitwood, 1997; Brooker, 2007). More recently, Froggatt (2006) has also highlighted the work of Nolan and his colleagues (2006) on relationship-centred care and on the development of the 'Senses Framework', which provides a therapeutic direction for relationship-centred care (see Box 5.4). Together, these approaches provide a basis for considering some of the ways in which gerontological social work with older people at the end of their life may best be undertaken.

## End-of-life care and critical gerontological social work

Currer (2001) highlights some specific skills that social work practice already does, and can, contribute to end-of-life care. Not surprisingly, these skills focus on the importance of active listening;

forming and developing relationships with people when they are likely to feel anxious and uncertain; working with systems to encourage communication in others; and promoting the rights of older people through effective advocacy. Alongside this, McMurray *et al.*, (2003) identify a number of core activities for any multi-professional team engaged in end-of-life and palliative services for older people. These are:

- social care and social support/therapeutic support;
- family work;
- challenging oppression and engaging in inclusive practice; and
- practical support.

Taken together, these skills and activities are a vital underpinning to gerontological social work practice with older people at the end of life, and as such we now consider them in more detail.

## Social care, social support and practical assistance

As we also argue in Chapter 8, gerontological social workers are well placed to explore actively in an assessment how an older person with complex needs perceives and defines well-being, or 'comfortable ageing' (Reed *et al.*, 2004). This is just as appropriate at the end of life and can give important insights into an older person's aspirations as well as the gaps between aspiration and experience. Active listening and the ability to form and develop positive relationships with older people provide opportunities to understand coping strategies, fears and worries, and changes in a person. Given that social workers are consistently valued for their ability to offer emotional support alongside practical assistance (Beresford, 2007c), they have a key role in enabling older people to articulate their wishes about end-of-life care and can signpost people towards, for example, the use of advance decisions (see Box 5.5).

These skills apply to all work with older people. Nevertheless, undertaking assessment, intervention and care planning with an awareness of end of life, alongside promoting a life of quality, should encourage practitioners to resist a focus on independence and autonomy at the expense of other elements of person-centred approaches to care and support. Interventions that seek to embrace an appropriate awareness of the importance of sustaining comfort and security, maintaining key attachments, spiritual and religious needs, and using biography as a means of promoting individualized care and support, should be a professional aspiration for working with older people with complex needs who face significant change and transition in this period of their lives.

## Box 5.5   Advance decisions

An advance decision (also known as an advance directive, advance statement or living will) allows a person to make his or her wishes known about treatment and health care in the event of that person becoming mentally incapacitated at some point in the future. These instructions cannot simply be ignored by a doctor unless:

■ The advance decision does not apply to the particular situation;
■ The advance decision is not clear; or
■ The conditions of the Mental Health Act can be applied to override the decision (www.mind.org.uk).

The Mental Capacity Act, 2005 (enforced in April 2007 in England and Wales) is the legal basis for advance decisions. To be valid, advance decisions must:

■ Be made by a person who is aged 18 or over and who has capacity to make an advance decision;
■ Is able to identify what treatment he or she wishes to refuse, and the circumstances in which the refusal would apply (this can be made in writing, recorded in medical notes, written in an electronic record – and includes a confirmation that the decision applies even if life is at risk); and
■ Not have been coerced by anyone else into making the decision (www.direct.gov.uk).

Lasting Power of Attorney (sections 9–14 Mental Capacity Act, 2005) is a legal document that enables a person to appoint someone as their attorney, to make decisions on their behalf. A Lasting Power of Attorney does not have legal standing until it is formally registered with the Office of the Public Guardian (www.publicguardian.gov.uk) and must be made while a person has capacity. Lasting Power of Attorney covers two key areas – property and affairs and personal welfare. The latter Lasting Power of Attorney means that a person can choose a legally appointed 'attorney' to make decisions about health care and care. This can include decisions to refuse or consent to treatment on the person's behalf (www.direct.gov.uk).

For information on advance decisions, mental health and mental capacity legislation in Scotland, refer to the Mental Health (Care and Treatment) (Scotland) Act, 2003.

For information on advance decisions, mental health and mental capacity legislation in Northern Ireland, refer to the *Bamford Review of Mental Health and Learning Disability (Northern Ireland): A comprehensive legislative framework* (2007)(www.northernireland.gov.uk).

## Family work

Gerontological social workers should also be encouraged and supported to use research and practice knowledge about the complexities of family structures and support networks, in assessment, intervention and care planning. This can illuminate, for example, the potential and particular challenges that older, co-resident carers may experience in providing end-of-life care and support at home for their spouse or partner. In this way, practitioners can assist family members to explore anxieties or concerns associated with supporting an older person nearing the end of their life, provide emotional support for people experiencing loss and change, and explore what, for example, having a number of formal agencies participating in care might mean. In addition, social workers are, of course, well placed to help carers to take time away from caring for a person whose care needs are complex or who is reaching the end of his or her life.

Social work has traditionally included a commitment towards welfare rights and social justice (Payne, 2006), and families providing care at home for an older person who is at the end of life are likely to incur extra expenditure for a range of resources, including, for example, heating costs, the cost of domestic help, informal carers' loss of earnings and income, or additional specialist equipment that is not available free of charge. Gerontological social workers, skilled in recognizing the potential hardships that a person and his or her family might face, can offer practical help and support regarding potential benefits as well as encouraging people to apply for the benefits to which they are entitled. Practitioners familiar with the geographical area in which they practice, are also often able to advise on the existence of voluntary and charitable organizations that may be able to respond to particular areas of need.

## Challenging oppression and engaging in inclusive practice

A fundamental part of gerontological social work means actively recognizing and responding to the ways in which older people at the end of their lives may be particularly marginalized. Challenging examples of marginalization may take many forms. For example, social workers can advocate for an older person to ensure that they receive services to which they are entitled, and can also work with other professionals to enable an older person to be able to continue to live where they want to live. Gerontological social workers should therefore seek to resist policies and procedures that create or reinforce existing oppressions for older people (Dalrymple and Burke, 2006).

This could mean resisting pressure to accept that a move to a care home is 'best', when other creative ways of managing risk and providing appropriate support at the end of life are possible.

Social workers also have skills that enable them to practice with people whose own communication skills may have been altered or compromised by physical illness, or sensory or cognitive impairment. To this end, gerontological social workers involved in planning care and interventions can contribute to sources of information about how, for example, a person communicates. They may also be in a position to provide biographical information from their own assessment, which can improve individualized care, or they can encourage family members to involve themselves in life-story work (see Chapter 4).

Above all, it is important that gerontological practitioners engage reflexively in a practice that seeks to make visible their own and others' personal assumptions, prejudices, fears and anxieties about ageing and dying. The knowledge and skills identified require, in our view, integration between the general skills and bodies of knowledge that should be of primary concern to all social work practitioners, with the specific gerontological knowledge that enhances practice in this area. This is not easy territory as it must necessitate, at times, resisting practices which run counter to good practice in end-of-life care, but which are firmly located in a managerialist agenda. It is fundamentally important that we seek to engage in practices that both challenge oppression and the marginalization of older people at the end of their life, and that we ensure that the older person remains at the centre of our assessments and interventions.

## Conclusion

There is an argument that it is not viable to consider social work practice in a palliative context outside a specialist setting, especially in the climate prevailing at the time of writing. However, taken together, it is clear that the social work value base, and our key skills and aspirations as practitioners, lend themselves to developing an already vital contribution to end-of-life care and older people. In reality, social work practitioners in general settings work every day with older people with complex needs who are likely to be experiencing the last phase of their lives. It follows, therefore, that we can make a vital contribution to the reconceptualization of end-of-life care and older people. Indeed, given the challenge of widening the availability of palliative care approaches in generalist settings, Small (2001, p. 284) highlights the need to 'spread the principles and values of palliative care to generalists in primary health and community care so that informed, integrated and best practice care is delivered equitably to those whose quality of life and death could be enhanced'. Clearly, then, the diffusion of palliative care concepts and practices through the whole health and social care system is a continuing task, and one in which critical gerontological social workers have a vital part to play.

## stop and think

- How do you think a 'reconceptualization of end of life' might help to promote good quality care for older people with serious long-term illness?
- How can social workers participate in improving end-of-life care for older people?
- How can you work on uncovering your own fears, assumptions and ideas about your own ageing and eventual death?
- How might social work practice contribute to developing end-of-life care in care homes?

taking it further

- Firth, P., Luff, G. and Oliviere, D. (2005) *Loss, Change and Bereavement in Palliative Care*, Buckingham: Open University Press.
- Hockley, J. and Clark, D. (2002) *Palliative Care for Older People in Care Homes*, Buckingham, Open University Press.
- National Council for Palliative Care and Policy Research Institute on Ageing and Ethnicity (2006) *Ethnicity, Older People and Palliative Care*, London, NCPC/PRIAE.
- Weinstein, J. (2008) *Working with Loss, Death and Bereavement: A Guide for Social Workers*, London, Sage.

# 6 Transitions and continuities

- Change and transition are features of all of our lives.

- A number of theoretical approaches have been developed in an attempt to theorize the experience of ageing as well as illuminating how older people might cope with and manage transitions commonly associated with older age.

- Traditional theories that seek to address the 'problem' of ageing have been critiqued. Other models, looking at adaptive and coping strategies, are relevant to social work practice and highlight the importance of, for example, recognizing and respecting the strengths, abilities, resources and continuities older people continue to use in coping with transition.

## Introduction

Transition and change are part of all of our lives. Often it is the continuities in our biography and life experience that provide us with a store of resources and skills from which we may be able to draw when faced with managing change and transition. In 1982, the Annals of the American Academy of Political and Social Science published a series of papers entitled 'Middle and Later Life Transitions', in which a distinguished collection of academics mapped out key transitions to be faced over the life course. This was a breakthrough publication for a number of reasons: it focused on the latter half of the life course rather than on childhood; it viewed transitions as a normal condition of life rather than seeing them as problem periods; and, in discussing transitions, it addressed social and environmental issues rather than psychiatric and psychological perspectives.

The definition of transition in this publication, taken from Golan

(1981), was: 'simply as moving from one stage or event in life to another with varying degrees of instability in the adaptive process'. Berardo (1982, p. 10) argues that such transitions can be classified in at least three ways: 'Those involving specific time intervals; those characterised by role shifts and those with clearly notable marker events'. Time interval transitions can be age-related, such as retirement (though this is much more flexible at the time of writing than it was in 1982); role shifts include marriage, widowhood and divorce (all of which may occur at any age); and notable marker events would encompass things such as the death of a close relative or friend. Geographical and socio-economic change, such as a change in location or income, may accompany these transitions and result in physical, emotional, social and practical adjustments.

Older people are, of course, likely to face numerous transitions. Some will be positive and welcomed (such as becoming a grandparent) while others, such as a move into a care home, taking on care-giving responsibilities, significant changes in physical and cognitive health and well-being, bereavement and loss, and end-of-life issues, are more likely to fall within the remit of social work attention. The focus of this chapter is therefore on what a critical gerontological approach can bring to social work in situations of change in older people's lives. We devote the first half of the chapter to looking at the range of theoretical perspectives that have been developed to assist us in comprehending the kinds of transitions people face as they grow older. To illustrate the ways in which our understanding of transitions may be broadened, we then focus on the theorizing and research that exists concerning two key transition experiences for older people: transitions associated with bereavement and loss; and those involved in moving to, and settling into, a care home. These discussions serve as a platform for considering the areas on which a critical gerontological social work approach might concentrate if it is to support and facilitate older people through such important periods in their lives.

## Theorizing transition

From a life-course perspective, Sugarman (2001) argues that adult life can be seen as a continual process of coping with, and adapting to, life events. This contrasts with traditional ideas about 'age and stage' transitions that were prevalent for many years and attempted to illuminate the experiences of ageing, and the transitions thought to accompany ageing in particular ways. Below, we consider the contributions that some of these traditional theories have made to our understanding of transitions.

## Disengagement and activity theory

Both disengagement theory (Cumming and Henry, 1961) and activity theory (Havighurst, 1963) were based on the premise that key later-life transitions (primarily retirement for men and widowhood for women) were inherently problematic and illustrated the wider 'problem' that old age and demographic ageing presented to society. This problem-orientated approach ran through much of the early history of gerontology, with transitions being seen as negative and with a primary focus on aspects of role loss and social dysfunction.

Disengagement theory, for example, proposed that old age is characterized by an inevitable and mutual disengagement between the individual and social organizations. Older people or, more accurately, older *men*, it was argued, retired from work, which was seen as universal, normal and normative from the theoretical perspective of disengagement theory – not just for the older person but also for a society that requires older people to step aside to enable younger people to take their places if it is to function properly. It was further argued that a reduction in roles such as engaging in paid employment would in fact benefit older people, and thus preserve their well-being. In fact, there has never been much empirical research evidence to support or substantiate this early, but widely accepted, theory. However, the sustained critique that followed in its wake was crucial in promoting critical gerontological theory (Estes *et al.*, 2003) and current critical approaches to understanding ageing and later life.

In contrast to disengagement theory, activity theory proposed that older people's adaptation to their own ageing could best be achieved by continued and enhanced participation in activities and valued social roles (Havighurst, 1963). While, on the surface, both the disengagement and activity theories might have an intrinsic and logical appeal, they both assume that old age and old people are homogenous, as well as reinforcing normative assumptions about what are right and proper goals, activities and aspirations in older age. Neither theory fully recognizes the diverse contexts in which older people may live, nor the differential life-course impacts on the experience of ageing. Drawing from the work of Townsend (1981), Sugarman (2001, p. 27) argues that 'the economic, political, legislative and social structure of society excludes older people from many significant roles, again making maintenance of an activity level associated with the middle years potentially problematic'.

## Continuity theory

Partly as a counter to the problems with both disengagement and activity theory, continuity theory evolved from psychological studies of adaptation in middle and later life. Robert Atchley (1999) has been a key figure in the development of continuity theory, and argues that, in the face of change, continuity remains the most prevalent form of adaptation to ageing. There is no assumption that an older person who seeks to use life-course continuities as a means of managing change will inevitably succeed, but, in general, Atchley (1999) maintains that people will try for continuity as their first effort to manage a change or transition. Rather than conceiving continuity as a set of patterns that are fixed, unchanging and rigidly applied across the life course, Atchley (1999, pp. 2–3) also argues that continuity should be conceptualized as: 'the persistence of general patterns rather than as sameness in the details contained within those patterns Religious values and beliefs may remain the same, but the meaning and interpretation that stand behind them evolve'. Continuity and change are therefore not mutually exclusive experiences, but rather co-exist.

Atchley (1999) identified key elements of continuity that evolve and develop across the life course:

- *Internal patterns* – for example, our identities, attitudes, beliefs and values, knowledge and skills, and coping strategies.
- *External patterns* – for example, social roles and activities, living arrangements and environments.
- *Continuity of relationships* – which highlights the importance of social support as a means of reinforcing internal patterns (such as identity) and external patterns (such as where we choose to live and the roles we undertake).
- *Developmental goals* – which focus on the notion that adults generally have goals that provide a direction or sense of purpose in life. Life experiences and cumulative biography are critically important in shaping the sorts of goals people may have and the activities they engage in to achieve those goals, in later as well as in earlier life.
- *Adaptive capacity* – which focuses on the strategies, resources and skills that people bring to bear on a situation of change or transition as a means of coping with and managing the change.

The importance of maintaining social relationships and networks across and throughout the life course has received considerable attention in gerontological research. For example, Antonucci (1990) proposed that, as we all move through the life course, we are accompanied by a 'convoy' of support: by those people to whom and from whom we give and receive social support. She conceived this support system as three concentric circles indicating the degree of attachment, closeness, importance and types of support provided. People who are closest to the individual, such as life-long partners, are located in the inner circle, while people with whom we are less closely connected, or who are of less importance to us, are located in the outer ring of the circle. This convoy and support network changes and fluctuates over time and, as Sugarman (2001, p. 196) comments:

> The boundaries between the circles of the network are permeable and, just as there can be flow into and out of the convoy, so, too, can there be movement across the circles as supportive relationships wax and wane. Those who become our partner or life-long friend are likely to have entered our support convoy at the outermost circle and over time moved towards the centre. Similarly, as we 'drift apart' from or 'fall out' with convoy members, they will move to less central positions in our convoy, or perhaps leave it altogether.

Similarly, Atchley (1999) argues that adaptive strategies also fluctuate and evolve across the life course but, critically, in adapting to change adults will, as a matter of course, seek to rely on the continuities they have spent time and energy developing. For example, if a person has developed strong expectations, borne out of positive experience, that close family members can be relied on for emotional support and practical assistance at times of stress, then this expectation will continue to be relied on when needed.

Continuity theory has an intuitive 'common-sense' appeal. It is not difficult to see, in our own lives, how important a sense of continuity is as a potential resource for managing change. It is also a means of communicating a sense of coherence in our identity. However, it is equally possible for people to rely on continuities that are not functional or positive. For example, a person may cling on to an abusive or unhappy relationship because of a belief, expressed as continuity, that the relationship is for life, whatever the difficulties or challenges associated with it. The research on which Atchley bases his findings comes, predominantly, from a homogenous community of older people who are, Estes *et al.* (2003, p. 31) argue, 'a population relatively unchallenged by uncertainty and significant socio-economic disruption of chosen life trajectories'. This casts some doubt on how generalizable Atchley's findings might be, especially since research has not yet addressed adequately the role of continuity when, for example, older people face significant disruption through changing, deteriorating or uncertain health.

## Selective optimization with compensation

In contrast, the selective optimization with compensation theory (Baltes and Baltes, 1990) emphasizes a more dynamic interaction and interrelationship between continued developmental gains and age-related losses. Significantly, this psychological theory highlights the potential for positive gains and ongoing adaptive strategies across the whole life course. Older people may engage in what Baltes and Baltes (1990) define as 'selective investment': concentrating on aspects of life that have a high priority for the individual. For example, an older person with mobility difficulties may forgo certain tasks requiring physical energy and strength in order to preserve their physical resources to go into town for shopping, say. The 'optimization' aspect of the theory refers to the sorts of strategies that people might use to maintain or enhance their functioning, and in-depth interviews with older people do indeed reveal the often complex and flexible strategies employed to preserve important activities and roles (Scharf *et al.*, 2004). 'Compensation' relates to the development of strategies that promote effective functioning, such as taking additional time for, or applying renewed effort to, a task. For example, a person may install a bath seat in order to continue to use the bath. Alternatively, if the person still feels unsafe or dislikes the use of a bath seat, he or she may abandon the goal of taking a bath and, if they have the resources, have a shower fitted instead. This may be interpreted as a positive development as it preserves independence, and personal hygiene standards are maintained.

Clearly, adaptive capacity is influenced by a number of structural factors, such as access to the social, physical, emotional and economic resources needed to adapt to change. Moreover, personal resources such as the ability to cope with change, make sense of change and make appropriate decisions in response to change, are all essential components in adaptive capacity. Here too, continuity theory comes into play in coping with change, as older adults will often orientate to coping strategies that reflect long-standing continuities.

## Successful ageing

The 'successful ageing' paradigm has also gained considerable attention since the 1990s and is sometimes used synonymously with phrases such as 'active ageing', 'ageing well' and 'productive ageing'. Rowe and Kahn (1997) define three conditions or characteristics that are necessary preconditions for successful ageing: the avoidance of disease and disability; the maintenance of high physical and cognitive functional capacity; and active engagement with life. Many current policies, particularly those relating to health improvement and 'health of the nation' targets, can be seen to include an orientation towards successful ageing (Department of Health, 2001; Department of Health, 2006; ODPM, 2006) and emphasize:

■ the importance of exercise in later life (for example, prescriptions for exercise);
■ life-long learning;
■ a healthy diet, including national targets for daily intakes of fruit and vegetables;
■ flexible retirement and the right to continue to work; and
■ targets to reduce obesity and smoking, and encourage active engagement.

However, from a critical gerontological perspective, Holstein and Minkler (2007) argue that successful ageing is not a neutral term. Fook's (2002) discussion of binary opposites highlights that the other side of any notion of 'successful' ageing would presumably be 'unsuccessful'. The construction of failure based on a normative definition of 'success' is likely to have the greatest impact on those older people who are already marginalized or oppressed. Holstein and Minkler (2007) also highlight the lack of attention given to the impact of gender, race and class on health and life chances. A failure to acknowledge these influences is crucially important, both in terms of life-course inequalities and the sharpening of inequalities that tend to persist in older age.

## Widening our understanding of key transitions

Clearly, the kinds of issues highlighted above will affect how people are able, or not, to manage significant transitions in their lives. However, traditional theorizing, while it is helpful in drawing attention to the ways in which we might conceptualize how people manage and experience transitions, also needs application to real-life experiences if it is to be useful for practitioners working with older people in complex and sensitive situations. In this context, we now focus our discussion on two key transition experiences: the experience of bereavement and loss; and the experience of moving into a care home or supported housing.

### Theorizing bereavement and loss

Given the likelihood of death coming at the end of a long life, it follows that older people are likely to experience significant losses in later life, particularly the loss of key relationships through death. While widowhood, or the loss of a long-standing partner, is the most obvious and significant bereavement likely to be experienced by older people, the death of siblings, friends and extended family are also important, though they remain relatively under-investigated. In respect of widowhood, differences in mortality rates, together with the reality that older women have tended to marry men older than themselves, have resulted in over half of women aged 65 and over being widowed, a proportion rising to four-fifths of women aged 85 and over (ONS, 2006a).

Widowhood, within the context of disengagement theory, was seen as marking the entry, for women, into old age and signalled their retreat from society. Any research that was carried out tended to reflect this orientation, and viewed widowhood itself as being essentially problematic. Chambers (2005, p. 6) highlights how research on widowhood focused primarily on loss and loneliness, while at the same time reporting heterogeneous and often contradictory sets of findings:

> 'Older widows suffer more than younger widows' versus 'younger widows suffer more than older widows'; 'widows have close friends' versus 'widows lose their friends'; 'sudden death is more difficult for the widow' versus 'prolonged death is more difficult for the widow' and so on.

More recently, there has been a greater interest in the ways in which older people cope with the transition to widowhood and, for some, the very positive experiences to which this can subsequently lead (Moore and Stratton, 2002; Chambers, 2005).

Traditionally, though, theoretical approaches to loss and bereavement focused on the primary task of mourning and 'letting go' of the deceased person. It was assumed that this was a necessary goal to enable the bereaved person to be able to move on to form and develop new relationships. Stage models, such as the influential work by Kübler-Ross (1969) (see Chapter 5), was characterized by a process that began with experiences of intense reaction to loss and concluded with a resolution of grief and a notion of 'getting over' or 'coming to terms' with the loss. However, as noted in Chapter 5, such linear models, along with the notion of 'recovery', were critiqued for their proposition that there was a uniformity to grief reactions and that any different behaviours were likely to be seen as abnormal, or even pathological (Quinn, 2005). Moreover, a purely linear model was not supported by client evidence or clinical observation.

By contrast, Stroebe and Schut's (1999, 2001) 'Dual Process Model' of bereavement and loss emphasizes the importance of dynamic coping processes. They identify two dimensions of experiencing loss: what they call a loss orientation with a focus on the past (grief intruding on life; doing grief work); and a restoration orientation with a focus on the present and future (for example, avoiding grief; taking up new roles/activities). Stroebe and Schut (2001) hypothesized that, during a bereavement transition, a bereaved person will alternate between loss versus restoration-focused approaches to coping. In terms of loss approaches to coping, bereaved people may sometimes confront their loss, or engage in 'grief work', while in respect of restoration-focused approaches, they may engage in new activities or roles, deny or avoid grief, or distract themselves from grief. This model is powerful in that it highlights that bereaved people will oscillate between the two types of stressors as a necessary passage to adaptive coping with bereavement and loss, together with factors that may contribute to individual resilience in the face of bereavement and loss (Machin, 2008).

Extract 6.1 reflects on how Hannah and Jenny think Bridget is reacting to her mother's death. As you read, consider how practice can respond flexibly to different reactions to grief and loss? How might you identify grief reactions that become more complex for a

## Extract 6.1 *Being bereaved*

Mum is upset. She prods and prods the fire and frowns. She asks me what I think of how Bridget is reacting to Grandma's death. I say that Grandma has only just died, I don't even know how I'm reacting myself. It seemed so sudden. After all this time it's a shock even though she'd been ill so long and was old. I say maybe Bridget is shocked. She doesn't really seem to have taken it in. She hasn't cried or anything. She doesn't seem anything but the Bridget she's always been. I tell Mum I don't think she should have nagged Bridget about the future like that. I say she probably can't bear to think about it, surely we don't want her to think about it? Mum asks why not. I say that it doesn't look too appetising to me, Bridget's future. What will she have? Work? Oh, yes that's good, it's a real career and she loves it, it would be terrible if she didn't have that, much, much worse. But what else? Did Bridget have masses of close friends? Did she hell. She had Karl and she'd just told us what she thought of him and how much he doesn't mean to her. And she has us but how much is that? We're not going to be a substitute, for Grandma. She doesn't love us totally, completely, as she did Grandma.
(Margaret Forster, *Have the Men Had Enough?*)
Seen from Hannah's perspective, p. 249.

bereaved person? What kinds of support or assistance might you be able to help a bereaved person to access?

Theoretical models of bereavement at the time of writing highlight that 'letting go' or 'recovering' from bereavement are erroneous goals. We do not 'recover'; rather, we adapt and accommodate and change. In reality, coping with the death of a close person may be a process that continues in different ways for the remainder of our lives (Silverman, 2003). This more nuanced theoretical work, along with biographical research on widowhood, has been helpful in reorientating our understanding of widowhood away from a problem-focused perspective. Research now highlights, in particular, the ways in which widowed older women make sense of 'who' they are following the death of their partners (Chambers, 2005, p. 241) and illustrates how older widows draw on:

> Personal, social and collective identity over the life course ... what becomes apparent in the revealing of these hidden lives is that older widows draw on a range of experiences derived from their multiple narratives, and the sub-plots within those narratives, in order to make sense of who they are in later life widowhood. In doing so, they are continually integrating the past and present.

Here, narrative is a means of structuring experience, biography and social and cultural perspectives. From a practice perspective, such research also highlights the importance of recognizing and working with:

- diversity in experiences and narratives;
- the cultural and social meanings of loss and bereavement;
- an acknowledgment that loss and bereavement happens to us all and is therefore about 'us' rather than 'them' (Silverman, 2003); and
- the importance of biographical threads and multiple narratives that are used to make sense of loss and bereavement.

There is clearly a relationship too between bereavement and stress, and coping styles. People use different coping strategies, and some people appear to cope with stress better than others. Lazarus and Folkman (1984) identified coping strategies that focused on appraising a problem and deciding what to do about it; reframing problems; and regulating emotions and distress that appear as a result of the threat. It is also argued that the ways in which people cope and respond to stress may be more significant to their assessment of their well-being, functioning and health, than the frequency or incidence of stressful events (Silverman, 2003). One such stress-inducing transition in the lives of many older people with whom social workers come into contact, is the move to a care home, and it is to this experience that we now turn.

## Moving into a care home

In April 2006 it was estimated that there were over 12,000 registered care homes, providing in the region of 468,000 places for older people in the UK (Age Concern, 2007). However, it remains the case that relatively small percentages of older people live in such care homes: 4 per cent of the UK population aged between 75 and 84; and 17 per cent of people aged 85 and over (ONS, 2006a). Despite the small numbers, it is still the case that social workers in this area of practice will be involved regularly in assisting an older person to move into a care home. This often happens when community resources have either been exhausted or are inadequate for a person with complex needs, or if someone requires support and assistance 24 hours a day. As a result, older people may be moved suddenly into a care home, without the benefit of preparation or participation in decision-making (Reed et al., 2004).

A move into a care home also means that older people often have to face the losses and challenges associated with leaving their permanent home, which can itself be analogous to being bereaved. Peace et al. (2005) have long highlighted the importance of 'home' for older people, and its contribution to identity maintenance and quality of life. Home, as a sense of place, is reinforced by associated continuities (for example, there is a history of events, experiences and stories associated with home), and familiarity and knowledge of the surrounding neighbourhood. Availability of resources, both in terms of care homes and financial resources, may mean that older people have little choice but to move into a care home that is not located within their own community or neighbourhood, and such a move may have an immediate impact on the loss of friends or neighbours.

Sometimes too, an older person may have to face being separated from his or her spouse or partner, if they are moving into a care home alone. This may constitute a fundamental change in the rhythms of a relationship that might have lasted for the whole of their adult life. Older people can also face other challenges and losses, such as being separated from much-loved pets. Morley and Fooks (2005) argue that, despite a wealth of research demonstrating the importance of pets in contributing to well-being, formal services and organizations often marginalize or disregard this bond. They go on to argue for a more 'pet-aware' development of policy and practice that includes, for example, the design of environments to allow for pets, and for practitioners to recognize the potential impact of pet loss and separation.

These important relationships can be 'lost' or marginalized where assessment and initial care planning are inadequate, especially when older people have moved as a result of a crisis. Where older people also have communication difficulties or cognitive impairments, the transition to a care home can be particularly challenging, and people may then find themselves in an unfamiliar environment where their needs, preferences and routines are poorly understood. Extract 6.2 illustrates these difficulties. As you read, consider what the move into a care home might be like for an older person such as Mrs McKay, and for her family. Current policy often portrays care homes and other supported environments (for example, retirement villages) as being a 'home for life'. To what extent do you think that this is a realistic goal for someone with dementia, like Mrs McKay? What is your view on whether people with dementia should live in 'specialist' settings or with other people not known to have dementia?

## Extract 6.2    *A home that suits people, or people to suit a home?*

We ended the tour back in the office ... Then we got down to the negotiations. Charlie said he had no doubts at all, he would like his mother put on the waiting list. Matron said it was not quite so simple. Mrs McKay would have to be assessed, as she had explained on the telephone. She could arrange for someone to come and make an assessment at Mrs McKay's home or we could bring her here. Charlie hesitated. I could see him wondering which gave us a better chance of getting his mother accepted. I used his pause to ask Matron what kinds of things were assessed, what St Alma's was looking for. She described the problem: St Alma's wanted pleasant personalities, people who would get along with other people. It was no good admitting anyone so deeply rooted in their family that they would never accept a substitute. And, although most of the old people they had were a little confused, they did not accept the severely demented since it put too much of a strain on the other occupants. Of course, if while at St Alma's they degenerated into severe dementia, then they would not be turned out: other arrangements would be made.

I really felt we might just as well forget it. It did seem a pleasant enough place but Grandma had about as much chance of getting in as she had of getting into a Cambridge college.
(Margaret Forster, *Have the Men Had Enough?*)
Seen from Jenny's perspective, p. 117.

## Box 6.1 Research into practice: requirements of residential care for people with dementia

| Characteristic | Examples of evidence |
|---|---|
| Social environment | ■ Friendships encouraged and nurtured<br>■ Supportive and caring relationships between people who live in the home and people who work there<br>■ A sense of belonging and attachment<br>■ Staff belong and are valued by managers and owners |
| A meaningful life | ■ Access to appropriate occupational opportunities and activities<br>■ Being able to do and enjoy 'ordinary' things (e.g. be outside, make a pot of tea, go to the shops)<br>■ A sense that life is lived rather than time just passing<br>■ A sense of agency and participation |
| Health | ■ Access to good quality health care and preventative services (e.g. dental treatment)<br>■ Skilled staff able to assess and respond positively to pain management<br>■ A decent and nutritional diet<br>■ Access to alternative therapies (e.g. yoga, exercise, massage) |
| Love and sex | ■ A staff group who do not stereotype older people as asexual<br>■ Facilities for couples (e.g. privacy, shared bedroom spaces)<br>■ Active encouragement to maintain existing relationships<br>■ Appropriate training and support for staff in addressing ethical issues (e.g. capacity and consent) |
| Recognition of biography | ■ Celebration of diversity among older people in approaches to care, support, routines and rhythms at home<br>■ Commitment to using biography appropriately for personalized and individualized care<br>■ Recognition that past trauma (e.g. domestic violence, sexual abuse) may have a serious impact on an older person's well-being |
| Reducing stress | ■ Recognition of biography, preferences and past issues that may disturb or distress a person (see above)<br>■ Avoidance of large, noisy spaces (unless it is situation specific)<br>■ Clashing stimuli (e.g. loud radio, TV on, chatting, staff talking loudly to each other)<br>■ Effective communication |

**Box 6.1** *continued*

| Characteristic | Examples of evidence |
|---|---|
| Spiritual needs | ■ Biographical assessment that recognizes potential religious or spiritual needs and how they may be met<br>■ Access to places or worship or ministers of worship appropriate to a person's religious affiliation<br>■ Care and support that are culturally competent and aware of religious and cultural requirements<br>■ Recognition and acceptance that care homes are a place where people die as well as live<br>■ Ensuring that people who live and work at the home are not excluded from a death that might affect them greatly |
| Appropriate built environment | ■ Environment should not disable (e.g. signposting to toilet facilities, finding one's own room, patterned carpets and wallpaper)<br>■ Purposes of rooms should be clear<br>■ Access to 'domestic' rooms such as a kitchen, homely bathrooms, personalized bedrooms<br>■ Shared space should be homely and accessible<br>■ Access to outdoors and outdoor spaces |

*Source*: (Alzheimer's Society, 2001; Marshall, 2001)

Difficult though such a transition undoubtedly is, some research has highlighted the strategies that older people use to manage this kind of change in their lives (Reed and Payton, 1996). One strategy is to construct a narrative of familiarity with the home, or aspects of it. This can be promoted by living close to the home, visiting friends or family at the home, getting to know members of staff, and developing new relationships with other people living in the home. Clearly, all of this implies a degree of planning ahead, though, as we know, very many older people move in response to crisis rather than as a pre-planned goal.

Once an older person has moved into a care home, there are also key requirements that should, if they are implemented properly, assist older people to adapt to their new circumstances. Box 6.1 highlights good practice issues with respect to residential care for older people with dementia, but the same requirements would apply equally to older people with other impairments.

## The contribution of critical gerontological social work

Much of what has been discussed in the preceding pages suggests to us that critical gerontological social workers have a key role to play in older people's transition experiences, particularly in relation to reorientating interventions and support around an approach that draws on continuities and strengths. We therefore consider a strengths-based approach in a little more detail here.

### Strengths-based approaches

While it might be argued that social work literature and practice does indeed highlight the importance of identifying service users' strengths and resources as part of an assessment, many such calls to attend to the capacities and competences of people are little more than professional rhetoric. In his analysis of strengths-based interventions, Saleebey (2002, p. 2) argues that 'practising from a strengths orientation means that everything you do as a social worker is predicated in some way on helping to discover, embellish and exploit people's strengths and resources in the service of assisting them to achieve their goals'. In the context of the kinds of transitions we have been considering, this would imply a need for critical gerontological social workers to be supported in their efforts to get to know and understand properly the older people with whom they work, and to utilize relevant research and literature to inform their practice.

A strengths-based approach also offers a robust critique to the commonly held view that people become service users simply as a result of deficit, dysfunction and individual pathology. A dysfunction-based approach to assessment and intervention has a number of consequences for both service user and practitioner:

- The person is seen as the problem or pathology.
- A language of pessimism and doubt develops, which may be reinforced by professional cynicism.
- Distance, power and inequality mark the boundaries between helper and helped.
- Service users are stripped of their individual context (for example, biographies and individual identities) (see, for example, Saleebey, 2002).

By contrast, the strengths perspective is underpinned by a number of fundamental principles and values of relevance to critical gerontological practice. First, a critical gerontological social worker will need to be committed to the belief that, regardless of the apparent complexity of circumstance or need, all individuals, groups, families and communities have strengths. Second, while the kinds of transitions we have considered may be stressful and difficult to endure, they may also constitute sources of opportunity for growth and development. Third, the approach of a critical gerontological social worker should be directed towards helping a person to develop their capacities to cope with transition experiences. This means recognizing what resources, skills and abilities are available, as well as the resources, skills and abilities that are potentially available (Trevithick, 2005). Finally, practitioners should avoid making assumptions about the upper limits of a person's or group's capacity to grow and change through these experiences.

Such an orientation runs counter to the reality of much practice current at the time of writing, which continues, in terms of assessment and interventions, to focus on and emphasize the functional difficulties a person has. It has been argued that so much emphasis is placed on functional limitations that an older person's quality of life is often reduced to nothing more than a list of activities of daily living and associated deficits (Fast and Chapin, 2002, p. 151). Critical gerontological practitioners must therefore make a conscious effort to ensure that what an older person wants, is doing, has done and can do, are essential components of strengths-based assessment and taken into account when assisting people through key transitions. This would extend to actual interventions and could, for example, be aimed at helping to rejuvenate or create anew natural helping networks even within institutional settings such as care homes.

Above all, then, this highlights the importance of a reflexive engagement with practice. Helping older people through difficult transitions associated with bereavement and loss, or a move into a care home, is complex and sensitive work. It brings practitioners face-to-face with the realities of life and death. Yet, in the face of these realities, it is also vitally important that critical gerontological social workers should, for example, be encouraged to confront their own fears about ageing, along with reflecting on the possibilities for continuing to find meaning and benefit in life despite the real potential of loss and change.

## Conclusion

This chapter has sought to examine some of the theoretical perspectives that have informed our thinking in respect of transitions in later life. A number of these theoretical perspectives have been critiqued because of their lack of application to the lived experience of ageing as well as the assumptions that underpin them about the 'problem' of older age. Over the years, other theoretical approaches have developed, which now highlight the importance of understanding transition and change as life-course experiences. They also draw attention to the fact that transitions are contextualized by factors such as biography, social settings, access to resources, and previous experiences of managing transitions. Clearly, there are some transition experiences for older people with which social workers are more likely to be involved, and here we have considered the experience of loss associated with bereavement or moving to a care home. Critical gerontological social work practitioners must continue to work with an older person's strengths, as well as recognizing the importance of life-course and biographical perspectives, if older people's experiences of change and transition are to be properly recognized and supported.

## stop and think

- How might social work practice assist an older person to manage the transition to living in a care home?
- What sorts of transitions do social workers often work with in practice with older people?
- How can a biographical understanding of an older person help in developing practice that supports a person to cope with a transition?

**taking it further**

- Machin, L. (2008) *Working with Loss and Grief: A New Model for Practitioners*, London, Sage.
- Peace, S. M., Kellaher, L. and Holland, C. (2005) *Environment and Identity in Later Life*, Buckingham, Open University Press.
- Saleeby, D. (ed.) (2002) *The Strengths Perspective in Social Work Practice*, (3rd edn), Boston, Mass., Allyn & Bacon.
- Sugarman, L. (2001) *Life-span Development: Frameworks, Accounts and Strategies*, Hove, Psychology Press.

# 7 Care-giving in diverse contexts

- Carers are diverse and care-giving is a diverse activity. Care can be defined by its complexity.

- Care is given as part of a relationship involving reciprocity and *inter*dependency.

- Care is central to all our lives and is something we all experience.

- The relationship that carers have with the person they care for will be individual and located in their own biography and life course. Taking a life-course approach to care is essential.

- Both carers and care recipients have rights as citizens.

- A critical gerontological approach challenges assumptions; adopts reflexivity; values diversity; addresses power differentials; and has in its repertoire of tools mediation and negotiation skills.

## Introduction

The notion of care and care-giving remains at the heart of social work, and as such is an area of crucial importance for critical gerontological social work. Through assessment and care management practice, social workers operate at the interface of care between (informal) carers and older people. Informal carers provide a major support system for older people with complex needs, yet the carers themselves have needs in their own right, and the two perspectives may sometimes be at odds. In addition, social workers bring their own values and approaches to care, often based on their own knowledge and experience as care recipients or care-givers. This mix makes for a complex area of work, and an area in which different voices and conflicting policies operate.

This chapter therefore considers the difficult issues that practitioners face in working with informal carers and the people they care for. It begins by revisiting briefly the now extensive literature on care and care-giving, and looking at the contested nature of the term 'care' and 'carer'. This exploration of care is interwoven with an examination of the changing conceptualization and theorizing which has taken place over recent years and which, in turn, has helped widen our understanding of the complexities associated with care-giving. Here we trace a move away from an emphasis on models of stress and burden and on carers as dependent, to a more rights-based approach to care and care-giving drawing on notions of power, citizenship and human rights. With this as a basis, we then explore how a critical gerontological social work approach might assist practitioners to create more empowering contexts for service users and carers, even when their needs and aspirations may conflict.

## The context of care

In order to develop social work practice with informal carers and older people, it is important to understand the assumptions underpinning the concept of care. The word 'care' has many different meanings, dimensions and values attached to it; definitions of care have proved contentious; and consensus has been difficult to achieve. One reason is that the borders surrounding concepts of care are unclear and it is therefore difficult to boundary 'care'. For example, much existing literature attempts to dichotomize care with major distinctions being drawn between whether care is formal or informal, paid or unpaid, professional or personal, provided in the domestic arena or in the market-place, in private or public spaces. Traditionally too, care was seen in the early research literature of the 1980s as a homogeneous activity focussed around the provision of instrumental support, and understood as one person 'doing care to' another (Finch and Groves, 1983). Relational aspects were largely ignored and there was a concentration on describing care situations with little theorizing around the notion of care (Lewis and Meredith, 1988; Nissel and Bonnerjea, 1982).

The literature is also replete with attempts to disaggregate different types of carers (by age and gender and, increasingly, by dimensions such as class, race and sexual orientation,) as well as by types of care (personal, financial, emotional) or by care recipient (older person, person with a learning disability, with mental health problems). For example, in early care-giving literature, care was frequently described in gendered terms: with men concentrating on the physical and instrumental tasks such as gardening and finance, while women provided the hands-on personal and emotional aspects (Wærness, 1992). Extract 7.1 reflects some of these views by illustrating different family perspectives about the appropriate care of 'Grandma': Mrs McKay. Consider how you might work with a group of siblings or family members like these who have differing views on who should be doing what in caring for, and supporting, an older family member? How can you work positively with an older person and a person who cares for them, when they have different aspirations or expectations of your role and what they each wish to achieve?

## Extract 7.1 *Carers' roles and responsibilities*

Bridget does not credit Charlie with any generosity in renting that flat. She sees it as guilt money, for not taking Grandma in, and it is. But Charlie did not have to rent that flat. He did not have to co-operate with Bridget, whatever the moral pressures. Stuart, the eldest, did nothing but then, in that respect, Bridget lets him off the hook. Policemen are not rich, not like 'something in the city'. What Bridget doesn't see is that money does not solve everything. True, Charlie can afford to rent the flat but he handles the maintenance too and that involves a great deal of trouble. The flat has ancient plumbing, cracks in the ceilings, all kinds of problems crop up and Charlie deals with them all. (p 29)

Stuart does not want to discuss anything, ever, regarding all forms of discussion as 'soft'. He thinks Charlie is mad to pay for Grandma's flat and foot the bills and generally manage her affairs. He let it be known, in an uncharacteristic outburst of at least four sentences, that he thought Grandma should be in a Home, that Home should be in Glasgow and a Council Home. Grandma had paid her taxes and was entitled and that was that. Her mind had gone and nothing could be done and he was very sorry but facts were facts and could not be dodged ... Stuart said he washed his hands of it all. That was five years ago and he has stuck to his resolution. (p 32–33)

Bridget already bears the brunt: compared to her we do hardly anything. What do I do after all: I bring Grandma along here for two hours three times a week; I shop for her; I do her laundry; I look after her on Sundays; I supervise the helpers. What does Charlie do: he pays the bills and looks after the flat ... Bridget sleeps with her two nights a week and lives beside her, always on the alert. Her life is dominated by Grandma. (p 33–34)

(Margaret Forster, *Have the Men Had Enough?*)

Seen from Jenny's perspective.

With the growth of feminist perspectives, the care-giving literature was given an added impetus as well as a language for articulating the sense of injustice between men and women over the burden of care (Twigg, 1998). Yet, while feminism helped highlight the gendered dimensions of care, there was still little theorizing about care beyond this. Indeed, carers – like Mrs McKay's daughter-in-law Jenny – were increasingly stereotyped as being predominantly women who were out of the labour market and providing care in the domestic 'home' setting. Likewise, care recipients were also seen primarily as passive dependents until this view was robustly challenged by the disability movement (Campbell and Oliver, 1996; Oliver, 2004).

Despite a developing recognition of the different contexts and intensities associated with caring, much of the early literature on carers, including that from a feminist perspective, framed them in a negative light with the emphasis on the experiences and outcomes of the stresses and burdens they faced (Parker, 1985). We now know a great deal about the 'costs' of caring: for example, financial costs stemming from a loss of income in addition to the increased costs of care such as incontinence aids; physical costs through risks of personal injury in lifting, fatigue and stress; and the mental, emotional and social costs through isolation and potential household conflict. This research focus contributed, we would argue, to a construction of a care giver as a person who is effectively pathologized by their need and who is a carer above all other aspects of their lives. Further, it is this literature which has primarily influenced social work practice and assessment over the years and which has meant, in turn, that carers' assessments have tended to focus predominantly on the deficits rather than the strengths of carers (Phillips *et al.*, 2006).

Alongside research, theorizing and practice, it is also important to note that the policy context around care and care-giving was undergoing considerable development throughout the 1970s and 80s (see Chapter 2). With the advent of new managerialism in social policy, the focus was firmly on family and individual responsibility. However, despite research highlighting the needs of carers and the 'burdens' they faced, carers' issues as they related to care of older people remained invisible in policy arenas, especially in comparison with care for young children. It was not until the introduction of the NHS and Community Care Act (1990) that carers became more prominent in policy and legislation.

## Widening our understanding of care

Howsoever we view it care, both informal and professional care, clearly involve a complexity of tasks, roles and relationships and has to be understood as a multi-faceted, difficult and demanding undertaking. Consequently, it is important that social workers wishing to engage in critical practice with older people are enabled to reflect upon and understand more recent developments in theory, research and policy. Below, we discuss how care is now being reconceptualized and theorized and the implications this has both for policy and the ways in which agencies work with carers.

## Reconceptualizing care and care practices

Although early feminist perspectives may have unwittingly reinforced the stereotyping of carers and care practices, more recent critical feminist theory applied to care has been important in helping to underline the fact that care-giving is legitimate work for both men and women; that the private and public arenas of care cannot be separated; and that the importance of care within the family should be valued publicly and not seen simply as a private responsibility (Martin-Matthews and Phillips, 2008).

Feminist perspectives have also highlighted that, in line with much social work practice, the issue of power is central to our understanding of care and care-giving practices. Ungerson and Kember (1997) drew on the early distinction between 'caring about' and 'caring for', and argued that men focus predominantly on the former and women the latter. 'Caring about' or 'taking care of', can mean caring in a more detached way than 'caring for' somebody (for example, caring about victims of famine in Africa). However, caring 'for' can also imply an action toward, and a passive dependence of one person on another, while 'care-giver' and 'care recipient' are terms similarly imbued with notions about who is powerful and who is powerless.

One of the most challenging writers on care is Tronto (1993), who argues that it is a political, as well as moral, concept through which we can make judgements about the public world by, for example, how well it cares. Fisher and Tronto (1990:127) outline 'an ethic of care' with four crucial elements: attentiveness (noticing the needs of others – caring about); responsibility (caring for); competence; and responsiveness (involving an awareness of one's vulnerabilities and interaction). Their contention is that all of these need to be present and integrated if care is to be of good quality. Fisher and Tronto (1990, p. 117) also argue that care is central to all our lives, is something we all experience, and it can therefore be viewed as a more positive concept and not focused solely on stress or burden. Tronto (1993, p. 102) also extends our understanding of care by defining the term as implying: 'a reaching out to something other than self: it is neither self-referring nor self-absorbing'. In other words, it is a disposition as well as a practice.

This more holistic understanding of care as something that pervades all human relationships and activity is also supported by other contemporary commentators (Martin-Matthews, 2008). In these formulations, care is seen as a central part of life, binding together families, friends and communities, and is embedded in social relations. These notions are in turn embodied in the principles of society through concepts such as obligation, duty, love and loyalty. Despite permeating all human relationships, it is also important to note that care is culturally specific. What constitutes 'good' quality care will also be culturally defined. We cannot assume that our ways of knowing and understanding are the same as those of others, and there is no universal 'truth' about care. In summary, then, an all-encompassing definition of care is elusive, and care can only be defined through its complexity.

### Dependency and interdependency; agency and power

The early literature, and indeed much early social policy around this issue, has largely missed out the relational component of informal care. In doing so, policy has tended to dichotomize the 'carer' and 'cared for', and assume a one-way relationship in which the 'cared for' person is dependent on the 'carer', and in policy and research terms, rendered virtually invisible. Moreover, as Henderson and Forbat (2002, p. 677) argue, policy 'circumvents people's own meanings of informal care' and ignores the interpersonal dynamics of the relationship, which is often, in fact, the valued component rather than the care-giving activity itself. A re-focusing on the interpersonal components of care allows for emotions to be expressed and for factors such as interdependence, reciprocity and exchange to be properly recognized. A practice that focuses on procedural approaches to assessment, for example, may mean that entire areas of need with regard to the caring relationship are neglected or overlooked.

As you read Extract 7.2, consider the ways in which caring takes place in the context of the relationships Mrs McKay has with members of her family. How might an understanding of family biographies help practitioners to understand present-day relationships in their practice with older people and their family carers? How might you, in your own practice, capture the importance of the relationship in which caring takes place in assessment, support and care planning? How can we be alert or sensitive in practice to the possibility that parent/child relationships have had a difficult history?

## Extract 7.2 Caring as a relationship

I said, 'Bridget loves your mother, Charlie.'

That is the difference. It is what gives Bridget the right which Charlie so resents. She fights her mother's corner, he does not. I know Charlie cannot stand up and say he loves his mother. He does not *not* love her but, if his love is analysed, it proves to be a token emotion. He likes his mother, he is greatly concerned with her welfare, he pities her, he admires her, but he does not *love* her as he loves his children, as he loves me. Nor is he loved by her, which has a great deal to do with it. Grandma would never use the word love of anyone but, if pushed, she would say she loved all her children the same, as any decent woman should, and had no favourites. She loves Stuart, Charlie and Bridget, all equally. Nothing would ever make her admit there is a difference in the interpretation of the word love when applied to Stuart or Charlie or Bridget. But the difference is so huge that there is no connection. Grandma loves Bridget with an all-consuming emotion, fiercely, completely, beautifully: she loves Charlie affectionately, distantly; she loves Stuart as a memory. And they all know it. Grandma gets back what she gives, it is as simple as that.

(Margaret Forster, *Have the Men Had Enough?*)

Seen from Jenny's perspective, p. 63.

## Models of care

A further way in which our understanding of care and care-giving has been widened is through an examination of the ways in which agencies work with carers. Here too, the notion of differentiated power is important to these developments. Twigg and Atkin (1994) sought to explore the way in which service providers respond to carers, and contended that service agencies and professionals generally lacked an explicit rationale for work with carers. Instead, they argued that providers and professionals tended to adopt one of four implicit models: carers as resources; carers as co-workers; carers as co-clients; and superseded carers.

Each of the 'models' reflected a different relationship that formal service providers adopt, often unwittingly, with carers. According to Twigg and Atkin (1994, p. 12), the *carers as resource* model reflects care provided by carers as a 'given' against which agencies operate: it is 'freely available' with no 'cost' attached to it. The 'cared for' person is the focus of intervention and the concern with carer welfare is

marginal. The primary focus of agency intervention is that of maintenance. Alternatively, the *carers as co-workers* model means that the
informal carer and paid worker are jointly involved in providing care.
In theory, the divisions of formal and informal care are transcended
in this joint enterprise and partnership is achieved. However, the
reality of the differing worlds of formal and informal care, with
potentially diverse values and expectations, means that this rarely
happens in practice (Twigg and Atkin, 1994, p. 14). In fact, the
primary aim of the formal care system in this model is to assist 'carers
as co-workers' to carry on caring.

By contrast, in the model of *carers as co-clients*, the aim of the
service system is primarily to support those carers who are most
stressed and heavily burdened. Carers are regarded as clients themselves, and the focus of attention is on the carer and her/his needs,
sometimes at the expense of the cared-for person. For example, a
social worker may support and encourage an older person to take a
respite care break even though it is against their express wishes, in
an attempt to support a family carer. Finally, the *superseded carer*
model is one in which informal care relationships are replaced by
formal care. This may be perceived as being in the best interests of
the person being cared for, or the family carer. This model is often
employed with parental carers of disabled adults, as a way of developing independence for the 'cared for' person. Older spousal carers,
however, may never see their role as 'giving up', and many care-
giving roles and responsibilities continue after the death of a
partner, being replaced by caring for others or caring in a formal
capacity.

While acknowledging that these models might be appropriate in
describing given circumstances, Nolan *et al.* (1996) suggest that
none of the models are adequate as a basis for intervention across
the interface of formal and informal care because they fail to truly
reflect ideals of empowerment, partnership and choice. Moreover,
they contend that underpinning Twigg and Atkin's framework is the
principle that all parties, both formal and informal care providers,
bring something of value to an encounter and share views in
moving towards a common goal (Nolan *et al.*, 1996; Brown *et al.*,
2001). The literature, they go on to argue, suggests that this is often
not the case, and that professionals and family carers frequently
have differing, and not necessarily complementary, goals and
sources of knowledge. Furthermore, what is needed is a working
model that reflects more adequately the goals of partnership and
empowerment inherent in policy and practice guidelines, and recognizes the power differentials of formal service provision and family
care.

This critique has led them to develop their 'Carers as Experts' model, which can be used as a basis for assessment and intervention (Nolan *et al.*, 1996). The model incorporates a number of basic assumptions that resonate very strongly with the critical gerontological social work approach that has been articulated in the preceding chapters of this book. First, important though the problems of caring are, a full understanding of carers' needs will not be achieved solely via an assessment of the 'difficulties' of caring, but instead must be grounded in knowledge of the expertise that is derived from a 'caring career'. This might include, for example, past and present relationships; the rewards of caring; coping skills; and resources. Second, assessment must incorporate the subjective experience of the carer and the carer's willingness and/or capacity to care. Third, a life-course approach to 'caring' is adopted that acknowledges temporality; that is, 'the changing demands of care and the way in which skills and expertise change over time' (Brown *et al.*, 2001, p. 31). Finally, if carers are conceptualized as 'experts', then it becomes possible to help them attain further competence, skills and resources, and thus enable them to provide quality care without detriment to their own health.

Alongside these assumptions, it is recognized that users are also experts in their situation, and a clash of agendas or hidden agendas may result between users and carers, making this a contested and tricky area in which to operate as social workers. Thinking both about 'carers as experts' and 'users as experts', what reaction do you have to Jenny's ploy in Extract 7.3 to get Grandma out of the car? Remember too the discussion in Chapter 4 about how effective communication means starting from where the person with dementia is, and ask yourself how you would interpret Mrs McKay's comment that her 'legs are stuck'? How can social workers ensure that the expertise of family carers is incorporated appropriately into the process of assessment, intervention and care planning?

We have seen that care and care-giving are understandably complex, contested in their definitions, and dynamic in the ways in which care can shift and change over time. Moreover, care takes place in the context of existing relationships, and the nature of those relationships will inevitably influence the experience of providing and receiving informal care. A critical gerontological social work approach therefore needs to build on these existing empirical and theoretical understandings, and it is to this that we now turn.

## Extract 7.3   *Carers as experts*

When we pulled up outside the Day Centre, ... Grandma refused to budge. She said her legs were stuck and she would have to go home ... I fingered the ten pence piece Susan had returned to me. Grandma was staring straight ahead, rigid. Carefully, I bent down and placed the coin about a foot from the car door. The sun made it shine most satisfactorily. Then I stood back. The shadow of my presence removed, Grandma turned to see where I had gone. The coin stood out quite unmistakably on the dirty pavement. 'Oh!' she exclaimed, and pointed. 'Look at that money – somebody's dropped it, will we take it to the police station?' I did not move. I said, 'It's only ten pence, not worth picking up.' 'In the name of God!' Grandma raged and struggled to be free. She swung her legs out of her own accord, muttering that it was alright for some, easy come, easy go, but if you looked after the pennies the pounds would take care of themselves and she never thought to see the day when silver wouldn't be worth picking up. I gave her a helping hand and steadied her while she bent to pick up the ten pence. She clutched it triumphantly. 'Will we take it to the police?' she asked. I closed the car door and without replying led her into the Day Centre where she approached each person she met in the corridor with the coin asking if it was theirs ...

It was just possible that dropping a coin outside the car door would always get Grandma out of it but the thought of such endless subterfuge wearied me. Everything is becoming a game ... As I drove home, I wondered if games, tricks, could do any damage. What was Grandma saying when she announced her legs were stuck? She was saying, in the only way she knew how, that she did not want to go to the Day Centre. Was this something she should be helped to overcome? Or, instead of responding with sleights of hand, should we respect her wish?'
(Margaret Forster, *Have the Men Had Enough?*)
Seen from Jenny's perspective, pp. 90–2.

## Care and the contribution of critical gerontological social work

Given the discussions thus far, a critical gerontological social work approach clearly needs to foreground the importance of negotiated solutions and resolutions to complex caring issues. With regard to informal carers, the critical practitioner would seek to provide appropriate support to enable them, for example, to cope with the demands of the role more effectively. However, they would also need to undertake such assessments in the context of an understanding of the whole family, and not just make assumptions about who cares for whom. This also means consciously avoiding a tendency to pathologize carers, and not seeking to provide help (for example, via carers' education) merely as a means of ensuring a carer's ongoing engagement. Moreover, practitioners should not assume that people needing care and support will want to be cared for by, typically, another family member (Phillips *et al.*, 2006). Rather, they should also at times seek to move action beyond the family level, and consider how to provide and advocate for high-quality funded care.

Consequently, we argue that there are a number of areas that provide a basis for action under a critical gerontological social work approach. In particular, we highlight the importance of revaluing carers, of building on the knowledge that carers and caring relationships are diverse, and for the need for practitioners to work with, rather than reinforce, the power differentials. Practitioners are also well placed to extend and develop their professional skills, particularly in the area of negotiation.

### Revaluing carers

The subjective experiences of carers, however similar their objective situations, will be different. It therefore follows that practitioners cannot simply assume that care is 'burdensome'. Indeed, social work assessment must take into consideration, and build on, the positive aspects of the care relationship, recognizing that both the 'carer' and the person receiving care are experts in their situations. Attention to carers' individual biographies, and the history of their relationship with the older person, is crucial if a thorough assessment is to take place, and appropriate care planning and services are to be provided. Beyond this, it must also be remembered that carers, of whatever sort, have lives too. People who are carers are also citizens with a multiplicity of roles – perhaps in the workplace and in their own homes, or perhaps as parents or volunteers. Consequently, a 'one size fits all' approach has to be resisted, and this means that practice must reflect an understanding of the diversity of caring relationships and family life.

Extract 7.4 highlights vividly the potential tensions and worries that can arise when carers strive to carve out time for themselves and their families. As you read, consider how easy or difficult it is for families to

## Extract 7.4   *Carers have lives too*

We're all going away tonight. Mum is so worried she's thinking of not going, she says we shouldn't all be away, because of Grandma. Dad is cross with her, he says he's paying Mary a fortune to stay with Grandma and what is the point if it doesn't free us. Mum says but what if anything happens, what if Grandma falls and Mary rings and no one is here, what then, what will Mary do? Dad says ring for an ambulance like anyone else ... Dad sighs, he says he will speak to Mary. He speaks. Mary says no one is to worry, she would cope ... Mum doubts it, she says Mary is too good. Then she has a brainwave. She says she will give Stuart's number to Mary. In an emergency Stuart would *have* to come, even if he never came again, even if he only did it once. Mum says she won't ask him, she'll just do it. Dad says he doesn't bloody care, just so long as she's agreeing to go with him.

They are going to a Silver Wedding party in Cambridge. Dad's best friend is a don there. Dad is looking forward to it no end, Mum not so much ... Adrian is going to the Barn, a place his school has in Somerset. He's doing some A-Level Geography field trip, will be away all weekend. All I'm doing is going to stay at Frinny's. I have to.

(Margaret Forster, *Have the Men Had Enough?*)
Seen from Hannah's perspective, pp. 166–7.

find someone to 'care' formally for someone they love: a person whom they can trust? How can critical gerontological social workers assist family carers to have a life of their own in the face of someone else's needs? To what extent would you see there being a social work role in helping to manage spousal tensions, as illustrated in the extract?

### *Recognizing, valuing and working with diversity*

The existing body of research and literature has also clearly demon-strated the diversity that exists among carers and in care-giving sit-uations. Increasing numbers of people from ethnic minorities are ageing, which means that the numbers of people who need care and support because of long-term illness is set to increase. However, while the expressed desire for family care may be high, families may be dislocated through both geographical distance and culture.

Globalization has transformed our notions and perceptions of space and place, and questioned the nature and extent of care provision. The now global nature of care for some people challenges our traditional concepts of care with new patterns of support emerging which cross continents. Critical gerontological social workers need to be aware that distance can, for example, have substantial negative impacts on personal contact with parents, particularly for distances greater than 100 miles (Parker *et al.*, 2001). The inability to visit regularly may create conflict, guilt or ambivalence for some carers (Baldock, 2000; Connidis, 2001). However, as distance increases between an older person and their adult offspring, extended family members and friends may well take on some of the care roles typically associated with adult children (DeWit *et al.*, 1988; Keeling, 2001). In addition, Campbell and Martin-Matthews (2003) found that there can be positives in distant care, as greater distance may be a legitimate reason for less physical and intimate care involvement but can lead to more regular emotional support via the telephone.

In order to take into account, and recognize and value such diverse experiences, research by Dunst *et al.* (1994) highlights a number of key issues of particular relevance to critical gerontological practitioners, which we note here:

- The importance of reflective listening skills as a basis for understanding the diverse needs and concerns of families.
- Help for families to prioritize aspirations as well as needs.
- The importance of proactive helping styles.
- Help that is compatible with the family's own culture.
- Help compatible with the family's definition of problems and circumstances.
- Help leading to the acquisition of competencies that promote independence.
- Help carried out in the spirit of co-operation and partnership to solve problems.
- The locus of decision-making resting with the family as a whole.

### Addressing power differentials

Throughout these discussions, it remains evident that acknowledging and addressing power differentials in care is a fundamental aspect of a critical gerontological social work approach. It is crucial that social workers acknowledge the power differentials in their relationship with carers and service users, and between carers and those for whom they care. At times, these relationships will inevitably be ambivalent or even conflictual. Not all carers are in harmonious relationships, and some may feel forced to provide care or feel that their own lives cannot be attended to appropriately. Critical gerontological practice, with its emphasis on an holistic systems approach, has much to offer in helping to uncover these tensions, and find practical and supportive strategies to tackle such difficulties. However, problem-solving in situations of conflict requires considerable negotiation skills, and it has to be accepted that social workers may not be able to resolve completely tensions between family members.

Rather, the purpose of negotiation is to reach some form of agreement, perhaps from a range of options, or to resolve a disagreement, conflict or injustice (Coulshed and Orme, 1998). Thompson (2002) has highlighted negotiation skills as being essential in promoting shared decision-making and partnership working. Negotiation therefore forms an important part of direct work with carers. While it is essential that the carer is kept fully in the picture, it is also highly likely that negotiations will extend beyond the carer to other key people in the system.

## Conclusion

Informal care, as we have seen, is complex, and is most commonly undertaken in the context of existing relationships and support networks. While this chapter has concentrated on what, historically, has been termed 'informal care', similar principles apply to the 'formal' care work sector. Simply supporting care, in whatever sphere, as a routine technical task requiring largely manual competencies will ensure that care retains low status in both sectors. A redefinition of both care and carer, along citizenship lines, will permit social workers to work in more equitable and empowering ways, embodying all the essentials of a critical gerontological practice. Moreover, if Tronto's 'ethic of care' is taken as a guiding principle for practice, care can then be valued as a transcending experience of life. Whether the 'ethic of care' will marry with the kinds of managerialist agendas adopted by health and social care agencies remains to be seen, but the emphasis placed in some countries of the UK on empowerment and participatory approaches, and on community development solutions (Department of Health, 2001; Welsh Assembly Government, 2003, 2006), gives us some cause for optimism.

- What are the current key components of a feminist approach to care?
- How do you view your own experiences of giving and receiving care across your life course?
- In what ways can practitioners create empowering contexts for service users and carers when their hopes and goals are in conflict?

taking it further

- Calasanti, T. (2003) 'Masculinities and Care Work in Old Age', in S. Arber, K. Davidson and J. Ginn (eds), *Gender and Ageing: Changing Roles and Relationships*, Buckingham, Open University Press, pp. 15–30.
- Chambers, P. and Phillips, J. (2008) 'Working Across the Interface of Formal and Informal Care of Older People: Partnerships between Carers and Service Providers' in J. Buchanan and R. Carnwell (eds), *Effective Practice in Health and Social Care: Working Together* (2nd edn), Buckingham, Open University Press.
- Martin-Matthews, A. and Phillips, J.E. (eds)(2008) *Aging and Caring at the Intersection of Work and Home Life – Blurring the Boundaries*, New York: Lawrence Erlbaum Associates.
- Phillips, J.E. (2007) *Care*, Cambridge, Polity Press.

# 8 Developing critical gerontological practice: new challenges

**main points**

- Older people, as with any other part of the life course, may experience trauma, abuse or life events that impact on their emotional and mental well-being.

- Social work can continue to have an important role in the recognition, assessment and support of older people experiencing emotional distress caused by trauma, abuse or other life difficulties.

- This means ensuring that social work skills are used beyond the current emphasis on care brokerage.

- Social workers can play an important role in the development of appropriate resources and services.

- The current knowledge and research base in respect of the three areas discussed in this chapter is limited; they are all developing fields.

## Introduction

Having explored insights from gerontological research and applied them to contemporary areas of social work practice with older people, we now turn our attention in this chapter – and in Chapter 9 – to a consideration of the challenges that still remain if we are truly to adopt critical gerontological approaches in both educational and practice arenas. To illustrate these challenges, we focus in this chapter on three areas that we contend are under-appreciated, under-researched and, as a consequence, poorly understood and with variable practice responses. The areas we focus on concern the unresolved traumatic life events experienced by older people, depression among older people, and safeguarding older people who may be experiencing abusive or neglectful relationships. These issues go to the heart of what being a reflexive practitioner and doing critical gerontological social work is about: they are complex, difficult and sensitive areas that require reappraisal and re-evaluation, both intellectually and practically. They also illustrate once again how important it is to build on the things we value about good social work with older people – for example, the core skills and values associated with interpersonal helping – while at the same time developing these into more robust and critical approaches.

Consequently, this chapter begins from the premise that, like all adults, older people may have emotional, social and psychological difficulties that are long-standing or that have emerged as a result of issues affecting them in later life. By focusing on unresolved traumatic life events, depression and safeguarding older people who may be experiencing abusive or neglectful relationships, we believe this provides sufficient evidence to challenge what we see as a drift towards a default position of responding to an older person, regardless of his or her situation, with practical 'care'. There is also a need to take seriously the case for social work practice being alert to, and intervening in, problems stemming from new or long-standing experiences that have had traumatic or problematic consequences for an older person. Critical gerontological practice should therefore embrace, as we have contended throughout, appropriate skills such as active listening in assessment, and interventions that address emotional as well as practical aspects, and timely referral of older people to other specialist services.

## Traumatic life events

Extract 8.1 illustrates the ways in which unresolved family events can have an effect on present experience, feelings and attitudes. As you read, consider to what extent social work assessment and practice might address this sort of issue? How, in your experience, can unresolved family events have an impact on present experiences and relationships?

It is now recognized increasingly that the kinds of events depicted in Extract 8.1 may result in enduring psychological and emotional difficulties and distress. Indeed, the term 'post-traumatic stress disorder' has entered our everyday language in the wake of wars and conflicts (Hunt, 1997) as well as major disasters such as the Paddington Rail crash and the London bombings. Despite this attention, our

## Extract 8.1   *Unresolved family dilemmas*

Stuart ... was eight when his father went off to the war and twelve when he was killed, but Stuart is taciturn on that subject, as on most. Stuart does not go in for memories ... Stuart does not want to discuss anything, ever, regarding all forms of discussion as 'soft' ... He let it be known, in an uncharacteristic outburst of at least four sentences, that he thought Grandma should be in a Home, that Home should be in Glasgow and a Council Home.
[Seen from Jenny's perspective, p. 32.]

Stuart: he makes no excuses, sees no reason why he should. He knows he is not cruel. He doesn't hate his mother, he doesn't wish her to be unhappy, but he thinks, as he constantly repeats, that she has 'had her day' and should be 'packed off'. Stuart's heart doesn't break when he looks at Grandma, he doesn't melt as Bridget does. He sees everything in practical terms.
[Seen from Hannah's perspective, pp. 50–1.]

As Grandma would say, I blame that Stuart. Why hasn't he brought his children up differently? Maybe he did his others, his older ones. Stuart's divorce is said in family lore to have devastated Grandma in her heyday. Mum says in many ways Grandma cast Stuart off before he cast her (Bridget says that is complete nonsense).
[Seen from Hannah's perspective, p. 70.]

(Margaret Forster, *Have the Men Had Enough?*)

understanding of the ways in which events can disrupt lives for decades or indeed, how people can appear to 'successfully cope or suppress the emotional pain for many years, only to find that it returns in later life and in ways that may be very difficult for persons affected and those around them to understand' (Hunt, 1997, p. 3), is still very limited.

The impact of traumatic life events is of potential relevance to work with older people in a number of ways. First, older people may experience traumatic and disturbing events *in* older age. For example, Scharf *et al.* (2004) found that 40 per cent of older people interviewed in areas of multiple deprivation had been a victim of crime. Second, like Grandma McKay, older people may have experienced long-standing psychological and emotional difficulties as a result of stressful events experienced earlier in the life course. Third, older people who appear to have functioned well through their life and apparently 'adjusted' to earlier trauma, may experience the emergence of emotional and psychological distress in later life, perhaps as the result of other age-related changes or losses that may precipitate symptoms associated with an earlier traumatic event (Elder and Clipp, 1988). Indeed, Hunt (1997) has highlighted that the consequences of struggling to come to terms with earlier traumatic experiences remains under-appreciated despite analyses estimating that, in Britain alone, 1.19 million people aged over 60 are likely to be affected by early life trauma (Hunt, 1997).

Busuttil (2004) also comments that structural inequalities such as poverty and poor housing, along with issues such as social isolation and loneliness, may exacerbate established chronic post-traumatic stress disorder. Presumably too, long-established difficulties associated with unresolved reactions to trauma may, in turn, have an impact on a person's ability to access financial resources or sustain intimate relationships, and may well serve as a risk factor to heightened vulnerability to chronic illness and disability. Joffe *et al.* (2003), in research with Holocaust survivors, observed that intuitively clinicians would expect people who survived the most serious and enduring types of persecution, accompanied by being the least psychologically resilient, would be the people most likely to experience adverse consequences in later life.

Unfortunately, the long-term implications of unresolved trauma are not well understood, so causal relationships between trauma and subsequent longitudinal life chances remain relatively speculative. Moreover, the consequences of endemic ageism and assumptions about ageing may make us less sensitive to the potential for an older person to remain or become deeply troubled or upset as a consequence of unresolved trauma.

Crocq (1997), in a reflection on his therapeutic work with veterans of the Second World War, has highlighted that older people referred for help include those who have unexpectedly experienced a re-emergence of distressing memories as a result of events that have received national attention, such as the 50th anniversary of the Normandy landings. This example also illustrates the 'health warning' that Coleman offers against the casual use of reminiscence as a pleasant pastime. Moreover, Coleman and Mills (1997) also warn of the danger of an approach to reminiscence which assumes that everyone will experience and recollect major events in the same way. Due regard needs to be paid to the possibility of people having different perspectives, experiences and interpretations of the same event. Consider, for example, the potential differences in experience of a child during the Second World War who lived in a rural environment and remained there with his or her parents, and a child who was evacuated to a rural environment, taken away from an inner city and his/her family.

It is evident then that the past may intrude without warning into work with older people (Coleman and Mills, 1997), and social workers and other caring professionals need to be alert to this possibility in various settings and situations. Some examples would include:

- Intimate and personal care triggering memories and fears associated with childhood sexual abuse, rape or torture.
- Collective care settings, such as noisy dining rooms, large and busy public areas and poor access to food in care homes may trigger memories of war (for example, bomb shelters; queuing and waiting for food; rationing; school dining rooms).
- Background 'noise' such as television programmes or 'background' music, can intrude on people with cognitive impairment and trigger unwelcome and frightening memories.

Moreover, while a great deal of work has been undertaken in respect of environments for people with dementia, there is nevertheless still huge scope for considering the ways in which the built environment can promote well-being more generally, particularly in collective care settings. However good the design principles are, though, it is the culture of care within a setting that is crucial. Thoughtless use of a radio for the benefit of staff, rather than the older people, is an example of how 'ill-being' can be promoted.

## Depression and ageing

Although traumatic life events may or may not lead to enduring emotional distress, we know that depression is the most commonly experienced mental health problem in older age. Extract 8.2 shows how Mrs McKay's memories of the war affect how she conducts herself and who she is today. As you read, think about how we can be sensitive to the potentially painful or difficult memories that older people are likely to have experienced through their lives. How might we develop our practice to be more alert to the possibility of older service users experiencing unrecognized or undiagnosed depression?

It is estimated that one in seven older people is affected by depression (Chew-Graham et al., 2004) and the prevalence is particularly high among those living in residential and nursing home settings (Manthorpe and Iliffe, 2005). As Godfrey and Denby (2004, p. 25) also argue, unrecognized and untreated depression increases the

## Extract 8.2  *Depressing memories*

The memory of all the wars she has lived through, real and imaginary, depresses Grandma. She says it as a boast in the beginning and then, the more she repeats it, the more real it becomes and the more miserable it makes her. She never talks about my grandfather being killed in the war. She can state it as a fact but that's all. I don't even know which battle he died in or exactly how. But these memories of surviving wars must surely be connected to that event. Poor Grandma. She's staring vacantly ahead, crumbling a bit of bread in her strong hands, thinking about war. But she never cries. Occasionally, watery eyes but tears never fall. It suddenly strikes me how extraordinary it is that my grandmother never cries. I have never seen her sob ... Adrian has stopped laughing. We all watch Grandma, willing her to cheer up. Her sadness is tearing at me, *I* could cry.
(Margaret Forster, *Have the Men Had Enough?*)
Seen from Hannah's perspective, p. 137.

risk of it having a major impact on health, well-being and quality of life:

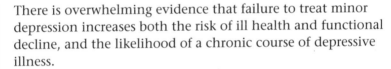

> There is overwhelming evidence that failure to treat minor depression increases both the risk of ill health and functional decline, and the likelihood of a chronic course of depressive illness.

The significance of depression in older age as a reflection of health inequalities in later life, alongside its importance as a public health issue, has been recognized in the National Service Framework for Older People (Department of Health, 2001) and other national policy initiatives (see, for example, CSIP, 2005, 2007). Nevertheless, despite increased policy attention, it remains the case that the assessment, diagnosis and treatment of depression in older age is often overlooked (Godfrey and Denby, 2004).

### Defining depression

From a medical perspective, essential diagnostic criteria for major depression are a depressed mood and/or a marked loss of interest or pleasure for at least two weeks (Butler *et al.*, 1998). Associated symptoms include difficulty in sleeping, changes in appetite and weight, feelings of fatigue or loss of energy, feelings of worthlessness, helplessness and guilt, decreased concentration and indecisiveness, and thoughts of death and suicide (Royal College of Psychiatrists, 2003). As well as the duration of symptoms, Manthorpe and Iliffe (2005) suggest that lack of fluctuation (that is, symptoms occur all the time, with little or no relief), together with intensity (symptoms are of a degree of severity that is not usual for the individual), provide a useful 'rule of thumb' in distinguishing depression from, for example, temporary and context-appropriate feelings of sadness.

Although anxiety disorders are reported as being less common among older people (Butler *et al.*, 1998), prevalence figures suggest that approximately 10 per cent of the older population are affected (Chew-Graham *et al.*, 2004), and symptoms of anxiety are commonly associated with depression. However, there is a tension to be managed between achieving an appropriate diagnosis of depression as against pathologizing an older person who is exhibiting signs of anxiety that are an appropriate response to a particular circumstance or life event:

> Anxiety symptoms are also part of normal experience, as part of a healthy and necessary 'fight or flight' reaction to danger, and are by no means inappropriate or a sign of mental ill-health. The older person being bullied, abused or exploited by others has every reason to be anxious, and should not be too speedily categorised as mentally ill. (Manthorpe and Iliffe, 2005, pp. 15–16)

Dysthymic disorder (often regarded as being less serious than depression) can also cause seriously debilitating and chronic difficulties, and symptoms include low self-esteem, poor concentration, appetite disorders, low energy, sleep disturbance and, commonly, feelings of sadness. However, sadness and feeling low are sometimes entirely appropriate reactions to life circumstances and events and, like anxiety, should not necessarily be regarded as a psychiatric illness (Lebowitz *et al.*, 1995). Consequently, older people may well present with different symptoms from younger people (Chew-Graham, 2004), and it has been argued, for example, that sadness may be less of a feature in older people, but appetite disturbance, changes in sleep patterns, or presentation of physical symptoms may be more apparent.

### Risk factors for depression

A number of factors have also been identified that may increase a person's likelihood of developing depressive disorders in later life. For example, higher rates of depression are found among older people living in sheltered housing, those in receipt of home care services, and those who are disabled (Bannerjee and MacDonald, 1996; Asthana and Halliday, 2006). In addition, a range of chronic illnesses and physical impairments may be associated with depression in older age, including coronary disease such as heart failure; neurological disorders such as Alzheimer's disease; metabolic disturbances such as diabetes mellitus; and cancer (Godfrey and Denby, 2004). Other conditions causing chronic pain and difficulties in managing bodily functions are also identified as significant risk factors.

Furthermore, adverse social and economic circumstances have been reported consistently as a risk factor for depression. For example, Harris *et al.* (2003) have shown that older people with no occupational pension are at greater risk of suffering from depression than their privately-pensioned counterparts, while the Survey of Psychiatric Morbidity (ONS, 2000) reveals that depression is more common among those in manual social classes and those with low incomes. Poor housing, impoverished communities characterized by declining resources and services, and a fear of crime and social isolation may also contribute to depression in later life (Asthana and Halliday, 2006). Unsurprisingly, then, this range of risk factors means that many older people with depression will in fact be known to social work and social care practitioners.

## *The impact of depression*

Depression in older age has a number of highly significant impacts in terms of costs to the older person's health, well-being and quality of life, to their family and social networks, and to care and support services, as well as the wider costs to health and social service resources. It is also evident that the impact of depression may be so severe that suicide becomes a significant risk factor. Suicide among older people accounts for one in eight persons who commit suicide (Manthorpe and Iliffe, 2005), and older people have a higher risk of successful suicide than any other age group (World Health Organization, 2002). Butler *et al.* (1998, p. 100) comment that, along with common methods such as overdose, hanging and the use of firearms, older people may accomplish suicide '"subintentionally" by ... means of not eating, not taking medicines, drinking too much, delaying treatment and taking risks physically'.

Although in absolute terms the numbers of older people who commit suicide appears to be small, it is reasonable to assume that behind these figures lie significant stories of mental distress and associated health and psychological costs. While not everyone who commits suicide is depressed, O'Connell *et al.* (2004, p. 896) conclude that: 'according to the psychological autopsy studies of suicides in elderly people, 71–95% of the people had a major psychiatric disorder at the time of death; depressive illnesses are by far the most common and important diagnoses'. Self-rated intensity of depressive feelings has also been shown to be a significant predictor of suicide (Ross *et al.*, 1990), while other risk factors include serious physical illness, pain and multiple morbidity; stressful life events; loneliness and isolation; and being widowed, single or divorced in later life (O'Connell *et al.*, 2004).

However, Manthorpe and Iliffe (2005) caution against adopting a simplistic understanding of risk factors, not least because many older people often experience all these things without attempting suicide. Nevertheless, there is clearly a need to be alert to the possibility that an older person experiencing depression, or acute feelings associated with loss and bereavement, might actively contemplate suicide. Social workers are again well placed to identify potential depression and risk of suicide, and have a significant role in referring older people for emergency assessment, and specialist assessment and treatment, as well as providing important psychosocial interventions.

## Abuse and neglect

As with depression, abuse of older people has received growing policy attention in recent years although it is still under-researched and, in practice terms, under-investigated and largely ignored (Select Committee on Abuse, 2004). The evidence base is also limited and, with some exceptions, the perspectives of victims remain substantially unexplored. As you read Extract 8.3, think about how you would respond if you were a social worker working with Mrs McKay and her family in this situation. How might we participate in challenging poor and potentially abusive practice in collective care settings such as care homes?

### Defining abuse

'No Secrets' (Department of Health, 2000, p. 9) defines abuse as:

> A violation of an individual's human and civil rights by any other person or persons ... Abuse may consist of a single act or repeated acts. It may be physical, verbal or psychological. It may be an act of neglect or an omission to act, or it may occur when a vulnerable person is persuaded into a financial or sexual transition to which he or she has not consented or cannot consent. Abuse can occur in any relationship and may result in significant harm to, or exploitation of, the person subjected to it.

## Extract 8.3  *Institutional abuse?*

Bridget pats her hands, which she is holding, both of them, in her own. She keeps saying, 'Mother, heh, Mother it's me.' Grandma makes no response. Bridget swears under her breath and then begins to rage about Grandma's clothes. 'What have they put on her? Where're her clothes? My God, what rubbish is this, where are her own slippers?' Grandma opens her eyes ... She struggles to speak but all that comes out is an unintelligible murmur ... Grandma mumbles. I only catch, 'legs'. Bridget examines them. (Grandma has stockings on but they're rolled down to the ankle.) She says, 'Bloody hell, she's bruised, she's *bruised*.' She tells me to stay where I am, she's going to see Sister Grice ...

It is a very awkward tableau ... And then it's like a tennis match. Bridget serves first.

My Mother doesn't seem happy to me.

Oh, goodness, she's fine, she's a bit in the dumps today, but they all have their days you know ...

... what I wanted to ask you about were those bruises.

What bruises?

There, and there.

Oh, they're nothing, they bruise easily at this age, I expect she knocked her leg on a chair.

But my sister-in-law says she doesn't walk on her own any more.

That's true, but we walk her, we keep her going, don't we Mrs McKay, don't we darling?

And I was wondering where her clothes are?

Being name-taped, they'll be back soon.

I'd like her to be in her own clothes.

But they're awkward, they're not as comfortable as these, not as easy, look you see, Velcro, easier for the old things.

(Margaret Forster, *Have the Men Had Enough?*)
Seen from Hannah's perspective, pp. 221–2.

Categories of abuse (financial, physical, sexual, psychological, neglect and discriminatory) are expanded in the policy guidance, along with potential indicators or 'symptoms' of different types of abuse. However, commentators have challenged the use of the term 'elder abuse', arguing that it is a demeaning label and questioning how helpful it is to coalesce a wide range of experiences into an umbrella term (Mowlam *et al.*, 2007). At the time of writing, elder abuse may encompass 'mis-care' as a consequence of stressful informal care relationships; systematic abuse over time of vulnerable older people in a collective care setting; or criminal activities against an older person/people. The Association of Directors of Social Services (ADSS) (2006) have also suggested that the commonly used term 'protection of vulnerable' adults, should be replaced by 'safeguarding adults' on the basis that vulnerability carries with it a number of inappropriate messages (for example, passivity and, potentially, an element of blame).

## Prevalence

Estimates of the prevalence of elder abuse have, until recently, tended to be based on small-scale studies or on figures gleaned from analysis of calls to helplines such as Action on Elder Abuse (Action on Elder Abuse, 2006). An earlier large-scale study (Ogg and Bennett, 1992) indicated that one in twenty older people had experienced verbal or financial abuse, and one in fifty physical abuse. However, a significant omission in that study was the exclusion of disabled adults and people living in collective care settings. In contrast, in 2006, Action on Elder Abuse reported on a 2-year project funded by the Department of Health, which aimed to investigate and analyse adult protection data from nine local authorities. Over the period of the investigation, 639 referrals were analysed and it was found that:

- Of the total number of referrals, 54.8 per cent related to older people.
- Physical abuse accounted for the largest number of referrals, followed by neglect.
- Institutional settings accounted for the highest number of alleged instigators of abuse.
- Only five of the total number of reported cases led to criminal proceedings, although there was police involvement in over forty of the investigations.
- The majority of investigated cases led to a decision for 'further monitoring', although Action on Elder Abuse raised concerns about the number of cases that led to 'No further action'.

More recently still, research funded by Comic Relief and the Department of Health (O'Keefe *et al.*, 2007) looked at data from 2,100 older people (aged 66 and over) living in private households (including sheltered accommodation) in England, Scotland, Wales and Northern Ireland. The researchers found that:

- 2.6 per cent of people aged 66 and over reported that they had experienced mistreatment involving a member of the family, a care worker or a friend in the year preceding the study, equating to 227,000 people. This increases to approximately 342,400 people when prevalence of mistreatment is widened to include neighbours and acquaintances.

■ The most common type of mistreatment was neglect (11 people in 1,000), followed by financial (7 people in 1,000), psychological mistreatment (4 people in 1,000), physical mistreatment (4 people in 1,000) and sexual abuse (2 people in 1,000).

■ Levels of mistreatment were reported to be higher for people who reported poor health status, a limiting long-term illness, lower quality of life and depression.

This study also argues that the incidence of abuse is likely to be very much higher than is either currently reported to, or coming to the attention of, adult protection services (O'Keefe *et al.*, 2007). Older people may be afraid, unable or unwilling to report experiences of mistreatment, especially if, for example, they rely on the person or institution for other forms of care, support or sustenance.

## Risk factors

Despite increased awareness of the issue, the sorts of risk factors that may make an older person more susceptible to mistreatment are still not well understood. Mowlam and colleagues (2007, p. 2) highlight the complexity of abusive situations, contending that:

> Mistreatment does not occur in isolation but against a backdrop of an individual's and their family's long history of relationships as well as events that are increasingly common as people age; increasing ill health or disability, limitations of daily activity, bereavement of partners, family members and friends.

It is further suggested that a combination of characteristics such as gender, age, health profile and where someone lives, may place a person at particular risk of abuse (Cambridge *et al.*, 2006). Moreover, where abuse or mistreatment has become endemic in an institutional setting, public enquiries such as that emanating from discoveries of poor and abusive care on Rowan Ward (CHI, 2003), have identified a number of common features leading to poor care and mistreatment:

■ poor/institutionalized environment (for example, rigid routines and routinized and task-orientated care for the benefit of staff, rather than based on individual need);

■ lack of occupation, stimulation and engagement;

■ low/inadequate staffing levels which encourage a culture of 'getting by' and doing the 'essentials' (that is, physical care) rather than accepting that, for example, time spent in conversation with a resident may count as doing 'care';

- high use of bank staff who may have little or no investment in the culture of care or the people living and working in the environment;
- little staff development, which means that long-standing or outdated practices may persist;
- poor supervision, providing few opportunities for learning by reflection, modelling, debating critical issues, or learning about new developments in care and support;
- lack of knowledge re: 'whistle blowing' and how to challenge poor, risky or unacceptable care practices;
- an inward-looking culture that discourages contact or relationships with organizations, agencies and people in the wider community; and
- a weak management structure (for example, poor evidence of investigation of unexplained bruising or untoward incidents).

In addition, depression was the single factor that emerged consistently in the UK prevalence study (O'Keeffe et al., 2007). However, while a causal relationship could not be established from the available data, other research has also highlighted an association between mistreatment and depression among older people (Pillemer and Prescott, 1989; Wolf, 1999; Dyer et al., 2000).

## Impact of abuse

If risk factors are poorly understood, then it is also the case that the impact of abuse remains relatively under-investigated, particularly with respect to the longer-term consequences of abuse (such as unresolved trauma leading to psychological and emotional difficulties), or how interventions may ameliorate the impact of the experience of abuse. The voices and experiences of older people who have been abused are also largely absent from research. Nonetheless, it is evident that abuse has an impact on older people's self-confidence and self-esteem, on their sense of independence, on physical and mental health, and on family relationships (Mowlam et al., 2007).

While the relationship between the experience of abuse and its potential consequences or implications is a complex one, a number of protective factors have also been identified that might increase an older person's resilience. The older respondents in Mowlam et al.'s (2007) research highlight the importance of effective social support and engagement, personal strengths, and the experience of coping with other difficult life events as factors that promoted their resilience and ability to cope with the difficulties of experiencing mistreatment. Conversely, factors that might worsen the impact and implications of mistreatment include the unpredictability, duration, intensity and frequency of mistreatment; the location of the perpetrator; the nature and type of abuse; the availability of access to support and help; and other factors (such as ill health) that might affect the quality of life of an older person. Similarly, the older people who had experienced abuse who participated in Pritchard's (2002) research, highlighted a number of key needs they would wish to have had addressed. These included being taken seriously; having someone to listen to and confide in; access to help and assistance, both at the time and afterwards; and access to financial help. Consequently, it is abundantly clear that older people require help, treatment and interventions that are supportive and individually tailored to their particular circumstances, and it is to these issues that we now turn.

## Critical gerontological social work in practice

Critical gerontological social workers, by virtue of their holistic approach to practice, are well placed to contribute actively to a range of interventions that could support older people experiencing the kinds of complex and sensitive situations we have explored in the previous pages. With these explorations as a basis, we now focus our discussion on a number of areas of importance to social work interventions with older people. We begin by examining the legislative and legal aspects, as they relate, in particular, to our discussion of abuse and neglect. We then go on to consider treatments for depression and other traumas (both medical and psychosocial); the importance of life-course and biographical perspectives on these issues; assessment, care planning and the intersection with community resources; and, finally, the importance of working with, and listening to, the older people themselves.

### Legislation and legal interventions

Given the complexity of the legal frameworks around abuse and neglect, it would be inappropriate to enter into detailed discussions here, particularly given the very full explanations of relevant legislation available elsewhere (for example, Brammer, 2007). However, it is important to draw attention to the fact that 'No Secrets' (2000) provides the main policy and practice context on the protection of all vulnerable adults and, while it was issued under Section 7 of the Local Authority Social Services Act (1970), it does not carry the full force of the law. Indeed, there is not at the time of writing any legislation intended specifically to protect and safeguard vulnerable adults in England, Wales and Northern Ireland (for the Scottish legislative framework, readers are referred to The Protection of Vulnerable Adults (Scotland) Act 2007). Despite the absence of specific legislation, however, a variety of existing laws may be used as a means of responding to the abuse of vulnerable adults; respect for the autonomy of the individual remains an essential principle; and any intervention should present a positive improvement of the situation as well as upholding an individual's rights (Brammer, 2007).

Moreover, the appropriateness of legal interventions will vary, depending on individual situations. For example, criminal or legal remedies are less likely to be of immediate relevance in neglect arising from the difficulties and stresses of an informal care relationship. Research by O'Keeffe *et al.* (2007) found that partners were the main perpetrators in the neglect of older people, but they reflect that this may not be as a result of deliberate actions. Rather, it may be a consequence of two older people with long-term illnesses or increasing disabilities trying to cope with a complex situation, with inadequate support or assistance.

As well as the 'No Secrets' guidance, the Mental Capacity Act (2005) is fundamentally important in providing additional guidance on the principles that should inform practice in safeguarding vulnerable adults. It starts from the premise that a person *has* capacity, unless it is proven otherwise, and it requires practitioners to make every effort to establish a person's capacity to make specific decisions and choices. This important principle is intended to protect people from the consequences of ill-judged or inappropriate assumptions that can be made by practitioners about, for example, the capacity of a very elderly person with cognitive impairment. In respect of adult protection, if a decision is made that a person lacks capacity to make a particular decision, then it is necessary to determine what protective action should be taken *in the person's best interests*. Decision-making and interventions that aim to protect a person from abuse must include every attempt to encourage and facilitate the participation of that person; must take into account the wishes, feelings, beliefs and values of the person, as well as the views of other people; must be non-discriminatory; and should interfere the least with the rights and freedoms of the person (see www.publicguardian.gov.uk).

## Medical and psychosocial treatments

Turning now to a consideration of treatment, interventions and management strategies for older people who may be depressed, anxious or suffering from the consequences of traumatic life events, it is evident that a range of possibilities now present themselves. While social workers clearly do not prescribe medications, it helps to be aware that the administration of, for example, anti-depressant medication is now often recommended in combination with other forms of psychosocial treatment (Royal College of Psychiatry, 2002). Bartels *et al.* (2002) have commented that combined treatments are far more likely to be effective in reducing the impact of depression, and other research has suggested that physical exercise as an adjunct to anti-depressive medication is also helpful (Mather *et al.*, 2002). Treatment outcome studies with respect to reducing the effects of unresolved or re-emergent trauma are lacking, however (Busuttil, 2004), and despite the significance of depression in older age, screening for symptoms, assessment, diagnosis and treatment also remains under-developed.

Yet, some research examining the impact of psychosocial or multi-faceted programmes of intervention appears to demonstrate promising results in improving a person's quality of life. For example, Unützer *et al.* (2002, cited in Chew-Graham *et al.*, 2002) undertook a randomized control trial with 1801 depressed older people. The participants were randomized into a 'usual care' group and a 'collaborative care' group. The 'collaborative care' group received treatment *and* psychosocial support from a care team, and results indicated that, after twelve months, almost half of the 'treatment' group was at least 50 per cent improved from baseline assessments, compared with only one in five in the control group. The research summarized in Box 8.1 shows similar improvements among depressed older people living in care homes. At the very least, then, critical gerontological social workers can encourage care homes to recognize the importance of psychosocial well-being for individual older people.

In addition, talking therapies and interventions, such as cognitive behavioural therapy, have received only limited attention with regard to their impact on depression in older people. This is an area for further development, and national policy has sought to recognize the challenge of providing at least equal mental health services to older people (CSIP, 2005). Hsleh and Wang (2003) undertook a systematic review that assessed the effect of reminiscence therapy on older adults with depression. Despite the current evidence being described as 'weak', Hsleh and Wang (2003) indicated that results were sufficiently encouraging to suggest there was value in reminiscence therapy as a therapeutic tool. It is clear, however, that understanding how reminiscence as therapy may have a positive impact on depression is still at an early stage with respect to an evidence base.

## Box 8.1 Research into practice: reducing depression among older people receiving care

This research examined the impact of individualized, person-centred interventions on depression among older people living in care homes. Eighty-seven older participants with depression (as defined by the Depression scale of the Geriatric Mental State Schedule) were assigned to care workers who were specially trained to plan and carry out individualized interventions and support plans. Initially, care workers undertook a detailed interview with the older participant in order to ascertain the person's likes/dislikes, life history/ biography, physical health, and relationships in the care home. The interview also sought to identify what improvements the older participant wanted in their own lives. Care plans were developed directly from the interviews to address individual needs and provide psychosocial support. Intervention goals included:

- visits to the supermarket;
- review of hearing and hearing aid equipment;
- resuming attendance at church;
- going to football matches; and
- being able to sit outdoors.

Results suggested that, on follow-up from baseline measurements of depression, participants showed significant improvement, including a number of people who had ceased to be identified as having 'clinical' symptoms of depression. Improvement was noted to be the most significant among older people who had initially exhibited the most severe symptoms of depression. Lyne et al. (2006, p. 4) comment that the approach: 'implements person-centred care through personalising interventions around the priorities and choices of each individual. It offers a means for implementing in attainable, practical ways the goals of 'well-being and choice', affirmed by the 2006 White Paper, "Our Health, Our Care, Our Say"'.

*Source:* Lyne *et al.*, 2006.

### Life course and biographical perspectives

In both recognizing and responding to unresolved trauma, depression, and abuse and neglect, it emerges that an over-emphasis on an older person's functional (in)abilities, rather than addressing biographical, social and psychosocial needs (see Lymbery, 2005; Phillips *et al.*, 2006) is critical. We have argued throughout this book that, in practice with an older person with complex needs or circumstances, it is often necessary to have an understanding of the relevance of a life-course perspective. Such an approach provides opportunities to understand how biography may have an impact on current circumstances (Bywaters, 2007), and Busuttil (2004) has argued, for example, that careful history-taking, including a screening question about exposure to trauma, may be especially helpful in old-age psychiatry. Clearly, such an approach could, in combination with active and empathic listening, and the development of a working alliance between social worker and service user, highlight important clues as to how an older person's biography has included traumatic experiences or possible symptoms of depression. Single assessment processes also provide opportunities for practitioners to request specialist assessments if there is evidence, for example, that an older person is experiencing emotional distress or suffering mental health problems.

Given the human and financial costs associated with mental health problems, together with the apparently entrenched difficulties in responding to older people with depression, it is further argued that a focus on prevention may be the most appropriate way to direct attention (Manthorpe and Iliffe, 2005). However, Asthana and Halliday (2006, p. 548) argue that preventative services, 'despite the rhetoric, are also still under-funded and underdeveloped, with resources continuing to focus on the most vulnerable rather than the wider older population'. In addition, the evidence base on 'what works' in preventing depression, for example, remains· poorly understood and under-investigated. With this in mind, Manthorpe and Iliffe (2005) have suggested that appropriate emotional and psychological support, provided at the time people receive 'bad news' (for example, diagnosis of a serious illness) may enhance adjustment. Second, they suggest that a more proactive approach to screening following bereavement might identify people who are depressed, or have developed depression or acute reactions, such as suicidal thoughts. In this context, members of older persons' teams are well placed to identify older people in receipt of services, or have been referred to services, who may be at risk of depression or experience difficulties in managing traumatic life events. Social workers can also participate proactively in commissioning and developing community services and responses, particularly in partnership with older people. The value of, for example, peer mentoring and support is an area that would merit further development and attention.

## Assessment, care planning and community resources

Critical gerontological social workers, orientated towards the development of a positive working alliance with service users, are theoretically very well placed to identify potential signs of depression, trauma, or abuse and neglect. Moreover, a relationship that is grounded in trust, empathy and respect may create an environment in which older people, often reluctant to talk about feelings and worries, may feel able to share these (Manthorpe and Iliffe, 2005). However, Chew-Graham (2004) has highlighted that, at the time of writing, practitioners have limited time to spend with older people who may have a number of co-existing difficulties, and are therefore less likely to spot, for example, symptoms of depression. By implication, this means that social workers engaged in practice with older people need to challenge robustly an orientation towards fast 'throughput' regardless of the complexity of their practice. In addition, of course, assessment skills are a vital component in the process of identifying a person's needs and context, and the Social Care Institute for Excellence has produced comprehensive guidance on the assessment of older people with mental health needs (Moriarty, 2005).

Care planning also provides an important opportunity to identify how an older person's social and emotional needs may be met. As we saw in the research reported in Box 8.1, significant gains in well-being and quality of life can be achieved by what appear to be deceptively simple interventions. Clearly, individual social workers cannot tackle the culture of a care home that appears to under-recognize the importance of psychosocial care. However, individual social workers can certainly ensure that initial care plans address, for example, individual interests and aspirations, and that they provide information about stressors and the ways in which an older person may cope with challenge. Moreover, they can, and should, resist practices that they know will reinforce or create further oppression for older people. This means engaging with practice that embodies the three strands of administrative, individualistic/therapeutic and collective traditions of social work (Lymbery, 2005), and which might include, for example, working with inspection services to identify examples of poor practice in care home and domiciliary care provision, or developing alliances with other professionals to provide the best response to an older person experiencing mental distress.

Beyond this, social service teams are often at the forefront of supporting and funding voluntary and private agencies, as well as local authority resources which provide social support to older people. This is an area that has potential to be developed by gerontological social workers familiar with local communities, in order to identify gaps in preventative services that could be dealt with by local commissioning, joint working and new projects (for example, partnership and older-people funding). The importance of community resources that promote opportunities for valued and valuable social interaction, occupation and relationships, can be a key feature in the promotion of mental health in older age.

## Listening to older people

A further persistent thread throughout our discussions has been the importance of active listening with older people. The research evidence highlights just how important it is for older people to feel that they are being listened to, and that their experiences are validated and responded to appropriately and with sensitivity (Mowlam *et al.*, 2007). The critical practice perspective of an 'open and not knowing approach' (Brechin, 2000), manifested in the ability to maintain an open mind about a person's risks, or assumptions about a person's guilt, are also of crucial importance (Cambridge and Parkes, 2004).

The listening skills and abilities of critical gerontological social workers are important in many situations, particularly when working with a person with particular communication needs; with a person who may be more tired at some times in the day than others; or when a person has particular routines and rhythms that are important to him/her. This may mean that the older person has specific needs in terms of enhancing their ability to participate in decisions about their lives.

From a wider perspective, critical gerontological social workers also need to be able to work with complex systems, and be able to respond to different agendas, concerns and perspectives on the same situation. The ability to cope with multiple perspectives is at the heart of critical practice. For example, one professional worker may view the apparently neglectful circumstances of an older person as needing the support of a full-time residential place, but the older person may want to remain at home with a partner who, for reasons of their own declining health, is struggling to provide appropriate care. The couple's son may want both parents to be taken care of in a care home. There are rarely any easy answers to these ethical dilemmas, and being prescriptive runs directly counter to a critical gerontological approach that highlights the importance of listening to the individual, and keeping him or her at the centre of practice.

## Conclusion

This chapter has discussed three challenging areas for critical gerontological social work where older people may be susceptible to their needs being unrecognized and under-appreciated. The importance of mental health as an essential part of healthy ageing is now included in much national policy, but there is still a long way to go with respect to, for example, recognizing and providing helpful interventions and support for older people with depression. Similarly, it remains the case that, despite the increased attention being focused on elder abuse, this is not supported by accompanying research or a clearly evolving practice base that identifies ways in which the distress and impact of abuse of older people may be addressed and ameliorated (Mowlam *et al.*, 2007). This means that critical gerontological social workers, along with other practitioners, are not able to draw easily on a well-developed research or evidence base to inform their practice. However, the picture continues to improve and develop, and, as with other areas of practice discussed in this book, this means that critical gerontological social workers should be well placed to make a vital contribution to the well-being of all older people with whom they work.

## stop and think

- How can interventions that address social issues such as loneliness, isolation or poor support networks be developed?
- What should a social worker do if he or she believes that an older person has depression?
- What kind of approaches would be helpful in identifying unresolved trauma, loss or grief in later life?
- How can practitioners try to ensure that they practice in a way that preserves the rights of an older person?

taking it further

- Brammer, A. (2007) *Social Work Law* (2nd edn), Harlow, Longman.
- Lyne, K. J. Moxon, S., Sinclair, I., Young, P., Kirk, C. and Ellison, S. (2006) 'Analysis of a Care Planning Intervention for Reducing Depression in Older People in Residential Care' in *Aging and Mental Health*, 10(4), pp. 394–403 (further information and related resources may be obtained from: http://www.well-beingand choice.org.uk/ReducingDepression.htm).
- Manthorpe, J. and Iliffe, S. (2005) *Depression in Later Life*, London, Jessica Kingsley.
- Social Care Institute for Excellence (SCIE) (2006) *Assessing the Mental Health Needs of Older People*, London, SCIE.

# 9 Pushing the boundaries

## Introduction

Our motivation in writing this book came first from a strong belief in, and commitment to, the importance of social work with older people. Such a role should, we believe, offer a robust challenge to responses to older people premised on the provision of practical care regardless of the person's presenting need. Second, we have, in the course of our teaching, research and contact with social workers, identified a number of areas of practice that seem to be especially relevant to the experience of older people, and throughout this book we have sought to examine the possibilities for social work in these areas. Finally, making the *case* for critical gerontological social work practice was a key aspiration for the book, especially in the light of the challenges that are apparent to the current and future social work role with older people. Despite variations in policy and practice across the four countries of the British Isles (see Chapter 1), our discussions are set in the context of what appears to be an increasingly beleaguered social work practice with older people.

Our views of the challenges facing social workers who work with older people are not exhaustive. Others may disagree with the topics we have prioritized, or the arguments we have mounted. Whatever your view as a reader, it is an inescapable reality that social workers continue to practice in increasingly complex contexts. It is also the case that older people often experience discrimination based on assumptions about what they should 'need'. As a result, older people are too often on the receiving end of services that might not meet their aspirations or needs, or enable them to feel as if their concerns are being appreciated fully and responded to appropriately.

This final chapter highlights some of the key contributions that social work practice may be able to make. The challenges or difficulties at the time of writing in developing these areas of practice are summarized, and goals for addressing those challenges are considered.

## The benefits and challenges of a social work role

There is a relative paucity of research examining what older people value about social workers, and their relationship with them (Manthorpe *et al.*, 2007). Not surprisingly, the research that does exist highlights that the social theories and approaches commonly associated with social work practice are frequently cited by service users in positive evaluations. Such approaches include moving away from assumptions grounded in a deficit model, towards valuing older people by starting from their frame of reference and recognizing the strengths, resources, experiences and continuities that older people facing change and transition possess (Older People's Steering Group, 2004). The National User Network (Beresford, 2007c, p. 5) identifies a number of key skills particularly valued by people who use social work services, including:

- advice and advocacy;
- negotiating with other agencies;
- counselling and psychotherapeutic support;
- practical guidance/help;
- accessing financial support; and
- signposting people to other agencies.

The positive quality of the relationship that can be achieved between a service user and social worker has also been cited in service user evaluations. Beresford (2007c, p. 5) and the National User Network emphasize the value of social worker relationships, which include:

- flexibility and person-centred approaches;
- continuity;
- empathy, warmth and genuineness;
- effective communication and active listening; and
- the ability to relate the personal to the social and political.

Evaluations from older people who have received social work services identified the benefits of practitioners who could recognize and support emotional need and distress in an empathic and constructive way (Manthorpe *et al.*, 2007) as well as being able to provide relevant emotional and practical assistance. Nevertheless, the same research, revealed a number of concerns and criticisms of social work practice, based on experiences of receiving social work services:

> Negative statements about social workers included references to unhelpful attitudes, guarding the council's money and rationing services, and being too slow to respond to requests for help or to undertake social care assessments, or in some cases, not responding at all. (Manthorpe *et al.*, 2007, p. 9)

Consultation with service user groups (Older People's Steering Group, 2004) is critical of social work practice that over-emphasizes an administrative approach (Lymbery, 2005) with an attendant focus on assessment and care brokerage, at the expense of wider needs and circumstances. This evidence challenges a social work practice that is constructed increasingly around purchasing care, regardless of need:

> The commodification of care – constructing 'care' as an entity to be bought and sold – has absorbed these practitioners' energies, filling time available for working with individuals and families. Community care practice has become an exercise in resource finding within a market economy. (McDonald *et al.*, 2007, p. 7)

A key premise of this book is that critical gerontological social workers should possess an appropriate knowledge base that reflects the complexities of social work practice in general, and practice with older people in particular. The kinds of skills that social workers are trained to have, such as the development of social understandings of complex situations, the ability to work with systems, drawing on eclectic theories and models to inform practice, and the importance of developing positive and participatory relationships with older people, have been severely challenged within the context of a practice that emphasizes the identification of problems as a means of managing finite resources and determining eligibility to receive services.

Chapter 1 outlined the current managerialist approach to practice with older people. The key practice changes that have arisen in the wake of the NHS and Community Care Act (1990) have resulted in significant changes to social work, including an increased focus on the notion of care brokerage and a growing separation between aspirations for social work as a professional project and an administrative model (see, for example, Gorman and Postle, 2003; Lymbery, 1998, 2005). A review of the roles and tasks of social workers (Blewitt *et al.*, 2007) has highlighted that it is not clear how, for example, social workers can use their knowledge and skill base to deliver person-centred assessment and interventions in the context of a standardized approach to assessment that is current at the time of writing.

There is growing evidence that social workers are being drawn into procedures and administrative processes at the expense of using (and developing) a knowledge base that would enhance capacity to respond to individual need and work with situations of complexity and uncertainty (McDonald *et al.*, 2007). Barriers to using appropriate knowledge have been identified by McDonald *et al.*, (2007) at three levels: structural, management and practitioner, evidenced by factors such as close attention to outcome at the expense of process; and the marginalization or loss of social worker ability to make use of theoretical frameworks to inform and shape their practice and decision-making.

In the context of the growth in interprofessional working, an apparent decline in professional knowledge and skill, combined with increased uncertainty about the professional role of social work carries a number of threats. Lymbery (2005), for example, has argued the potential for other professionals to define the social work role; for other professional workers to lay claim to activities that traditionally fall within a social work role; and for the managerialist agenda to define the role of social work so narrowly that, in effect, a professional qualification is deemed to be unnecessary. It is essential that social workers with older people can identify the skills and knowledge base they bring to social work with older people as well as their distinct contribution to the overall skill, knowledge and value mix that makes up interprofessional practice.

Social workers are well placed to make visible, and intervene in addressing the structural inequalities and forms and processes of discrimination often experienced by older people. Fundamentally, this means challenging 'essentialism' and the assumptions that underpin a 'tick box' and reductionist approach to practice with older people. As we have discussed, the impact of poverty, age-based discrimination, racism and gender-based oppressions should be within the purview of a social work practitioner. Training that highlights the importance of human growth and development across the life course can assist social workers to understand the potential for sharpening inequalities in older age, and the potential impact of cumulative disadvantage in later life – as well, of course, as the potential for growth, change and development throughout the *whole* of the life course.

Social work training should lend itself to taking an holistic approach in practice with older people. In Chapter 3 we discussed the importance of adopting a critical perspective for commonly used terms to define and construct older people (for example, frailty, risk, dependency). We argued that such terms are often not objective statements about an older person's total experience, but rather are used to communicate information about eligibility and the 'giving' of finite amounts of 'care'. Social work with older people has a distinct contribution to make in challenging assumptions about older people that are grounded in an oppressive frame of reference (such as the inevitable dependency of very old people; or adopting a risk-averse or minimization approach). A social work focus on systems could also mean that social workers are in a position to advocate for an older person in the context of conflicting perspectives and ideas about how best to assist an older person deemed to be vulnerable or 'at risk'.

Moreover, critical practice should make a positive and discernible difference to older people. Dalrymple and Burke (2006) highlight the role of social work in enabling service users to gain, or regain, control. Social work practice, using the skills and abilities that are evaluated positively by older people and the wider service-user community, could enable older people to participate actively and lead on decisions that are fundamental to their lives. This means that social workers need to be able to build relationships that facilitate the genuine participation of older people, and challenge attempts to intervene in an older person's life without having due regard for their individual biography and the strengths, capacities, resources and aspirations that older people use to manage and cope with change and transition. Moreover, social workers should be able to work with older people to encourage an active role in developing services and community responses which chime with the aspirations of older people. This is an area that needs considerable attention as older people, particularly those who have traditionally been excluded from opportunities to participate (such as people with dementia), have a history of exclusion from rather than inclusion in democratic approaches to participation (Beresford, 2007b). Mental Health Media (2004) as one example, provide powerful and positive illustrations of the benefits that older people with depression derived from democratic participation in community resources developed to provide opportunities for social participation, peer mentoring and emotional and practical support.

Social work practitioners can potentially participate in this area of work in a number of ways. They can, for example:

- Listen to the needs of older people and their aspirations beyond physical need/assistance.
- Signpost people to community resources which support participation.
- Challenge managers to develop the participation of older people in the evaluation and development of community resources.
- Record and highlight the issue of unmet need.
- Highlight information about collective needs (community need).
- Feed into commissioning processes in the development of resources and facilities.

A critical gerontological practice would also question and keep an open mind about ideological positions underpinning current policy focus in social care. The emphasis on independence and autonomy, with its focus increasingly towards a personalization agenda, is undoubtedly of importance to many older people. But it is also a political aspiration that is encompassed in most social policy about older people (for example, the National Service Framework for Older People, Department of Health, 2001). Ferguson (2007) discusses the importance of uncovering the assumptions that underpin the emphasis on individualization, and the transfer of risk from the state to the individual. Autonomy, for example, is linked with choice. It remains the case, however, that older people often do not have a choice about the services they receive, when and how they receive them, and the extent to which a person can 'vote with his or her feet' and reject the service offered. A response to the difficulties in establishing choice has in part been responded to via an increased policy attention towards direct payments and individualized budgets. However, Ellis (2007, p. 418) has commented that 'the largest group of potential recipients – older people – were assumed not to want the bother of direct payments or to lack the gumption to manage them'. There is clearly work to be done in challenging social workers' assumptions about what older people can/should have access to in response to their needs.

However, the emphasis on autonomy and agency increasingly characterized by the so-called individualization agenda, should not mean acting for oneself under conditions of oppression, disadvantage or discrimination. Simply 'giving' care services to an older person while they continue to live in poverty or with unmet emotional needs fails to recognize the proper meaning of agency and the importance of advocacy, relationships and support in challenging oppression. Ferguson (2007, p. 401) has argued that:

> Overcoming a sense of powerlessness ... will involve moving beyond the individualism and market-based solutions of personalisation theory. It will require the development and strengthening of collective organisation both amongst those who use services and amongst those who provide them.

It is imperative that the concern for autonomy and independence does not exclude other rights that may be as important for older people who are living with serious long-term illness, uncertain futures or at the end of their lives. Other factors such as comfort and security, preserving attachments and reciprocal relationships, are also essential and must be included in social work practice if the goal of social models of understanding and holistic perspectives are to be realized.

## Discussion

There is now a significant evidence base confirming the challenges that face a future social work role with older people (Lymbery, 1998,

2005; Gorman and Postle, 2003; McDonald *et al.*, 2007). The emphasis at the time of writing on purchasing services in the context of increasingly proceduralized processes, calls into question the areas of knowledge and skill that could reasonably be identified as areas where social workers would have a distinct, valuable, and indeed viable, contribution to make to the quality of life of an older person.

In Chapters 1 and 2, we identified the relative invisibility of social work with older people in social work training in a North American context. The evidence base in Britain about the value, content and importance attributed to social work with older people in an educative context also remains sparse. Indeed, the lack of research may of itself be an indicator of the degree of interest in this area of practice. Research by Quinn (1999) reflected the assumptions often made by students about the undesirability of social work practice with older people. Based on current evidence, there is a case for raising the visibility of social work practice with older people in social work education and training. The involvement of older people and older peoples' community groups in social work teaching and assessment is a key element in encouraging students to engage with opportunities that may uncover assumptions and prejudices about ageing, and develop interest in this area of practice. Social work education should include an appropriate gerontological focus, which can enhance student capacity and confidence in developing appropriate theoretical and knowledge frameworks to apply to practice. This should include specific attention to the forms and processes of oppression that older people may experience, and ways in which social work may challenge such oppression. Critically, students should be encouraged to understand the complexities and diverse range of knowledge and skills required to work effectively with older people.

Anecdotally, in-service training with a practice (and process) focus with the aim of developing professional knowledge and skill, has been marginalized in favour of mandatory training with an emphasis on topics such as briefing about new procedures and reorganization of services. This is a loss and we cannot help but question its potential impact on practitioners' abilities to develop their knowledge and skill in the delivery of social work to older people (McDonald *et al.*, 2007). The dangers of a supervision practice that focuses increasingly on workload management and checking the achievement of performance criteria at the expense of assisting social workers to explore difficult areas of practice has also been raised (by, for example, Sawdon and Sawdon, 2003; McDonald *et al.*, 2007). Practitioners engaged in post-qualifying awards should be able to access gerontological research, theories and knowledge as a means of enhancing their professional practice.

Greater visibility of social work with older people in a research context is also needed. The Economic and Social Research Council (ESRC) recognizes social work as a research discipline that increases the scope for developing the social work research base as well as raising the visibility of social work practice in specific areas of practice, including gerontological practice. Developing the research base with respect to older people and social work must include the active participation and involvement of the older people who use and experience both formal services and social work services. Throughout this book, gaps in research (and thus also in the knowledge base) have been identified repeatedly; for example, research that is convened by older people, or reflects the concerns and interests of older people; the experience of older people with depression; strategies and interventions in response to mistreatment of older people; and the views and experiences of social workers in practice with older people are just some examples.

It seems to us that there is also an urgent need to raise the profile of social work with older people. Our contact with social workers confirms that they often feel devalued within their organization, but also in terms of the lack of importance that is attached to social work with older people. At an individual level, social work practitioners can contribute to raising the profile of social work with older people by, for example, publicizing creative or new developments in their practice; evaluating their practice; and highlighting to colleagues the skills and knowledge base that practitioners bring to gerontological social work. Active participation in professional bodies and organizations can also contribute to raising the profile of gerontological social work.

Nationally, the review of the roles and tasks of social work (GSCC, 2007) may illuminate further the future direction for social work within a broad range of practice areas. Organizationally, it is inevitable that the agenda for change will continue unabated. Beresford (2007c) has commented that social work managers and policy-makers would do well to listen to the voices of service users, including older people, about the kinds of services they both value and want. Treading the path between the management of finite resources and fast-paced change against the value of professional practice, is undoubtedly difficult. It is important that managers recognize the resource they have in social workers and the role that social workers play day-in and day-out in the practice, support and management of increasingly complex and demanding workloads. Valuing the contribution of social work staff and trying to ensure that their support needs are not overlooked – by providing decent supervision and opportunities for development – can contribute significantly to the well-being of staff. Making progress in developing frameworks for the participation of older people in the evaluation of existing services, and learning from examples of good practice in this area, is essential if the voices of older people are to influence the debates about the social work profession (Manthorpe *et al.*, 2007) and the kinds of services, support and assistance that are important to their well-being and quality of life.

McDonald *et al.*, (2007) have argued that:

> Both academic and practice agendas need to support and sustain the commitment and enthusiasm of all practitioners by debating and seeking to resolve structural, management and individual barriers to ethical and effective practice.

This highlights the importance of the social work role as being of concern to us all. We are all likely to grow old, and a good number of us may need the assistance of a practitioner whom we would wish to listen to our concerns; understand our emotional distress; offer practical assistance; signpost us to other services; and work with the life experiences, qualities and resources we have carried through our lives. This person may be a social worker. We need to do what we can to ensure that the role of social work with older people has a future, and a future that recognizes and responds to the stated requirements of older people.

# Useful website addresses

Age Concern: www.ageconcern.org.uk
Alzheimer's Society: www.alzheimers.org.uk
BASW (British Association of Social Work): www.basw.co.uk
BSG (British Society of Gerontology): www.britishgerontology.org
CPA (Centre for Policy on Ageing): www.cpa.org.uk
CCWALES (Care Council for Wales): www.ccwales.org.uk
CSCI (Commission for Social Care Inspection): www.csci.org.uk
CSIP (Care Services Improvement Partnership): www.csip.org.uk
DWP (Department of Work and Pensions): www.dwp.gov.uk
GSA (Gerontological Society of America): www.geron.org
GSCC (General Social Care Council): www.gscc.org.uk
Help the Aged: www.helptheaged.org.uk
HO (Home Office): www.homeoffice.gov.uk
Housing 21: www.housing21.co.uk
IFSW (International Federation of Social Work): www.ifsw.org
King's Fund: www.kingsfund.org.uk
MRC (Making Research Count):
    www.makingresearchcount.keeleuniversity.org
National Audit Office (formerly Audit Commission): www.nao.org.uk
National Council for Palliative Care: www.ncpc.org.uk
NICE (National Institute for Clinical Excellence): www.nice.org.uk
NIA (Northern Ireland assembly): www.niassembly.gov.uk
NISCC (Northern Ireland Social Care Council): www.niscc.info/
ODPM (formerly Office of the Deputy Prime Minister):
    www.communities.gov.uk
ONS (Office of National Statistics): www.statistics.gov.uk
PRIAE (Policy Research Institute for Ageing and Ethnicity): www.priae.org
SA (Scottish Assembly): www.scottish.parliament.uk
SSSC (Scottish Social Services Council): www.sssc.uk.com
WAG (Welsh Assembly Government): www.wales.gov.uk
WHO (World Health Organization): www.who.int

# Bibliography

Achenbaum, W. A. (1995) *Crossing Frontiers: Gerontology Emerges as a Science*, Cambridge, Cambridge University Press.

Achenbaum, W. A. (1997) 'Critical Gerontology', in A. Jamieson, S. Harper and C. Victor (eds), *Critical Approaches to Ageing and Later Life*, Buckingham: Open University Press.

Achenbaum, W. A. and Levin, J. S. (1989) 'What Does *Gerontology* Mean?', *The Gerontologist*, 29(3), pp. 393–400.

Action on Elder Abuse (2006) *Adult Protection Data Collection and Reporting Requirements*, London, Action on Elder Abuse.

Adams, T. and Bartlett, R. (2003) 'Constructing Dementia', in T. Adams and J. Manthorpe (eds), *Dementia Care*, London, Arnold, pp. 3–21.

Adams, T. and Manthorpe, J. (eds) (2003) *Dementia Care*, London, Arnold.

Adams, T. and Gardiner, P. (2005) 'Communication and Interaction within Dementia Care Triads: Developing a Theory for Relationship Centred Care', *Dementia*, 4(2), pp. 185–205.

Age Concern England (2004) *Grandparents*, London, Age Concern.

Age Concern England (2005) *Dying and Death*, London, Age Concern. Available at: www.ageconcern.org.uk.

Age Concern England (2006a) *Hungry to be Heard: The Scandal of Malnourished People in Hospital*, London, Age Concern.

Age Concern England (2006b) *Just Above the Breadline: Living on a Low Income in Later Life*, London, Age Concern/IFF Research. Available at: www.ageconcern.org.uk.

Alaszewski, A. (2000) Balancing Act, *Openmind*, 101, pp.10–11.

Allan, K. (2001) *Communication and Consultation: Exploring Ways for Staff to Involve People with Dementia in Developing Services*, York, Joseph Rowntree Foundation.

Aldred, H., Gott, M. and Gariballa, S. (2005) 'Advanced Heart Failure: Impact on Older Patients and Informal Carers', *Journal of Advanced Nursing*, 49(2), pp. 16–24.

Alexander, C. (2002) 'Beyond Black: re-thinking the colour/culture divide', *Ethnic and Racial Studies*, 25 (4), pp. 552–571.

Allcock, N., McGarry, J. and Elkan, R. (2002) 'Management of Pain in Older People Living in the Nursing Home: A Preliminary Study', *Health and Social Care in the Community*, 10(6), pp. 464–71.

Allen, N. H., Burns, A., Newton, V., Hickson, F., Ramsden. R., Rogers, J., Butler, S., Thistlewaite, G. and Morris, J. (2003) 'The Effects of Improving Hearing in Dementia', *Age and Ageing*, 32, pp. 189–93.

Alzheimer's Society (2001) *Quality Dementia Care in Homes: Person Centred Standards Report* London, Alzheimer's Society UK

Alzheimer's Society (2004) *Neuroleptics/Antipsychotic Drugs*, Policy Positions, London, Alzheimer's Society. Available at: www.alzheimers.org.uk.

Anderson, D., and Wiscott, R. (2004) 'Comparing Social Work and Non Social Work Students' Attitudes to Aging: Implications to Promote Work with Elders, *Journal of Gerontological Social Work*, 42(2), pp. 21–36.

Andersson, L. and Stevens, N. (1993) 'Associations between Early Experiences with Parents and Well-being in Old Age', *Journal of Gerontology*, 48(3), pp. 109–16.

Antonucci, T. C. (1994) 'Attachment in Adulthood and Aging', in M. B. Sperling and W. H. Berman (eds), *Attachment in Adults: Clinical and Developmental Perspectives*, New York, Guilford Press, pp. 256–72.

Antonucci, T. C. (1990) 'Social Supports and Social Relationships', in R. H. Binstock and L. K. George (eds), *Handbook of Aging and the Social Sciences* (3rd edn), San Diego, Calif., Academic Press.

Arber, S. and Ginn, J. (eds) (1991) *Gender and Later Life. A Sociological Analysis of Resources and Constraints*, Sage, London.

Arber, S and Ginn, J. (1995) *Connecting Gender and Ageing*, Buckingham, Open University Press.

Ariès, P., (1983) *The Hour of Our Death*, Harmondsworth, Penguin.

Aronson, J. (1999) 'Conflicting Images of Older People Receiving Care: Challenges for Reflexive Practice and Research', in S. Neysmith (ed.), *Critical Issues for Future Social Work Practice with Aging Persons*, New York, Columbia Press, pp. 47–70.

Association of Directors of Social Services (ADSS) (2006) *Position Statement: Safeguarding Adults*, London, ADSS.

Asthana, S. and Halliday, J. (2006) *What Works in Tackling Health Inequalities?* Bristol, Policy Press.

Atchley, R. C. (1999) *Continuity and Adaptation in Aging: Creating Positive Experiences*, Baltimore, Md., Johns Hopkins University Press.

Audit Commission (2000) *Forget-me-not; Mental Health Services for Older People*, London, Audit Commission.

Baars, J. (1991) 'The Challenge of Critical Studies', *Journal of Aging Studies*, 5, pp. 219–43.

Baars, J., Dannefer, D., Phillipson, C. and Walker, A (2006) 'Introduction: Critical Perspectives in Social Gerontology', in J. Baars, D. Dannefer, C. Phillipson and A. Walker (eds), *Aging, Globalization and Inequality: The New Critical Gerontology*, Amityville, NY, Baywood, pp. 1–16.

Baldock, C. V. (2000) 'Migrants and their Parents: Caregiving from a Distance', *Journal of Family Issues*, 21, pp. 205–24.

Baltes, P. B. and Baltes, M. M. (1990) 'Psychological Perspectives on Successful Aging: The Model of Selective Optimization with Compensation', in P. B. Baltes and M. M. Baltes (eds), *Successful Aging: Perspectives from the Behavioural Sciences*, New York, Cambridge University Press, pp. 1–34.

Banerjee, S. and MacDonald, A. S. (1996) 'Mental Disorder in an Elderly Home Care Population: Associations with Health and Social Services', *British Journal of Psychiatry*, 168, pp. 750–6.

Bartells, S. J., Aricca, M. D., Duns, R., Thomas, B. A., Oxman, E., Lon, M. D., Schneider, M. D., Arean, P. A., Alexopoulis, G. S. and Jeste, D. V. (2002) 'Evidence-based Practice in Geriatric Mental Health Care', *Psychiatric Services*, 53, pp. 1419–31.

BASW (British Association of Social Work) (2002) *Code of Ethics*. Available at: www.basw.co.uk.

Beckett, C. and Maynard, A. (2005) *Values and Ethics in Social Work: An Introduction*, London, Sage.

Bell, V. and Troxel, D. (2001) *The Best Friends Staff: Building a Culture of Care in Alzheimer's Program*, Baltimore, Md., Health Professions Press.

Ben-Shlomo, Y., White, I. R. and Marmot, M. (1996) 'Does the Variation in the Socioeconomic Characteristics of an Area Affect Mortality?', *British Medical Journal*, 312(8037), pp. 1013–14.

Berardo, D. H. (1982) 'Divorce and Remarriage at Middle Age and Beyond: Middle and Late Life Transitions', *Annals of the American Academy of Political and Social Science*, 464 (November), pp. 132–9.

Beresford, P. (2007a) 'The Role of Service User Research in Generating Knowledge Based Health and Social Care: From Conflict to Contribution', *Evidence and Policy*, 3(3), 329–41.

Beresford, P. (2007b) 'Service Users Do Not Want Care Navigators', *Community Care*, 12–18 April. Available at: www.communitycare.co.uk.

Beresford, P. (2007c) *The Changing Roles and Tasks of Social Work from Service Users' Perspectives: A Literature Informed Discussion Paper*, London, Shaping our Lives, National User Network.

Bernard, M. (1998) 'Backs to the Future? Reflections on Women, Ageing and Nursing', *Journal of Advanced Nursing*, 27, pp. 633–40.

Bernard, M. (2000) *Promoting Health in Old Age: Critical Issues in Self-Health Care*, Buckingham, Open University Press.

Bernard, M. (2001) 'Women Ageing: Old Lives, New Challenges, *Education and Ageing*, 16(3), pp. 333–52.

Bernard, M. and Phillips, J. (eds) (1998) *The Social Policy of Old Age – Moving into the 21st Century*, London, Centre for Policy on Ageing.

Bernard, M. and Phillips, J. (2000) 'The Challenge of Ageing in Tomorrow's Britain', *Ageing and Society*, 20(1), 33–54.

Bernard, M., Phillips, J., Machin, L. and Harding Davies, V. (eds) (2000) *Women Ageing: Changing Identities, Challenging Myths*, London, Routledge.

Biggs, S. (1993) 'User Participation and Interprofessional Collaboration in Community Care', *Interprofessional Care*, (7)2, 151–60.

Blewitt, J., Lewis, J. and Tunstill, J. (2007) *The Changing Roles and Tasks of Social Work: A Literature Informed Discussion Paper*, London, GSCC. Available at: www.gscc.org.uk.

Bond, J. (2001) 'Sociological Perspectives', in C. Cantley (ed.), *Handbook of Dementia Care*, Buckingham, Open University Press, pp. 44–61.

Bornat, J. (2000) *Oral History, Health and Welfare*, London, Routledge.

Bowlby, J. (1969) *Attachment and Loss*, London, Hogarth.

Bowling, A. (1983) 'The Hospitalisation of Death: Should More People Die at Home?, *Journal of Medical Ethics*, 9(3), 158–61.

Bradbury, J. (1989) 'The Policy Implications of Differing Concepts of Risk', *Science, Technology and Human Values*, 14(4), 380–99.

Brammer, A. (2007) *Social Work Law* (2nd edn), Harlow, Longman.

Braye, S. and Preston-Shoot, M. (1995) *Empowering Practice in Social Care*, Buckingham, Open University Press.

Brechin, A. (2000) 'Introducing Critical Practice'. in A. Brechin, H. Brown and M. A. Eby (eds), *Critical Practice in Health and Social Care*, London, Open University/Sage, pp. 25–47.

Brechin, A., Walmsley, J., Katz, J. and Peace, S. (eds) (1998) *Care Matters, Concepts, Practice and Research in Health and Social Care*, Sage, London.

British Geriatrics Society (2006) *Palliative and End of Life Care for Older People*, London, British Geriatrics Society.

Brodaty, H., Green, A., Koschera, A. (2003) 'Meta-analysis of Psychosocial Interventions for Caregivers of People with Dementia', *Journal of the American Geriatrics Society*, 51, pp. 657–664.

Brooker, D. (2004) 'What Is Person Centred Care in Dementia?', *Reviews in Clinical Gerontology*, 13, pp. 215–22.

Brooker, D. (2007) *Person-centred Dementia Care: Making Services Better*, London, Jessica Kingsley.

Brown, J., Nolan, M. and Grant, G. (2001) 'Who's the Expert? Redefining Lay and Professional Relationships', in M. Nolan, S. Davies and G. Grant (eds), *Working with Older People and Their Families*, Buckingham, Open University Press

Browne, C. J. and Shlosberg, E. (2005) 'Attachment Behaviours and Parent Fixation in People with Dementia: The Role of Cognitive Functioning and Pre-morbid Attachment Style', *Aging and Mental Health*, 9(2), pp. 1–9.

Browne, C. J., and Shlosberg, E. (2006) 'Attachment Theory: Ageing and Dementia, a Review of the Literature', *Aging and Mental Health*, 10(2) pp. 134–142.

Busuttil, W. (2004) 'Presentation and Management of Post Traumatic Stress Disorder and the Elderly: A Need for Investigation', *Psychiatry*, 19(5), pp. 429–39.

Butler, I. and Drakeford, M. (2005) 'Trusting in Social Work', *British Journal of Social Work*, 35(5), pp. 639–53.

Butler, R. (1980) 'Ageism: A Foreword', *Journal of Social Issues*, 36(2), pp. 8–11.

Butler, R. N. (1963) 'The Life Review: An Interpretation of Reminiscence in the Aged', *Psychiatry*, 26 February, pp. 65–76.

Butler, R. N., Lewis, M. I and Sunderland, T. (1998) *Aging and Mental Health: Positive Psychosocial and Biomedical Approaches* (5th edn), Boston, Mass., Allyn & Bacon.

Bytheway, B., Ward, R., Holland, C. and Peace, S. (2007) 'The Road to an Age-inclusive Society', in M. Bernard and T. Scharf (eds), *Critical Perspectives on Ageing Societies*, Bristol, Policy Press, pp. 105–24.

Bywaters, P. (2007) 'Tackling Inequalities in Health: A Global Challenge for Social Work', *British Journal of Social Work*, published on line 29 August 2007.

Cambridge, P. and Parkes, T. (2004) 'Good Enough Decision Making?', *Social Work Education*, 23(6), pp. 711–29.

Campbell, J. and Oliver, M. (1996) *Disability Politics: Understanding Our Past, Changing Our Future*, London, Routledge.

Campbell, L. and Martin-Matthews, A. (2003) 'The Gendered Nature of Men's Filial Care', *Journals of Gerontology Series B: Psychological Sciences and Social Sciences*, 58, pp. S350–S358.

Cantley, C. (2001) 'Understanding the Policy Context', in C. Cantley (ed.), *A Handbook of Dementia Care*, Buckingham, Open University Press, pp. 199–220.

Catt, S., Blanchard, M., Addington-Hall, J., Zis, M., Blizard, R. and King, M. (2005) 'Older Adults' Attitudes to Death, Palliative Treatment and Hospice Care', *Palliative Medicine*, 19, pp. 402–10.

Challis, D. and Davies, B. (1986) *Case Management in Community Care: An Evaluated Experiment in the Home Care of the Elderly*, Aldershot, Gower.

Chamberlayne, P., Bornat, J. and Wengraf, T. (eds) (2000) *The Turn to Biographical Methods in Social Science*, London, Routledge.

Chambers, P. (2004) 'The Case for Critical Social Gerontology in Social Work Education and Older Women', *Social Work Education*, 23(6), pp. 745–58.

Chambers, P. (2005) *Older Widows and the Life Course: Multiple Narratives of Hidden Lives*, Aldershot, Ashgate.

Chambers, P. and Ray, M. (2006) *Revisiting the Case for Critical Gerontology in Social Work with Older People*, Joint Social Work Conference: Crossing Boundaries: Personal, Professional and Political, Cambridge University, 13 July.

Chew-Graham, C., Baldwin, R. and Burns, A. (2004) 'Treating Depression in Later Life', *British Medical Journal*, 329, pp. 181–2.

CHI (Commission for Health Improvement Investigations) (2003) *Investigation into Matters Arising from Care on Rowan Ward, Manchester Mental Health and Social Care Trust*, London, The Stationery Office. Available at: www.tso.co.uk/bookshop.

Clark, H., Gough, H. and MacFarlane, A. (2004) *It Pays Dividends: Direct Payments and Older People*, Bristol, Policy Press.

Clarke, D. and Seymour, J. (1999) *Reflections on Palliative Care*, Buckingham, Open University Press.

Cole, T. R. and Sierpena, M. (2006) 'Humanistic Gerontology and the Meaning(s) of Aging', in J. M. Wilmoth and K. F. Ferraro (eds), *Gerontology: Perspectives and Issues*, New York, Springer, pp. 245–65.

Coleman, P. and Mills, M. A. (1997) 'Listening to the Story: Life Review and the Painful Past in Day and Residential Care Settings', in L. Hunt, M. Marshall and C. Rowlings (eds), *Past Trauma in Late Life: European Perspectives on Therapeutic Work with Older People*, London, Jessica Kingsley, pp. 171–83.

Connidis, I. (2001) *Family Ties and Aging*, Thousand Oaks, Calif., Sage.

Cornes, M. and Clough, R. (2004) 'Inside Multi-disciplinary Practice: Challenges for Single Assessment', *Journal of Integrated Care*, 12(2), pp. 18–29.

Costello, J. (2001) 'Nursing Older Dying Patients: Findings from an Ethnographic Study of Death and Dying in Elderly Care Wards', *Journal of Advanced Nursing*, 35, pp. 59–68.

Coulshed, V. and Orme, J. (1998) *Social Work Practice: An Introduction* (2nd edn), London, Macmillan/BASW.

Cox, E. and Dooley, A. (1996) 'Care Receivers' Perception of Their Role in the Care Process', *Journal of Gerontological Social Work*, 26(1), pp. 133–52.

Crocq, L. (1997) 'The Emotional Consequences of War 50 Years On: A Psychiatrist's Perspective', in L. Hunt, M. Marshall and C. Rowlings (eds), *Past Trauma in Late Life: European Perspectives on Therapeutic Work with Older People*, London, Jessica Kingsley, pp. 39–48.

CSCI (Commission for Social Care Inspection) (2006a) *The State of Social Care in England 2005–06*, London, CSCI.

CSCI (Commission for Social Care Inspection) (2006b) *Relentless Optimism: Creative Commissioning for Personalised Care: Report of a Seminar held by the CSCI on 18th May 2006*, London, CSCI.

CSCI (Commission for Social Care Inspection) (2006c) *Handled with Care? Managing Medication for Residents of Care Homes and Children's Homes – a Follow Up Study*, Newcastle, CSCI.

CSCI (Commission for Social Care Inspection) (2006d) *Highlight of the Day? Improving Meals for Older People in Care Homes*, March.

CSCI (Commission for Social Care Inspection) (2008) *The State of Social Care in England 2006/2007*, London, CSCI.

CSIP (Care Services Improvement Partnership) (2006) *National Social Inclusion Programme: Second Annual Report* London, CSIP/National Social Inclusion Programme.

CSIP (Care Services Improvement Partnership) and National Institute for Mental Health in England (2005) *Mental Health: New Ways of Working for Everyone: Developing and Sustaining a Capable and Flexible Workforce*, London, New Ways of Working in Mental Health/Department of Health.

CSIP (Care Services Improvement Partnership) and National Institute for Mental Health in England (2007) *Mental Health: New Ways of Working for Everyone: Developing and Sustaining a Capable and Flexible Workforce, Progress Report*, London, New Ways of Working in Mental Health/Department of Health.

Cumming, E. and Henry, W. (1961) *Growing Old: The Process of Disengagement*, New York, Basic Books.

Currer, C. (2001) *Responding to Grief: Dying, Bereavement and Social Care*, Basingstoke, Palgrave.

Dalrymple, J. and Burke, B. (2006) *Anti-Oppressive Practice: Social Care and the Law*, Maidenhead, Open University Press/McGraw-Hill Education.

Davies, C. (2003) 'Workers, Professions and Identity', in J. Henderson and D. Atkinson (eds), *Managing Care in Context*, Buckingham, Open University Press, pp. 189–210.

Davies, E. and Higginson, I. J. (eds) (2004) *Better Palliative Care for Older People* Copenhagen, World Health Organization Europe (WHO).

DeBraggio, T. (2002) *Losing My Mind: An Intimate Look at Life with Alzheimer's*, New York, The Free Press.

Department of Health (1991) *Care Management and Assessment: Summary of Practice Guidance*, London, Department of Health.

Department of Health (2000) *No Secrets: Guidance on Developing and Implementing Multi-agency Policies and Procedures to Protect Vulnerable Adults from Abuse*, London, Department of Health.

Department of Health (2001) *National Service Framework for Older People*, London, Department of Health.

Department of Health (2002a) *Getting the Best for Best Value: Sharing the Experience of Applying Best Value in Social Care*, London, Department of Health.

Department of Health (2002b) *Fair Access to Care Services: Guidance on Eligibility Criteria for Adult Social Care*, LAC circular (2002)13, London, Department of Health.

Department of Health (2002c) *Requirements for Social Work Training*, London, Department of Health.

Department of Health (2002d) *Care Homes for Older People: National Minimum Standards*, London, Stationery Office. Available at: www.doh.gov.uk/ncsc.

Department of Health (2005) *Independence, Well Being and Choice*, London, Department of Health.

Department of Health (2006) *Our Health, Our Care, Our Say: A New Direction for Community Services*, London, Department of Health.

Department of Health (2007) *Putting People First: A Shared Vision and Commitment to the Transformation of Adult Social Care*, London, Department of Health.

Department for Work and Pensions (2005) *Opportunity Age: Meeting the Challenges of Ageing in the 21st Century*, London, Department for Work and Pensions.

DeWit, D., Wister, A. and Burch, T. (1998) 'Physical Distance and Social Contact between Elders and their Adult Children', *Research on Aging*, 10, pp. 56–80.

Douglas, M. (1992) *Risk and Blame: Essays in Cultural Theory*, London, Routledge.

Dunst, C., Trivette, C. and Deal, A (1994) *Supporting and Strengthening Families: Vol. 1: Methods, Strategies and Practices*, Cambridge, Mass.: Brookline.

Dyer, C. B., Davlick, V. N., Murphy, K. P. and Hyman, D. J. (2000) 'The High Prevalence of Depression and Dementia in Elder Abuse and Neglect', *Journal of the American Geriatric Society*, 48(2), pp. 205–8.

Eames, M., Ben-Shlomo, Y. and Marmot, M. G. (1993) 'Social Deprivation and Premature Mortality: Regional Comparison across England', *British Medical Journal*, 307, pp. 1097–102.

Elder, G. H. and Clipp, E. C. (1988) 'Wartime Losses and Social Bonding: Influences across 40 Years in Men's Lives', *Psychiatry*, 51, pp. 177–198.

Ellis, K., (2007) 'Direct Payments and Social Work Practice: The Significance of "Street-level Bureaucracy" in Determining Eligibility', *British Journal of Social Work* 38(3), pp. 405–422.

ESDS (Economic and Social Data Service) *British Crime Survey (SN 5755) 2006–2007*, ESDS. Available at: www.esds.ac.uk/government/bcs.

Estes, C. (1979) *Aging Enterprise: A Critical Examination of Social Policies and Services for the Aged*, San Francisco, Jossey-Bass.

Estes, C., Biggs, S. and Phillipson, C. (2003) *Social Theory, Social Policy and Ageing: A Critical Introduction*, Buckingham, Open University Press.

Farmer, E. and Meyers, C. (2005) *Children Placed with Family and Friends: Placement Patterns and Outcomes, Executive Summary*, Bristol, DFES/ University of Bristol.

Fast, B. and Chapin, R. (2002) 'The Strengths Model with Older Adults: Critical Practice Components', in D. Saleeby (ed.), *The Strengths Perspective in Social Work Practice*, Boston, Allyn & Bacon, pp. 144–161.

Feldman, D. (2002) *Civil Liberties and Human Rights in England and Wales* (2nd edn), Oxford, Oxford University Press.

Ferguson, I. (2007) 'Increasing User Choice or Privatising Risk: The Antinomies of Personalisation', *British Journal of Social Work*, 37, pp. 387–403.

Field, D. (1989) *Nursing the Dying*, London, Routledge.

Finch, J. and Groves, D. (eds) (1983) *A Labour of Love*, London, Routledge & Kegan Paul.

Fine, M. and Glendinning, C. (2005) 'Dependence, Independence or Inter-dependence? Revisiting the Concepts of "Care" and "Dependency"', *Ageing and Society*, 25(4), 601–21.

Firth, S. (2001) *Wider Horizons: Care of the Dying in a Multicultural Society*, London, The National Council for Palliative Care.

Fisher, B. and Tronto, J. (1990) 'Toward a Feminist Theory of Caring', in E. Abel and M. Nelson (eds), *Circles of Care. Work and Identity in Women's Lives*, Albany, NY, State University of New York Press.

Fischer, J (1973) 'Is Casework Effective: A Review', *Social Work*, 18(1), pp. 5–20.

Fook, J. (2002) *Social Work: Critical Theory and Practice*, London, Sage.

Forbat, L. and Nar, S. (2003) 'Dementia's Cultural Challenge', *Community Care*, 25 September. Available at: www.communitycare.co.uk.

Foster, J. (2005) *'Where Are We Going'? The Social Work Contribution to Mental Health Services*, London, SCIE/NIMHE/Skills for Care/GSCC/ADSS/BASW/ DH.

Fox, N. (1999) 'Postmodern Reflections on "Risk", "Hazards" and Life Choices', in D. Lupton (ed.), *Risk and Sociocultural Theory: New Directions and Perspectives*, Cambridge, Cambridge University Press, pp. 12–33.

Friedell, M. (2002) 'Awareness: A Personal Memoir on the Declining Quality of Life in Alzheimer's', *Dementia*, 1(3), pp. 359–66.

Froggatt, K. (2001) 'Life and Death in English Nursing Homes: Sequestration or Transition?', *Ageing & Society*, 21, pp. 319–32.

Froggatt, K. (2004) *Palliative Care in Care Homes for Older People*, London, National Council for Palliative Care.

Froggatt, K. and Payne, S. (2006) 'A Survey of End-of-life Care in Care Homes: Issues of Definition and Practice', *Health and Social Care in the Community*, 14(4), pp. 341–48.

Gauthier, S. (ed.) (2006) *Clinical Diagnosis and Management of Alzheimer's Disease*, Abingdon, Informa Healthcare.

Gearing, B. and Dant, T. (1990) 'Doing Biographical Research', in S. Peace (ed.), *Researching Social Gerontology: Concepts, Methods and Issues*, London, Sage.

Gibson, F. (1994) *Reminiscence and Recall: A Guide to Good Practice*, London, Age Concern.

Giddens, A. (1991) *The Consequences of Modernity*, Cambridge, Polity Press.

Gilbert, P. (2004) 'Integration of Health And Social Care: Promoting Social Care Perspectives within Integrated Mental Health Services', notes from an SPN study day, 20th April. Available at: www.spn.org.uk.

Godfrey, M. and Denby, T. (2004) *Depression and Older People*, Bristol, Policy Press.

Golan, N. (1981) *Passing Through Transitions: A Guide for Practitoners* New York, Free Press.

Goldberg, E. M. and Connelly, K. (1982) *The Effectiveness of Social Care for the Elderly: An Overview of Recent and Current Evaluative Research*, London, Heinemann Educational Books.

Goldsmith, M. (1996) *Hearing the Voice of People with Dementia: Opportunities and Obstacles*, London, Jessica Kingsley.

Gorer, G. (1955) 'The Pornography of Death', *Encounter*, October pp. 49–52.

Gorman, H. and Postle, K. (2003) *Transforming Community Care: A Distorted Vision?*, Birmingham, Venture Press.

Gott, M., Seymour, J., Bellamy, G., Clark, D. and Ahmedzai, S. (2004) 'Older People's Views about Home as a Place of Care at the End of Life', *Palliative Medicine*, 18,pp. 460–7.

Green, J. (1997) *Risk and Misfortune*, London, UCL Press.

Grenier, A. (2007) 'Constructions of Frailty in the English Language, Care Practice and the Lived Experience', *Ageing and Society*, 27(3), 425–45.

GSCC (General Social Care Council) (2004) *Code of Practice for Social Care Workers and Code of Practice for Employees of Social Care Workers*, London, GSCC. Available at: www.gscc.org.uk.

GSCC (General Social Care Council) (2007) *Describing Social Work Toles and Tasks: A Record of the Work that Took Place at the Stakeholder Event in London* (report compiled by L. Moore and R. Donovan) February London, GSCC.

Gunuratnam, Y. (2006) *Ethnicity, Older People and Palliative Care*, London, National Council for Palliative Care/Policy Research Institute on Ageing and Ethnicity.

Guttuso, S. and Bevan, C. (2001) 'Mothers, Daughters, Patients and Nurses: Women's Emotional Labour in Aged Care', *Journal of Advanced Nursing*, 31, pp. 892–9.

Harris, A. I. (1968) *Social Welfare for the Elderly. Government Social Survey No. SS366.* London, HMSO.

Harris, T., Cook, D. G., Victor, C., Rink, E., Mann, A. H., Shah, S., DeWilde, S. and Beynton, C. (2003) 'Predictors of Depressive Symptoms in Older People – a Survey of Two GP Populations', *Age and Ageing*, 32, pp. 510–18.

Havighurst, R. J. (1963) 'Successful Aging', in R. H. Williams, C. Tibbitts and W. Donahue (eds), *Processes of Aging, Vol 1*, New York, Atherton, pp. 299–320.

Help the Aged (2006) *Older People, Decent Homes and Fuel Poverty*, London, Help the Aged.

Help the Aged (2007) *Less Equal than Others*, London, Help the Aged.

Henderson, J. and Forbat, L. (2002) 'Relationship-based Social Policy: Personal and Policy Constructions of Care', *Critical Social Policy*, 22(4), pp. 669–87.

Hockey, J. (1990) *Experiences of Death*, Edinburgh, Edinburgh University Press.

Holstein, M. and Minkler, M. (2007) 'Critical Gerontology: Reflections for the 21st Century', in M. Bernard and T. Scharf (eds), *Critical Perspectives on Ageing Societies*, Bristol: Policy Press, pp. 13–26.

Hopkinson, J. B., Hallett, C. E. and Luker, K. A. (2003) 'Care for Dying People in Hospital', *Journal of Advanced Nursing*, 44(5), pp. 523–33.

Horowitz, A. (1999) 'Aging and Disability in the New Millennium', in S. Neysmith (ed.), *Critical Issues for Future Social Work Practice with Aging Persons*, New York, Columbia Press, pp. 97–126.

House of Commons Health Committee (2004) *Elder Abuse: Second Report of Session 2003/04, Vol.1*, London, Stationery Office.

Hsieh, H. and Wang, J. J. (2003) 'Effect of Reminiscence Therapy on Depression in Older Adults: A Systematic Review', *International Journal of Nursing Studies*, 40(4), pp. 43–53.

Hughes, B. (1995) *Older People and Community Care: Critical Theory and Practice*, Buckingham, Open University Press.

Hunt, L. (1997) 'The Past in the Present: An Introduction to Trauma (Re)-emerging in Old Age', in L. Hunt, M. Marshall and C. Rowlings (eds), *Past Trauma in Later Life*, London, Jessica Kingsley, pp. 1–15.

Iliffe, S. and Manthorpe, J. (2004) 'The Debate on Ethnicity and Dementia: From Category Fallacy to Person-centred Care?', *Aging and Mental Health*, 9(4), 283–92.

Innes, A. and Capstick, A. (2001) 'Communication and Personhood', in C. Cantley (ed.), *A Handbook of Dementia Care*, Buckingham, Open University Press, pp. 135–45.

James, A. A. and Hockey, J. (1993) *Growing Up and Growing Old: Ageing and Dependency in the Life Course*, London, Sage.

Joffe, C., Brodaty, H., Luscombe, G. and Ehrlich, F. (2003) 'The Sydney Holocaust Study: Posttraumatic Stress Disorder and other Psychosocial Morbidity in an Aged Community Sample', *Journal of Traumatic Stress*, 16(1), pp. 39–47.

Johnson, J. and Bytheway, B. (1993) 'Ageism: Concept and Definition', in J. Johnson and R. Slater (eds), *Ageism and Later life*, London, Sage, pp. 200–6.

Johnson, M.L. (1979) *Relations and Relationships*, Block 1, Unit 4, An Ageing Population, Buckinghamshire, Open University Press.

Johnson, M.L. (1990) 'Dependency and Interdependency', in J. Bond and P. Coleman (eds), *Ageing in Society: An Introduction to Social Gerontology*, London, Sage, pp. 209–28.

Jutlla, K. and Moreland, N. (2007) *Twice a Child III: The Experiences of Asian Carers of Older People with Dementia in Wolverhampton, West Midlands*, Wolverhampton Dementia Plus, West Midland.

Kastenbaum, R. (1975) 'Time, Death and Ritual in Older Age', in J. T. Fraser and N. Lawrence (eds), *The Study of Time II*, New York, Springer.

Keady, J. and Gilliard, J. (2001) 'Testing Times: The Experience of Neuropsychological Assessment for People with Suspected Alzheimer's Disease', in P. Harris (ed.), *Pathways to the Person: The Subjective Experience of Alzheimer's Disease*, Baltimore, NJ, Johns Hopkins University Press, pp. 3–28.

Keady, J., Nolan, M. R. and Gilliard, J. (1995) 'Listen to the Voices of Experience', *Journal of Dementia Care*, 3, pp. 15–17.

Keating, N., Otfinowski, P., Wenger, C., Fast, J. and Derksen, L. (2003) 'Understanding the Caring Capacity of Informal Networks of Frail Seniors: A Case for Care Networks', *Ageing and Society* Concept Forum, 23(1), pp. 115–27.

Keeling, S. (2001) 'Relative Distance: Ageing in Rural New Zealand', *Ageing & Society*, 21, pp. 605–19.

Kemshall, H. (2002) *Risk, Social Policy and Welfare*, Buckingham, Open University Press.

Kemshall, H., Parton, N., Walsh, M. and Waterson, J. (1997) 'Concepts of Risk in Relation to Organisational Structure and Functioning within the Personal Social Services and Probation', *Social Policy and Administration*, 31(3), pp. 213–32.

Killick, J. and Allan, K. (2001) *Communication and the Care of People with Dementia*, Buckingham, Open University Press.

Kittay, E. (1999) *Love's Labour: Essays on Women, Equality and Dependency*, New York, Routledge.

Kitwood, T. M. (1993) 'Towards a Theory of Dementia Care: The Interpersonal Process', *Ageing & Society*, 13(1), pp. 51–67.

Kitwood, T. M. (1997) *Dementia Reconsidered: The Person Comes First*, Buckingham, Open University Press.

Knapp, M. and Prince, M. (2007) *Dementia UK: Summary of Key Findings*, London, London School of Economics/Kings College London/Alzheimer's Society.

Kübler-Ross, E. (1969) *On Death and Dying*, New York, Macmillan.

Lazarus, R. S. and Folkman, S. (1984) *Stress, Appraisal and Coping*, New York, Springer.

Lebowitz, B. D., Martinez, R. A., Niederehe, G. and Pearson, J. (1995) 'Treatment of Depression in Late-life', *Psychopharmacology*, 31(1), pp. 185–202.

Lewis, J. and Meredith, B. (1988) *Daughters Who Care. Daughters Caring for Mothers at Home*, London, Routledge.

Lipman, V. (2005) 'Rights for the Invisible: Older People and the Human Rights Project', *Generations Review*, 15(4), pp. 42–7.

Lloyd, L. (2004) 'Mortality and Morality: Ageing and the Ethic of Care', *Ageing and Society*, 24, pp. 235–56.

Lock, A. and Higginson, I. (2005) 'Patterns and Predictors of Place of Cancer Death for the Oldest Old', *Palliative Care*, 4, p. 6 http://biomedcentral.com/1472-684x/4/6 on 11 June 2007.

Lupton, D. (1999) *Risk*, London, Routledge.

Lymbery, M. (1998) 'Care Management and Professional Autonomy: The Impact of Community Care Legislation on Social Work with Older People', *British Journal of Social Work*, 28(6), pp. 863–78.

Lymbery, M. (2001) 'Social Work at the Crossroads', *British Journal of Social Work*, 31, pp. 369–84.

Lymbery, M. (2005) *Social Work with Older People: Context, Policy and Practice*, London, Sage.

Lyne, K. J. Moxon, S., Sinclair, I., Young, P., Kirk, C. and Ellison, S. (2006) 'Analysis of Care Planning Intervention for Reducing Depression in Older People in Residential Care', *Aging and Mental Health*, 10(4), pp. 394–403.

Macdonald, G. and Sheldon, B. (1992) 'Contemporary Studies of the Effectiveness of Social Work', *British Journal of Social Work*, 22 (6), pp. 615–43.

Machin, L. (2008) *Working with Loss and Grief: A New Model for Practitioners*, London, Sage.

Maciejewski, C. (2001) 'Psychological Perspectives', in C. Cantley (ed.), *A Handbook of Dementia Care*, Buckingham, Open University Press, pp. 26–42.

Manthorpe, J. and Adams, T. (2003) 'Social Policy and Dementia Care', in T. Adams and J. Manthorpe (eds), *Dementia Care*, London, Arnold, pp. 34–47.

Manthorpe, J. and Iliffe, S. (2005) *Depression in Later Life*, London, Jessica Kingsley.

Manthorpe, J., Moriarty, J., Rapaport, J., Clough, R., Cornes, M., Bright, L., Iliffe., S. and OPRSI (Older People Researching Social Issues) '"There Are Wonderful Social Workers but It's a Lottery": Older People's Views about Social Workers', *British Journal of Social Work*, Advance Access published on-line February 9, 2007.

Marshall, M. (1983) *Social Work with Old People*, London, Macmillan Education.

Marshall, M. (2001) *Is There Bird Food on the Bird Table? Some Reflections on Quality of Life for Older People in Long Term Care*, British Society of Gerontology conference proceedings, Stirling, University of Stirling.

Marshall, M. (2005) 'Perspectives on Rehabilitation', in M. Marshall (ed.), *Perspectives on Rehabilitation*, London, Jessica Kingsley, pp. 13–19.

Marshall, M. and Tibbs, M. A. (2006) *Social Work with People with Dementia: Partnerships, Practice and Persistence*, Bristol, BASW/Policy Press.

Martin-Matthews, A. (2008) 'Introduction', in A. Martin-Matthews and J. Phillips (eds), *Ageing at the Intersection of Work and Family Life: Blurring the Boundaries*, New York: Taylor & Francis.

Mather, A. S., Rodriguez, C., Guthrie, M. F., McHarg, A. and Reid, I. C. (2002) 'Effects of Exercise on Depressive Symptoms in Older Adults with Poorly Responsive Depressive Disorders', *British Journal of Psychiatry*, 180, pp. 411–15.

Mayer, J. E. and Timms, N. (1970) *The Client Speaks: Working Class Impressions of Casework*, London, Routledge & Kegan Paul.

McCarthy, H. and Thomas, G. (2004) *Home Alone: Combating Isolation with Older Housebound People*, London, Demos.

McDonald, A. and Taylor, M. (2006) *Older People and the Law* (2nd edn), Bristol, BASW/Policy Press.

McDonald, A., Postle, K. and Dawson, C. (2007) 'Barriers to Retaining and Using Professional Knowledge in Local Authority Social Work Practice with Adults in the UK', *British Journal of Social Work*, doi:10.1093/bjsw/bcm/042, Advance access published online 25 April 2007.

McKeith, I, and Fairbairn, A. (2001) 'Biomedical and Clinical Perspectives', in C. Cantley (ed.), *A Handbook of Dementia Care*, pp. 7–23.

McLelland, R. J. (2007) *The Bamford Review of Mental Health and Learning Disabilities: A Comprehensive Legal Framework*, Northern Ireland Executive.

McMurray, A. (2004) 'Older People', in D. Oliviere and B. Monroe (eds), *Death, Dying and Social Differences*, Oxford, Oxford University Press, pp. 63–78.

McMurray, A., Theobald, K. and Chabayer, W. (2003) 'Researching Continuity of Care: Can Quality Outcomes Be Linked to Nursing Care?', *Contemporary Nurse*, 16(1–2), pp. 51–61.

Means, R. and Smith, R. (1998) *From Poor Law to Community Care: The Development of Welfare Services for Elderly People, 1939–1971*, Bristol, Policy Press.

Means, R., Morbey, H. and Smith, R. (2003) *From Community Care to Market Care? The Development of Welfare Services for Older People*, Bristol, Policy Press.

Mellor, P. A. (1993) 'Death in High Modernity', in D. Clark (ed.), *The Sociology of Death: Theory, Culture and Practice*, Oxford: Blackwell, pp. 11–30.

Mellor, P. A. and Shilling, C. (1993) 'Modernity, Self-identity and the Sequestration of Death', *Sociology*, 27(3), pp. 411–31.

Mental Health Media (2004) *Listen to the Voice of Experience* (Video), London, Mental Health Media.

Miesen, B. (1992) 'Towards a Psychology of Dementia Care: Awareness and Intangible Loss', in G. M. M. Jones and B. M. L. Miesen (eds), *Care Giving in Dementia: Research and Applications*, pp. 183–213.

Milligan, C. (2000) 'Bearing the Burden: Towards a Restructured Geography of Caring', *Area*, 32(1), pp. 49–58.

Mills, M. A., Coleman, P. G., Jerome, D., Conroy, M. C., Meade, R., Miesen, B. M. L. (1999) 'Changing patterns of dementia care: the influence of attachment theory in staff training', in J. Bornat, P. Chamberlayne and L. Chant (eds), *Reminscence: Practice, Skills and Settings*, London, Open University Press, pp. 15–20.

Milne, A., Gearing, B. and Warner, J. (2007) *Ageism, Age Discrimination and Social Exclusion*, London, Social Care Institute for Excellence (SCIE).

Minkler, M. (1996) 'Critical Perspectives on Ageing: New Challenges for Gerontology', *Ageing and Society*, 16(4), pp. 467–87.

Minkler, M. and Estes, C. (eds) (1991) *Critical Perspectives on Aging: The Political and Moral Economy of Growing Old*, Amityville, NY, Baywood.

Minkler, M. and Fadem, P. (2002) '"Successful Aging": A Disability Perspective', *Journal of Disability Policy Studies*, 12(4), pp. 229–35.

Mitchell, W. and Glendinning, C. (2007) *A Review of the Research Evidence Surrounding Risk Perceptions, Risk Management Strategies and Their Consequences in Adult Social Care for Different Groups of Service Users*, York, University of York, Social Policy Research Unit.

Moody, H. R. (1992) *Ethics in an Aging Society*, Baltimore, Md., Johns Hopkins University Press.

Moody, H. R. (1993) 'Overview: What is Critical Gerontology and Why Is It Important?', in T. R. Cole, A. Achenbaum, P. Jakobi and R. Kastenbaum (eds), *Voices and Visions of Aging – Toward a Critical Gerontology*, New York: Springer.

Moody, H. R. (1997) *The Five Stages of the Soul: Charting the Spiritual Passages That Shape Our Lives*, New York: Anchor Books/Doubleday.

Moody, H. R. (ed.) (2005) *Religion, Spirituality, and Aging: A Social Work Perspective*, Binghamton, NY: Haworth Press.

Moore, A. J. and Stratton, D. C. (2002) *Resilient Widowers: Older Men Speak for Themselves*, New York, Springer.

Moriarty, J. (2005) *Assessing the Mental Health Needs of Older People: Messages for Research*, London, SCIE. Available at: www.scie.org.uk.

Morley, C. and Fook, J. (2005) 'The Importance of Pet Loss and Some Implications for Services', *Mortality*, 10(2), pp. 127–43.

Moss, P. (2003) 'Getting beyond Childcare: Reflections on Recent Policy and Future Possibilities', in J. Brannen and P. Moss (eds), *Rethinking Children's Care*, Buckingham: Open University Press, pp. 25–43.

Mountain, G. (2004) 'Rehabilitation for People with Dementia: Pointers for Practice from the Evidence Base', in M. Marshall (ed.), *Perspectives on Rehabilitation and Dementia*, London, Jessica Kingsley, pp. 50–72.

Mowlam, A., Tennant, R., Dixon, J. and McCreadie, C. (2007) *UK Study of Abuse and Neglect of Older People: Qualitative Findings*, August, London, Comic Relief/Department of Health.

Mulkay, M. (1993) 'Social Death in Britain', in D. Clarke (ed.), *The Sociology of Death*, Oxford, Blackwell.

Mullen, J. and Dumpson, J. R. (1972) *Evaluation of Social Intervention*, San Francisco, Jossey-Bass.

Murphy, J., Tester, S., Hubbard, G., Downs, M. and MacDonald, C. (2005) 'Enabling Frail Older People with a Communication Difficulty to Express Their Views: The Use of Talking Mats™ as an Interview Tool', *Health and Social Care in the Community*, 13(2), pp. 95–107.

Murray, S. A., Boyd, K., Kendall, M., Worth, A., Benton, T. F. and Clausen, H. (2002) 'Dying of Lung Cancer or Cardiac Failure: Prospective Qualitative Interview Study of Patients and their Carers in the Community', *British Medical Journal*, 325, p. 929.

National Council for Palliative Care (NCPC) (2005) *The Palliative Care Needs of Older People*, London, NCPC.

National Council for Palliative Care (NCPC) (2007) *Palliative Care Explained*, London, NCPC.

National Institute for Clinical Excellence (NICE) (2006) *Nutrition Support in Adults: Oral Nutrition, Enteral Tube Feeding and Parenteral Nutrition*, Clinical Guideline 32, London, NICE.

National Institute for Clinical Excellence (NICE)/Social Care Institute for Excellence (SCIE) (2006) *Dementia: Supporting People with Dementia and Their Carers in Health and Social Care*, Clinical Guidelines 42, London, NICE/SCIE.

Needham, J. (2000) 'Research and Practice: Making a Difference', in R. Gomm, G. Needham and A. Bullman (eds), *Using Evidence in Health and Social Care*, London, Open University/Sage, pp. 131–51.

Neill, J. (1976) *Social Work and Personal Social Services for the Elderly in Great Britain, Report for the DHSS*, London, National Institute of Social Work.

Neysmith, S. and MacAdam, M. (1999) 'Controversial Concepts', in S. Neysmith (ed.), *Critical Issues for Future Social Work Practice with Aging Persons*, New York, Columbia University Press, pp. 1–26.

Nissel, M. and Bonnerjea, L. (1982) *Family Care of the Handicapped Elderly. Who Pays?*, No. 602, London, Policy Studies Institute.

Nolan, M., Grant, G. and Keady, J. (1996) *Understanding Family Care*, Buckingham, Open University Press.

Nolan, M., Brown, J., Davis, S., Nolan, J. and Keady, J. (2006) *The Senses Framework: Improving Care for Older People through a Relationship-centred Approach. Getting Research into Practice (GRiP), Report No. 2*, Sheffield, University of Sheffield.

Northern Ireland Assembly (2005) *Ageing in an Inclusive Society*. Available at: www.ofmdfmni.gov.uk.

O'Connell, H., Chin, A.-V., Cunningham, C. and Lawlor, B. A. (2004) 'Recent Developments: Suicide in Older People', *British Medical Journal*, 329, pp. 895–9.

ODPM (Office of the Deputy Prime Minister) (2006) *A Sure Start to Later Life: Ending Inequalities for Older People*, London, ODPM.

ODPM (Office of the Deputy Prime Minister) (2005) *Performance Indicators and Performance Standards Order, 2005*, London, ODPM.

Ogg, J., and Bennett, G. (1992) 'Elder Abuse in Britain', *British Medical Journal*, 305, pp. 998–9.

O'Keefe, M., Hills, A., Doyle, M., McCreadie, C., Scholes, S., Constantine, R., Tinker, A., Manthorpe, J., Biggs, S. and Erens, B. (2007) *UK Study of Abuse and Neglect of Older People: Prevalence Survey Report*, London, Comic Relief/Department of Health.

Older People's Steering Group (2004) *Older People Shaping Policy and Practice*, York, Joseph Rowntree Foundation.

Oliver, M. (2004) 'The Social Model in Action: If I Had a Hammer', in C. Barnes and G. Mercer (eds), *Implementing the Social Model of Disability: Theory and Research*, Leeds: The Disability Press.

Olsen, C. J. (2002) 'A Curriculum Development Model Enhances Students' Gerontological Practice Related Knowledge and Attitudes', *Journal of Social Work Education*, (special edition, Enhancing Gerontological Social Work Education), 39(1/2), pp. 159–76.

ONS (Office of National Statistics) (2000) *Psychiatric Morbidity Among Adults Living in Private Households*, London, ONS. Available at: www.statistics.gov.uk.

ONS (Office of National Statistics) (2006a) *Population Ageing*. Available at: www.statistics.gov.uk.

ONS (Office of National Statistics) (2006b) *National Projections*. Available at: www.statistics.gov.uk.

ONS (Office of National Statistics) (2006c) *Death Registrations, 2005: UK Snapshot*, London, ONS. Available at: www.statistics.gov.uk.

Ormel, J., Rijsdijk, F., Sullivan, M., van Sonderen, E. and Kempen, G. (2002) 'Temporal and Reciprocal Relationship between IADL/ADL Disability and

Depressive Symptoms in Later Life', in *Journals of Gerontology, Series B: Psychological Sciences and Social Sciences*, 57, pp. 338–47.

Ovrebo, B. and Minkler, M. (1993) 'The Lives of Older Women: Perspectives from Political Economy and the Humanities', in T. R. Cole, A. Achenbaum, P. Jakobi and R. Kastenbaum (eds), *Voices and Visions of Aging: Towards a Critical Gerontology*, New York: Springer.

Parker, G. (1985) *With Due Care and Attention*. London: Policy Studies Institute.

Parker, M. W., Call, V. R. and Kosberg, J. (2001) *Geographic Separation and Contact between Adult Children and Their Parents*, Paper presented at the IAG 17th World Congress, Vancouver, Canada.

Patmore, C. and McNulty, A. (2005) *Making Home Care for Older People More Flexible and Person Centred*, University of York, Social Policy Research Unit.

Payne, M. (2006) *What Is Professional Social Work?* Bristol, Policy Press.

Peace, S. M., Kellaher, L. and Holland, C. (2005) *Environment and Identity in Later Life*, Buckingham, Open University Press.

Perrin, T. and May, H. (2000) *Wellbeing in Dementia: An Occupational Approach for Therapists and Carers*, London, Harcourt.

Phillips, J. (2000) *Reconstructing Knowledge about Older People Through Social Work Research*, Conference proceedings of 'What Works as Evidence for Practice? The Methodological Repertoire in an Applied Discipline', Cardiff, Social Care Institute for Excellence, 27 April.

Phillips, J. (2003) *Gerontology: Research Based or Policy Driven?*, Presentation at Regional Making Research Count launch, London, May.

Phillips, J., Ray, M. and Marshall, M. (2006) *Social Work with Older People*, Basingstoke, Palgrave.

Phillipson, C. and Walker, A. (1987) 'The Case for a Critical Gerontology', in S. De Gregorio (ed.), *Social Gerontology: New Directions*, London, Croom Helm.

Phillipson, C., Alhaq, E., Ullah, S. and Ogg, J. (2000) 'Bangladeshi Families in Bethnal Green, London: Older People, Ethnicity and Social Exclusion', in A. Warnes, L. Warren and M. Nolan (eds), *Care Services for Later Life: Transformations and Critiques*, London, Jessica Kingsley, pp. 273–290.

Phillipson, C., Bernard, M., Phillips, J. and Ogg, J. (2001) *The Family and Community Life Of Older People: Social Networks and Social Support in Three Urban Areas*, London, Routledge.

Pillemer, K. A. and Prescott, D. (1989) 'Psychological Effects of Elder Abuse: A Research Note', *Elder Abuse and Neglect*, 1, pp. 65–74.

Postle, K. (2002) 'Working "Between the Idea and the Reality": Ambiguities and Tensions in Care Managers Work', *British Journal of Social Work*, 32, pp. 335–51.

Poverty website (undated) *Older People: Take Up of Benefits*, New Policy Institute. Available at: www.poverty.org.uk.

Priestley, M. (2003) *Disability: A Life Course Approach*, Cambridge, Polity Press.

Pritchard, J. (2002) 'The Abuse of Older Men', *Journal of Adult Protection*, 4(3), pp. 14–23.

Pritchard, J. (1997) 'Vulnerable People Taking Risks: Older People and Residential Care', in H. Kemshall and J. Pritchard (eds), *Good Practice in Risk Assessment and Risk Management (2) Protection, Rights and Responsibilities*, London, Jessica Kingsley.

Quinn, A. (1999) 'The Use of Experiential Learning to Help Social Work Students Assess Their Attitudes Towards Practice with Older People', *Social Work Education*, 18(2), pp. 171–81.

Quinn, A. (2005) 'The Context of Loss, Change and Bereavement in Palliative Care', in P. Firth, G. Luff and D. Oliviere (eds), *Loss, Change and Bereavement in Palliative Care*, pp. 1–17.

Quinton, A. (1973) *The Nature of Things*, Routledge, London.

Qureshi, H., Patmore, C., Nicolas, E. and Bamford, C. (2000) *Learning from Older Community Care Clients*, Research Findings from the Social Policy Research Unit, University of York, Social Policy Research Unit.

Ray, M. (2007) 'Redressing the Balance? The Participation of Older People in Research', in M. Bernard, and T. Scharf (eds), *Critical Perspectives on Ageing Societies*, Bristol, Policy Press, pp. 73–87.

Ray, R. E. (1996) 'A Postmodern Perspective on Feminist Gerontology', *The Gerontologist*, 36(5), pp. 674–80.

Ray, R. E. (2007) 'Narratives as Agents of Social Change: A New Direction for Narrative Gerontologists', in M. Bernard and T. Scharf (eds), *Critical Perspectives on Ageing Societies*, Bristol, Policy Press, pp. 59–72.

Reed, J. and Payton, V. R. (1996) 'Constructing Familiarity: A Way of Adapting to Life in a Care Home', *Ageing and Society*, 16(5), pp. 543–60.

Reed, J., Stanley, D. and Clarke, C. (2004) *Health, Well-being and Older People*, Bristol, Policy Press.

Reinharz, S. (1986) 'Friends or Foes: Gerontological and Feminist Theory', *Women's Studies International Forum*, 9, pp. 503–14.

Richards, S. (2000) 'Bridging the Divide: Elders and the Assessment Process', *British Journal of Social Work*, 30, pp. 37–49.

Rosen, A. L., Zlotnik, J. L. and Singer, T. (2002) 'Basic Gerontological Competence for All Social Workers: The Need to Gerontologize Social Work Education', *Journal of Social Work Education* (Special edition: *Advancing Gerontological Social Work Education*), 39(1/2), pp. 25–37.

Ross, R. K., Bernstein, L., Trent, L., Henderson, B. E., and Paganini-Hill, A. (1990) 'A Prospective Study of Risk Factors for Traumatic Death in the Retirement Community', *Preventive Medicine*, 19, pp. 323–334.

Rowe, J. W. and Kahn, R. L. (1997) 'Successful Aging', *The Gerontologist*, 37, pp. 433–40.

Rowlings, C. (1981) *Social Work with Elderly People*, London, Allen & Unwin.

Royal College of Psychiatrists (2003) *All About Depression*. Available at: www.rcpsych.ac.uk

Russell, C. (1987) 'Ageing as a Feminist Issue', *Women's Studies International Forum*, 10, pp. 125–32.

Saleeby, D. (2002) 'The Strengths Approach to Practice', in D. Saleeby (ed.), *The Strengths Perspective in Social Work Practice* (3rd edn), Boston, Mass., Allyn & Bacon, pp. 80–93.

Sawdon, C. and Sawdon, D. (2003) 'The Supervision Partnership: A Whole Greater than the Sum of Its Parts' in J. Reynolds, J. Henderson, J. Seden, J. Charlesworth and A. Bullman (eds), *The Managing Care Reader*, London, Routledge, pp. 306–14.

Scharf, T. and Bartlam, B. (2006) 'Rural Disadvantage: Quality of Life and Disadvantage Amongst Older People – a Pilot Study', London, Commission for Rural Communities.

Scharf, T., Phillipson, C. and Smith, A. E. (2005) *Multiple Exclusion and Quality of Life Amongst Excluded Older People in Disadvantaged Neighbourhoods*, Social Exclusion Unit, Office of the Deputy Prime Minister, London, Stationery Office.

Scharf, T., Phillipson, C. and Smith, A. (2004) 'Poverty and Social Exclusion – Growing Older in Deprived Urban Neighbourhoods', in A. Walker and C. Hennessy (eds), *Growing Older: Quality of Life in Old Age*, Buckingham, Open University Press, pp. 81–106.

Scharlach, A., Damon-Rodriguez, J., Robinson, B. and Feldman, R. (2000) 'Educating Social Workers for an Aging Society: A Vision for the 21st Century', *Journal of Social Work Education*, 36(3), pp. 521–38.

SCIE (Social Care Institute for Excellence) (2006) *Using Qualitative Research in Systematic Reviews: Older People's Views of Hospital Discharge*, London, SCIE.

Scottish Assembly (1999) 'Framework for Co-operation between DoH and the Departments Concerned with Health and Social Care in the Devolved Administrations'. Available at: www.scotland.gov.uk.

Scottish Assembly (2001) *Health and Social Care Bill*. Available at: www.scotland.gov.uk.

Scottish Assembly (2005) *The Role of the Social Worker in the Twenty-first Century: A Literature Review*. Available at: www.scotland.gov.uk.

Seale, C. F. (1995) 'Dying Alone', *Sociology of Health and Illness*, 17, pp. 378–94.

Seymour, J., Gott, M., Bellamy, G., Ahmedzai, S. and Clark, D. (2002) 'Planning for End of Life: The Views of Older People About Advance Care Statements', *Social Science and Medicine*, 59, pp. 57–68.

Shakespeare, T. (2000) *Help*, Birmingham, Venture.

Sheard, D., Ray, M. and Burrows, S. (2001) *Time to Listen*, Coventry, Health Authority/Social Services.

Sheldon, B. and Chilvers, R. (2000) *Evidence Based Social Care: A Study of Prospects and Problems*, Lyme Regis, Russell House.

Silverman, P. R. (1982) 'Transitions and Models of Intervention', F. Berardo (ed.), *Middle and Late Life Transitions*, The Annals of the American Academy of Political and Social Science, November, pp. 174–88.

Silverman, P. R. (2003) 'Social Support and Mutual Help for the Bereaved', in I. B. Corless, B. B. Germina and M. A. Pittman (eds), *Dying, Death and Bereavement: A Challenge for the Living* (2nd edn), New York, Springer, pp. 247–65.

Sims, A., Radford, J., Doran, K. and Page, H. (1997) 'Social Class Variation in Place of Cancer Death', *Palliative Medicine*, 11 (55), pp. 369–73.

Smale, G. and Tuson, G., with Brehal, N. and Marsh, P. (1993) *Empowerment, Assessment, Care Management and the Skilled Worker*, London, National Institute for Social Work.

Small, N. (2001) 'Social Work and Palliative Care', *British Journal of Social Work*, 31, pp. 961–71.

Stevenson, O. (1989) *Age and Vulnerability*, London, Edward Arnold.

Stroebe, M. S. and Schut, H. (1999) 'The Dual Process Model of Coping with Bereavement: Rationale and Description', *Death Studies*, 23, pp. 197–224.

Stroebe, M. S. and Schut, H. (2001) 'Models of Coping with Bereavement: A Review', in M. S. Stroebe, R. O. Hansson, W. Stroebe and H. Schut (eds), *Handbook of Bereavement Research: Consequences, Coping and Care*, Washington, DC, American Psychological Association, pp. 375–405.

Stroebe, M. S., Hansson, R. O., Stroebe, W. and Schut, H. (2001) 'Introduction: Concepts and Issues in Contemporary Research on Bereavement', in M. S. Stroebe, R. O. Hansson, W. Stroebe and H. Schut (eds), *Handbook of Bereavement Research: Consequences, Coping and Care*, Washington, DC, American Psychological Association, pp. 3–22.

Sugarman, L. (2001) *Life Span Development: Frameworks, Accounts and Strategies* (2nd edn), Hove, Psychology Press.

Swain, J., French, S. and Cameron, C. (2003) *Controversies in a Disabling Society*, Buckingham, Open University Press.

Tanner, D. (1998) 'The Jeopardy of Risk', *Practice*, 10(1), pp. 15–28.

Tanner, D. (2001) 'Sustaining the Self in Later Life: Supporting Older People in the Community', *Ageing and Society*, 21(3), pp. 255–78.

Thompson, N. (2002) *People Skills*, Basingstoke, Palgrave Macmillan.

Tibbs, M. A. (2001) *Social Work and Dementia: Good Practice and Care Management*, London, Jessica Kingsley.

Tornstam, L. (1997) 'Gerotranscendence: The Contemplative Dimension of Aging', *Journal of Aging Studies*, 11, pp. 143–54.

Tornstam, L. (1999) 'Gerotranscendence and the Functions of Reminiscence', *Journal of Aging and Identity*, 4(3), pp. 155–66.

Townsend, P. (1962) *The Last Refuge – A Survey of Residential Institutions and Homes for the Elderly in England and Wales*, London, Routledge & Kegan Paul.

Townsend, P. (1981) 'The Structured Dependency of the Elderly: A Creation of Social Policy in the 20th Century', *Ageing and Society*, 1, pp. 5–28.

Townsend, P. (2006) 'Policies for the Aged in the 21st Century: More "Structured Dependency" or the Realisation of Human Rights?', *Ageing and Society*, 26(2), pp. 161–80.

Townsend, P. (2007) 'Using Human Rights to Defeat Ageism: Dealing with Policy-induced "Structured Dependency"', in M. Bernard and T. Scharf (eds), *Critical Perspectives on Ageing Societies*, Bristol: Policy Press, pp. 27–44.

Trevithick, P. (2005) *Social Work Skills: A Practice Handbook* (2nd edn), Buckingham, Open University Press.

Trinder, L. and Reynolds, S. (2000) *Evidence Based Practice: A Critical Appraisal*, Oxford, Blackwell Science.

Tronto, J. (1993) *Moral Boundaries: A Political Argument for an Ethic of Care*, London, Routledge.

Truax, C. B. and Carkhuff, R. R. (1967) *Towards Effective Counselling and Psychotherapy*, Chicago, Aldine.

Twigg, J. (1998) 'Informal Care', in M. Bernard and J. Phillips (eds), *The Social Policy of Old Age*, London: Centre for Policy on Ageing, pp. 128–41.

Twigg, J. and Atkin, K. (1994) *Carers Perceived: Policy and Practice in Informal Care*, Buckingham, Open University Press.

Ungerson, C. and Kember, M. (1997) *Women and Social Policy: A Reader*, London, Macmillan.

Unützer, J., Katon, W., Callahan, C. M., Williams, J. W. Jr, Hunkeler, E., Harpole, L., Hoffing, M., Della Penna, R. D., Noël, P. H., Lin, E. H. B., Areán, P. A., Hegel, M. T., Tang, L., Belin, T. R., Oishi, S., Langston, C. for the IMPACT Investigators (2002) 'Collaborative Care Management of Late Life Depression in the Primary Care Setting', *Journal of the American Medical Association*, 288(22), pp. 2836–45.

UPIAS (Union of Physically Impaired Against Segregation) (1976) *Fundamental Principles of Disability*, London, UPIAS.

Vallely, S., Evans, S., Fear, T. and Means, R. (2006) *Opening Doors to Independence: Older People with Dementia and Extra Care Sheltered Housing*, Bristol, Housing 21.

Wærness, K. (1992) 'On the Rationality of Caring', in A. Showstack Sassoon (ed.), *Women and the State*, London, Routledge.

Waine, B. and Henderson, J. (2003) 'Managers, Managing and Managerialism', in J. Henderson and D. Atkinson (eds), *Managing Care in Context*, London, Routledge/Open University, pp. 49–74.

Walker, A. (ed.) (2005) *Understanding Quality of Life in Old Age*, Buckingham, Open University Press.

Wanless Review Team (2005) *Social Care Needs and Outcomes: A Background Paper for the Wanless Social Care Review*, London, Kings Fund.

Webb, S. (2006) *Social Work in a Risk Society*, London, Jessica Kingsley.

Welch, B. (1990) *Care Management: Managers Guide*, London, SSI.

Welsh Assembly Government (2003) *The Strategy for Older People in Wales*, Cardiff, Welsh Assembly Government.

Welsh Assembly Government (2006) *Fufilled Lives, Supportive Communities: A Strategy for Social Services in Wales over the Next Decade*, Cardiff, Welsh Assembly Government.

Williams, F. (2001) 'In and Beyond New Labour: Towards a New Political Ethics of Care, *Critical Social Policy*, 21, pp. 467–93.

Wolf, R. S. (1997) 'Elder Abuse and Neglect: Causes and Consequences', *Journal of Geriatric Psychiatry*, 30(1), pp. 153–74.

Woods, S. P. and Ashley, S. (1995) 'Simulated Presence Therapy: Using Selected Memories to Manage Problem Behaviours in Alzheimer's Disease Patients', *Geriatric Nursing*, 16(11), pp. 9–14.

World Health Organization (2002) *Active Ageing: A Policy Framework WHO Noncommunicable Disease Prevention and Health Promotion, Ageing and the Lifecourse*, Geneva, WHO. Available at: www.who.int.

# Glossary

**Active ageing**
Optimizing opportunities for healthy ageing by behaviours that support healthy lifestyles, and by participation and engagement in activities, occupational opportunities and life-long learning with the aim of promoting quality of life.

**Activities of daily living**
Personal care activities necessary for everyday living (for example, washing, dressing, eating, cooking).

**Advance statement**
A written and signed statement drawn up by a person indicating how he or she would wish to be treated if he or she were to become ill in the future (this can include wishes about *not* being actively treated).

**Best Value**
As part of the government modernization agenda and continuous improvement framework, Best Value sets out the requirement that services provide the best value to people, based on the principles of equity, efficiency and effectiveness.

**Care management/care managers**
The allocation of support and interventions for an individual deemed to be eligible to receive services, based on an assessment of need and a written care plan. Monitoring and reviewing of the goals and interventions laid out in the care plan are integral to the care management framework.

**Case load**
The number of cases a social work practitioner is responsible for at any one time. Increasingly, the allocation of work is undertaken using workload management models. This means that social workers are allocated work that reflects an allocation of time for specific types of work and the complexity of the work against the amount of time a practitioner has available to undertake casework.

### Code of practice (BASW)
A statement of rules, ethical codes, value positions and professional standards that underpin the roles and responsibilities of professional social work.

### Co-morbidity
Having two or more illnesses or conditions at the same time; the interaction or relationship between the two conditions is likely to be important (for example, the impact of having both osteoarthritis and being obese).

### Competence framework
Competence to practice as a social worker is assessed within predefined key roles which reflect the roles and responsibilities required of a social work practitioner.

### Direct payments
Payments made directly to service users to enable them to purchase their own support and assistance requirements. The provision of direct payments is still based on assessment of need and the individual meeting local eligibility bands within Fair Access to Care (see below).

### Eligibility criteria
Criteria set out in Fair Access to Care which determine levels of eligibility to receive support and interventions from social services.

### Fair Access to Care
The government framework for standardizing eligibility decisions. The framework is based on risk to independence and has four bands of eligibility (critical, substantial, moderate and low). It is anticipated that assessments which determine eligibility should not just consider immediate need but also the potential deterioration of a person's situation without support or assistance.

### Iatrogenic artefact
An adverse outcome from a treatment or intervention aimed at improving a person's condition.

### Managerialism
The performance of an organization enhanced by the application of effective management skills.

### National Occupational Standards (NOS)
Statements which define the requirements of competent work/practice in a specific occupation (for example, social work).

### Neuroleptic medication
Tranquilizing medication which can be prescribed, among other things, in the treatment of various behavioural symptoms in dementia.

**Normal ageing**
The process of growing old, characterized by gradual changes in biological function. The process is characterized by diversity in the experience of ageing.

**Palliative care**
A holistic approach to the care, support and treatment of people with life-threatening or terminal illness. Palliative care seeks to provide effective pain control, to enhance comfort, and to address psychological, social and emotional concerns alongside physical treatments.

**Performance criteria**
Goals that set standards for determining effectiveness and efficiency. Performance criteria may be set by national government and, through processes of audit and inspection, used as tools to evaluate the effectiveness and efficiency of public agencies.

**Personal social services**
There is no absolute definition of this term but, broadly speaking, it covers the provision of social care and social services.

**Post-qualifying**
Post-qualifying awards are intended to enable registered practitioners to remain up-to-date with their practice, and to develop their practice skills and associated knowledge/theory base. Post-qualifying awards and courses are accredited by the General Social Care Council, which is responsible for the registration of social work practitioners.

**Service user movement**
User-led campaigns with a variety of goals. For example, campaigning and pressure to change approaches to service delivery; active participation in developing user-led services and research; user-led development of theory and models; development of advocacy and self-advocacy services.

**Social model of disability**
While disabled people recognize that they may have physical, intellectual or emotional impairments, these issues become disabling because of the barriers and prejudices that society imposes on disabled people. For example, a person with impaired mobility experiences disabling consequences if an environment is designed to accommodate to people without such impairments (for example, stairs; no access to a lift; uneven paving; long corridors).

**Welfare state**
A number of major policy changes were initiated by the government after the Second World War with the aim of committing to the

public provision of a National Health Service; Social Security provision; and education and employment initiatives. The policies resulted in considerable investment in state and public bodies created to provide, develop and oversee the developments, along with a widening of state responsibility for intervention.

# Index

Learning Resource
Centre